Beyond

AMBITION

ROBERT E. KAPLAN

with
WILFRED H. DRATH and
JOAN R. KOFODIMOS

Beyond
AMBITION

How Driven Managers Can
Lead Better
and
Live Better

 Jossey-Bass Publishers

San Francisco • Oxford • 1991

BEYOND AMBITION
How Driven Managers Can Lead Better and Live Better
by Robert E. Kaplan with Wilfred H. Drath and Joan R. Kofodimos

Library of Congress Cataloging-in-Publication Data

Kaplan, Robert E.
    Beyond ambition : how driven managers can lead better and live
better / Robert E. Kaplan with Wilfred H. Drath and Joan R.
Kofodimos.
        p.   cm. — (The Jossey-Bass management series)
    Includes bibliographical references (p.   ) and index.
    ISBN 1-55542-315-9
    1. Executives — Psychology.   2. Leadership.   3. Success.
I. Drath, Wilfred H.   II. Kofodimos, Joan R.   III. Title.
IV. Series.
HD38.2.K37   1991   91-12695
658.4'09 — dc20   CIP

JACKET DESIGN BY BETH A. LOUDENBERG

FIRST EDITION
Code 9173

The Jossey-Bass Management Series

Consulting Editors
Organizations and Management

Warren Bennis
University of Southern California

Richard O. Mason
Southern Methodist University

Ian I. Mitroff
University of Southern California

Contents

ix

Preface

What do organizations do when a senior manager doesn't perform up to expectations? Probably the most common response is to remove the individual from his or her job, through internal transfer or outright termination. Turnover among senior managers is estimated to be as high as 33 percent.[1] The cost of replacing a failed senior manager from outside the organization is exorbitant, running into the hundreds of thousands, or even millions, of dollars.[2] When there is no alternative but to transfer or "outplace" an executive, then presumably the high price of deselection is worth paying.

Removal, however, is not the only recourse taken by organizations in response to performance problems with executives. *Development* is also a possibility, though traditionally less likely for executives than for managers at lower levels. When organizations do opt for development, problematic executives are given the opportunity to receive constructive feedback on their behavior and then to modify the offending behavior. The idea is to change the way they make decisions, handle people, press for results, and so forth. Although the behavioral approach can be effective under the right conditions, it suffers from overuse.

The field of management development, in general, has stuck faithfully to training methods aimed at observable behavior and has almost superstitiously steered clear of training methods that "get personal."

Basis of the Book

This book is predicated on the value of taking the person into account in making sense of the performance problems of an executive and in solving those problems. As Samuel Butler said, "Every man's work . . . is always a portrait of himself."[3] An executive we worked with commented: "You are who you are. The question is, how can you be a better you?" In a nutshell, that's what this book is about.

By the way, I do not mean "better you" in a moral sense. I mean it as it applies to executives who get into trouble by being so driven to achieve and succeed that they go to self-defeating extremes. Ironically, such executives are so ambitious to prove themselves that they end up undercutting themselves and undermining the organization. In order for executives to be better, in my terms, they must develop their goals beyond raw ambition for themselves.

Two sets of defenses discourage a personal approach to leadership and leadership development.[4] There are organizational defenses, which act to keep discussion and action on an impersonal level. And there are personal defenses, which resist attempts by others to delve into private motives. These defenses are activated by the idea of personal development in an organization. They are formidable, but can be overcome with a strong commitment to development and with a workable method for going about it.

Purpose of the Book. The purpose of this book is to propose a personal approach to fostering the development of senior managers. The personal approach is not intended to replace the behavioral method; rather, they are to be used in conjunction with each other. When used in tandem, these two methods have the potential to bring about real and lasting change.

A caution: Personal development is no panacea. It's certainly not a solution to all performance problems. But I do think it is an option that should be considered more often. In addition, this sort of development need not be reserved for executives in trouble. It can have appreciable payoffs for executives with no glaring performance problems.

The idea of personal development is something of a paradigm shift for a management development field dominated by the behavioral approach. The book will develop this rather controversial idea by showing how critical a part the person plays in the exercise of executive leadership and by explaining and illustrating personal development in driven senior managers. Many times, personal development takes the form of an inner shift that allows the individual to move beyond an excessive ambition to excel.

Research Background. This book is the outgrowth of a long expedition into the comparative wilderness of executive development that I conducted with my colleagues Bill Drath and Joan Kofodimos. We set out with simple questions: What makes executives tick? What sorts of performance problems do executives encounter, and what, if anything, can be done about them, especially by way of development? Can executive development work in the face of formidable obstacles, such as the executive's high position and success? What kind of development would be expressly suited to managers in high positions?

We attempted to answer these questions by studying executives in depth. We avoided studying a given executive only from his or her own point of view. Instead, we also talked with the individual's superiors, subordinates, and peers. To get a complete picture of the executive, we did not confine ourselves to the work setting but also talked with family members. We achieved unusual access to the lives and psyches of these highly placed individuals who typically manage to escape scrutiny because we gave something back—all the data we collected, in anonymous form. At the time of this writing, I personally have worked with more than forty executives on this basis. See the appendix for a more detailed description of the research method.

Put simply, the lesson we have learned is that leadership and leadership development are thoroughly *personal*. An executive's basic character powerfully affects the way he or she runs an organization. Managerial expertise and business knowledge matter, but it is a mistake to look upon leadership and leaders primarily in terms of their surface properties. To comprehend leadership fully, we must not confine ourselves to observable behavior, as the strong behavioral tradition in organizational science would have it. We must delve beneath the surface and look at the profound effects of basic character on leadership.

Why go below the surface? the reader may ask; after all, isn't it the case that adults cannot change their basic natures? Why not stick to behavior, which can be changed? There are two reasons. First, when attempts to alleviate performance problems are restricted to behavioral methods, the results are often disappointing because the troublesome behaviors prove to be stubbornly rooted in the person's character. Second, we have found that, while difficult, it *is* possible for executives to change in basic ways. Such changes are the evolutions—not revolutions—that many adults go through in the course of their lives. When managers undergo such an evolution—I call it a *character shift*—their performance noticeably improves. Not only that, they feel happier and better adjusted.

Who Should Read This Book? This book is written for three audiences. First, the book is meant to help executives (and those who aspire to become executives) to grow, improve, and find fulfillment. We have reason to believe that executives can identify with and learn from what we learned. We hope the book will provide fresh insights into their inner workings. Second, the book is for professionals and managers interested in promoting the development of executives. We hope we can highlight the neglected potential of personal development as a key to unlocking a senior manager's potential. Our third audience is comprised of students of management, who we believe generally pay too little attention to the deeply personal aspects of leadership and leadership development.

Overview of the Contents

The book begins with a chapter that gives a rationale for executive development and makes a case for the importance of the person in executive leadership and executive development.

The rest of the book is divided into three parts. Part One examines the challenge of gaining self-awareness. Chapter Two is a case study of an executive whose particular character gets in the way of self-awareness. Chapter Three explains why executives tend to have difficulty with self-awareness: first, because their elevated situations impede the flow of constructive criticism to them and, second, because their typically expansive natures lead them to resist indications of their flaws.

Part Two traces performance problems of executives to expansive character, as it is magnified by their elevated positions. Chapter Four illustrates what expansive character is and is not. Chapter Five is a case study showing the relationships between a "fix-it" executive's expansive character and his configuration of strengths and weaknesses. Chapter Six shows how expansiveness taken to an extreme results in various performance problems and explores the origins of expansiveness. Chapter Seven makes the point that certain extremely expansive executives redeem themselves by getting outstanding results. Finally, Chapter Eight considers the effects of expansive character on the lives of executives outside of work.

Part Three makes a case for personal development for executives. In Chapter Nine, the limitations of behavioral methods are discussed and an alternative approach is proposed. Chapter Ten conceptualizes personal development in driven executives as a shift in character. Chapter Eleven is a case study of a senior manager who underwent such a character shift. Chapter Twelve describes the process by which managers, senior or otherwise, can "reorganize" themselves by combining personal development and behavioral change.

The book concludes with Chapter Thirteen, which restates the challenge of helping managers, especially high-level men, make lasting improvements in the way they lead. I formulate this challenge acknowledging executives' doubts about whether they can change in the first place and their worry that if they do they will lose their effectiveness.

Throughout the book, I use stories of real people to enliven concepts and conclusions. I hope to convey meaning by bringing to life the executives and their developmental challenges and struggles. In addition to numerous brief examples, each of the book's three parts contains a chapter devoted entirely to a case illustrating the theme of that part. To help the reader remember who is who in what will grow to be a sizable cast of characters, a list of cases appears just before Chapter One.

Acknowledgments

This book is the product of a highly collaborative venture with a number of different people. First of all, we owe a debt to the executives who participated in this project and were willing to have us write anonymously about them. We have not so much studied them, as we have learned with them. Second, we are grateful to the adventurous human resource managers in a handful of companies who had the courage to team up with us to experiment with this research-and-service project. To protect the confidentiality of the executives with whom we worked, these brave souls will have to remain unnamed. Third, we thank those colleagues at the Center for Creative Leadership and at KRW International who also served as staff in this work and contributed to the design of the service. They include Diane Ducat, Barry Gruenberg, Rebecca Henson, Frank Kalgren, Fred Kiel, Eric Rimmer, Jeff Staggs, Joan Tavares, and Kathryn Williams. Fourth, we would like to single out Alice Warren, who from the inception of the research has served as a research assistant. She has contributed greatly by reviewing literature, collecting and analyzing data, critiquing drafts, and asking hard questions. This book has benefited from her hard work, fine mind, and encouraging collegiality. Fifth, we would like to express our appreciation to the Center for Creative Leadership for its support of what must at first have seemed a dubious undertaking. In particular, we thank David DeVries, the Center's executive vice-president, who consistently supported our work despite his occasional misgivings.

Many people took considerable trouble to review earlier drafts and provide wise counsel. They include Clayton Alderfer, Chris Argyris, William Campbell, Sally Carr, Laura Coburn, Susan Dorn, Diane Ducat, Douglas Hall, Keith Halperin, Rebecca Henson, Marcia Horowitz, Pauline Hodson, Rebecca Kaplan, Manfred Kets de Vries, Fred Kiel, T. J. Kofodimos, Michael Lombardo, Marie McKee, Leroy Malouf, Jim Melvin, Jennifer Morrow, Roland Nelson, David Noer, Stanley Pylipow, Eric Rimmer, Marian Ruderman, Leonard Sayles, Terrence Smith, Jeff Staggs, Glen Swogger, Joan Tavares, Stephen Wall, and Martin Wilcox.

We also appreciate the assistance of Frank Freeman and Peggy Cartner of the Center's library in painstakingly constructing the index for the book.

I would like to recognize the yeoman efforts of Jill Fields in typing the first draft, typing a considerably altered second draft, and then finally typing Bill Drath's close editing of the revision. I am grateful for her cheerfulness as much as her speed and accuracy.

I had the good fortune to draft the book while on sabbatical for six months in Oxford, England, in late 1989 and early 1990. (I have Robert McHenry to thank for arranging an appointment at Oxford University's Oriel College.) While I enjoyed writing at Oriel and in the study of the Shakespeare professor's house my family and I rented, I preferred holing up at the coffee shop that was part of the Straw Hat Bakery in North Oxford. Back in the States, it has been a bit of a comedown to do much of the revision at McDonald's.

Greensboro, North Carolina   Robert E. Kaplan
July 1991

*I dedicate this book to
Rebecca Kaplan,
whose love and competence
have helped me fulfill my ambitions
and move beyond them.*

The Authors

Robert E. Kaplan is a senior fellow at the Center for Creative Leadership in Greensboro, North Carolina. He has a B.A. degree in English (1965) and a Ph.D. degree in organizational behavior (1973) from Yale University. Before coming to the Center, he was on the organizational behavior faculty at Case Western Reserve University. In addition to various articles on management, individual and team development, and organizational change, he has coauthored, with Morgan McCall, the book *Whatever It Takes: The Realities of Managerial Decision Making*.

Wilfred H. Drath is publications director and a research associate at the Center for Creative Leadership in Greensboro, North Carolina. He holds an A.B. degree in literature from the University of Georgia. He has been engaged in research on executive character and development since 1983.

Joan R. Kofodimos is an independent consultant, researcher, and writer based in Greensboro, North Carolina. She received a B.A. degree (1979) in psychology and an M.A. degree (1979) in sociology from Stanford University and a Ph.D. degree in organizational behavior (1986) from Yale University. Prior to establishing her own practice, she worked with Manus Associates, a consulting firm specializing in strategic planning and executive development. Before that, she held the position of behavioral scientist in the Executive Leadership Group at the Center for Creative Leadership in Greensboro, North Carolina, where she remains on the adjunct staff. Her current practice and research focus on strategic leadership, top management teams, personal development of executives, and balancing work and family.

List of Cases

Rich Bauer (Chapter 5), a self-vindicator/fix-it leader

Hank Cooper (Chapter 9), who had no luck using behavioral methods to ameliorate an abrasive style

Chris Cramer (Chapter 10), who learned to live without his Superman suit

Diana Dowling (Chapter 10), who transcended the sense that she was nobody unless she was a high achiever and a member of the in-group

Bill Flechette (Chapter 12), whose acute concern with doing well and looking good made it difficult for him to accept criticism; a striver-builder

John Holland (Chapter 7), an ideal leader who got great results *and* handled people exceptionally well

Lee McKinney (Chapter 11), a perfectionist-systematizer who underwent a shift in character that showed up at work and at home

Mac Michaelson (Chapter 7), highly effective in bottom-line terms but at a human cost

Mark Tabor (Chapter 7), admired for his management of people but faulted for not getting the most from his organization

Russ Wright (Chapter 12), the beneficiary of a surprising amount of support after receiving a hard-hitting feedback report

Beyond
AMBITION

Chapter One

Driven Managers: Taking the Person into Account

It's fine telling people to change. But the real
measure of change is: Can you change
yourself?
—an executive

Executive development is important because most executives
need to improve. This is partly because they are human, falli-
ble, limited. "No one has it all," the chief executive officer (CEO)
of a medium-sized organization said. "We can all derail." But
more is involved than just making mistakes from time to time.
Many executives repeatedly mishandle certain types of situations. They chronically pull rank, or get into fights with higher-
ups, or avoid risks, or fail to follow through. Becoming a successful executive means that attitudes and behavior that used
to be nothing more than idiosyncrasies or quirks are suddenly
magnified for everyone to see. Problems never before evident
suddenly surface with increases in job scope, visibility, power,
and isolation. In other words, some executive fallibility is attributable not to the *human* condition but to the *executive* condition. Our umbrella term for this problem is "elevation."[1] One

1

executive offered a bit of down-home wisdom about the effects of elevation: "As my daddy said, the higher up the pole you are, the more your rear end is exposed."

Executive development is also important because organizations today are increasingly being forced to change themselves to keep pace with rapidly changing environments. They are revamping strategy, reshuffling divisions, merging or acquiring or divesting businesses, going global, flattening their hierarchy, or stepping up the emphasis on innovation or quality or responsiveness to customers. What's important here is that when organizations change, the executive in charge play a central role in engineering that change.

For the organization to adapt, the executive must also adapt. Sometimes this means little more than becoming computer-literate to gain access to a new management information system. Other times, such as when a change in the organizational culture is at hand, the executive must modify his or her style in a more personal sense.

Thus, as organizations struggle to adapt to a new order, executives must struggle to play the part required of them in the new order. As William Torbert argued, "A manager either leads the organization through those fundamental changes by equally fundamental changes in his or her own style at the appropriate times, or else he or she does not last. Many managers today do not last."[2] In this spirit one upper-level manager, taking part in a discussion with a few of his peers about the changes each of their organizations was going through, offered this summary comment: "We're all concerned with the change around us, change that we see as being needed. We're also concerned with our changing to do that. Each of us worries: Am I changing fast enough to make a difference?"

One popular misconception is that an organization's leader can introduce change as if they are manipulating an object outside of and independent of themselves. Senior managers who labor under this misconception don't learn to play their complementary part and therefore unconsciously undermine the reorganizations or cultural changes they initiate. Rarely can an executive institute a major change at arm's length, untouched by the change itself. More often, to usher in a new scheme of things requires the executive to change in some way along with the rest of the organization. Senior managers need to learn the simple lesson that a colleague, Bill Zierden, taught his executive clients about effecting organizational change: "Changing you means changing me." In the same spirit, Tolstoy once observed: "Everybody thinks of changing humanity and nobody thinks of changing himself."

Gone are the days when, as one senior manager put it, "you can tell an organization it has to change, and the organization is everyone but you." Practically nothing is more counterproductive than senior managers calling for a new managerial practice and then contradicting that call in their own actions.

One executive, "Harry," had a blind spot that got in the way of organizational change. The year before, the top management of his old-line company had started a campaign for greater employee involvement. Harry, a newly minted executive, said all the right things about sharing power, but his actions did not match his words. Some of his subordinates expressed their disillusionment with him by saying he had a good "textbook understanding" of management practice.

His problem could be described as a difficulty in delegating responsibility under stress. In general, Harry was quite capable of handing off responsibility. The problem was that when anything resembling a crisis occurred, Harry jumped back in with both feet. By taking over in every crisis, he hurt the corporate initiative to push power down the line, and he damaged his credibility with his own staff, who themselves held high-level functional jobs. Unfortunately, Harry couldn't see the contradiction, even when a subordinate had the nerve to point it out to him. Therefore, the problem persisted.

The first step in improving one's performance is to identify a need for improvement. But, as in Harry's case, such self-knowledge can be extremely difficult to come by. Consequently, one of the most basic challenges that executives face is to learn where they really stand.

Highly placed managers who are blind to their problems put their effectiveness and careers at risk. A recent study found that what distinguished executives who succeeded in their careers from those who derailed was *not* absence of weakness. Successful executives were not free of weaknesses. What made the difference was the ability to learn from one's experience, including from mistakes and failures.[3] A replication of this study with women executives obtained the same finding. Executive women who derailed were less likely to become aware of their faults, sometimes because they rebuffed other people's attempts to apprise them of those faults.[4] A CEO told us, "No matter how talented [an executive] you are, you are going to have problems, and the more you're in touch with those, the better prepared you'll be, and the more successful you'll be."

Like the rest of us, executives are fundamentally ambivalent about knowing themselves better. We all become possessive of ourselves as we are, so any attempt to call this self into question flies in the face of our investment in this present self and our belief in the rightness of it. Abraham Maslow called this ambivalence about self-awareness "the need to know and the fear of knowing."[5]

To make matters worse, even if executives want a clearer sense of themselves, their environment may not cooperate. Honest and constructive input about how they conduct themselves can be hard to get from superiors, peers, or subordinates. This can also stem in part from their own reluctance to make themselves vulnerable in the politicized settings at the higher reaches of large organizations. As one executive told us, "If you show any kind of weakness, you've let your shield down, you've taken your armor off." The irony is that because many executives hold back and are deprived of counsel about themselves, they may labor under the illusion that they're alone in having to deal with personal complexities and perplexities.

When performance problems are acknowledged — if they are — these problems are typically understood in surface, behavioral terms. I feel there is much to be gained — if a significant breakthrough in effectiveness is sought — by looking beyond behavior to the character of the person. I deliberately use the term *character* rather than *personality*. Personality suggests a set of traits, perhaps even disconnected traits. By character I mean to refer to a person's deep structure, including the basic driving forces. Character suggests a *unified* notion of the person's makeup. In this book, I define character as the set of deep-seated strategies used to enhance or protect one's sense of self-worth.

In our research we have seen over and over again that many executives depend on achievement and success as a means of obtaining and reinforcing a sense of self-worth. They rely so heavily on a strategy of worth-through-mastery that I have called this type of character *expansive.* The term is meant to convey the considerable extent of these executives' ambitions for themselves. Executives desire a sense not merely of adequacy but of high personal worth, and they seek it not by doing an acceptable job but by doing an exceptional job. Expansive executives see themselves, perhaps unconsciously, as heroes. Like heroes, they want to execute some masterstroke, or accomplish prodigious amounts of work, or adhere to the highest standards.

The term *expansive* is used here in a special sense. It does not have the usual meaning of jovial or benevolent (as in the expression, "she's in an expansive mood"). It does not mean receptive to change. Instead, it refers to someone who is vitally concerned with gaining mastery over his or her environment. All of human existence, according to one early personality theorist, is a "process of self-expansion."[6] The tendency to self-expansion is simply greater in the executive population.

One way to understand the expansive character is to compare it to another basic character type, one that I call *relational.* The relational person seeks first and foremost to establish a connection with other people. Relational types want to be included, they want to please other people, and they are interested in close personal relationships and self-disclosure. Rather than wanting to differentiate themselves as independent achievers, they want to integrate themselves into interdependent relationships. Relational people are thus those who are driven to seek communion or connectedness in order to feel good about themselves.

No one is a pure version of either of these types. In life, people blend the two, commonly giving one more weight. Executives, however, are typically more expansive than relational.

The very impulse to heroics in expansive executives is also the genesis of much of the counterproductive behavior found at upper organizational levels. No one can argue with wanting to be the best. One can only argue with wanting too badly to be the best. It is when executives go too far in pursuing their ambitions that trouble comes.

The concept of expansive character is fundamental to this book. It is in terms of this concept that I make the link between the person and leadership. Performance problems are understood as issuing largely from expansiveness taken to extremes. Personal development is understood chiefly as a moderation of excessive expansiveness. In the case of Harry, he could thank his intense ambition for his quick ascent up the corporate hierarchy and for some notable accomplishments along the way. But his effectiveness in his current job was impaired by his overblown need to do well. Any time he saw a crisis coming — and he was quick to perceive a crisis — he took over the reins from his immediate subordinates. One astute subordinate called this "the crisis cycle." Being so overwhelmingly concerned with doing well, Harry panicked when a crisis loomed. When he panicked, he took over. By taking back the responsibility he had delegated, he frustrated and demoralized his people. But it was so important to him to save the day that he brushed aside their objections.

This book is not, however, primarily about the challenge executives face in gaining awareness. Nor is it primarily about understanding performance problems in terms of underlying character. It is chiefly concerned with *how executives can improve as managers by growing as human beings.*

In the case of expansive executives, such personal development entails a moderation of their excessive ambition for accomplishment. They undergo a *character shift* that allows them to retreat from an overreliance on accomplishment as a means of fostering self-worth. They find ways to become more comfortable with themselves. They stop being so caught up in the effort to prove themselves. They shift themselves into a kind of overdrive that allows them to continue to move at high speeds but at lower rpms. They assume what management expert Larry Wilson calls an attitude of "relaxed concentration."

Such an inner shift is much easier to describe than to do. It is usually the result not just of soul searching on the executive's part but also of some powerful, often disturbing event or period in life. Furthermore, it usually requires the active involvement of other people in the executive's life. This sort of personal evolution is almost inevitably accompanied by a certain amount of pain. By stepping outside of themselves, these highly ambitious people see more clearly the price they have paid and the damage they have done. It is through such painful acknowledgment that they generate the thrust needed to escape the powerful gravity of the past.

I see executives as highly specialized human beings, gifted and unevenly developed. I am frankly awed by what they are able to do, fascinated by what they cannot do, and profoundly interested in their struggle to grow as managers and people. I have no interest in making superhumans out of them, or in treating them as monsters.

Yet some readers, depending in part on their own stance toward such authority figures, may find the book's view of executives tilted toward the negative. The book may give the impression that we seem to be looking for flaws in effective, successful executives.

One reason for this is that we chose not to take any executive's excellent reputation and aura of efficacy and confidence at face value. We dug beneath the surface and found what we would find in any normal and well-functioning adult: a fair share of conflicts, doubts, and compulsions, all of which take a toll on effectiveness. Outwardly, good adjustment can make executives appear perfectly normal and mask the neurotic components of their personality.[7] As one executive observed about the extensive feedback he had received, "It's like peeling an onion; when you peel enough, you reach flaws." A second reason for the book's slant toward the negative is its focus on development. After all, the book is dedicated to understanding what can go wrong for executives, why it goes wrong, and how it can be put right. In a sense the book is about the negative effects of executives' exceptionally well-developed strengths. There are some management experts like Peter Drucker and Warren Bennis who seem to argue that overcoming weaknesses doesn't pay and that the real payoff is in building on strengths. But the reality is that the weaknesses in executives are often strengths taken to extremes. So to fully capitalize on strengths inevitably means grappling with the weaknesses that issue from overdeveloped strengths.

A final reason for the stance taken toward executives is personal. My psyche and my intellect influenced the conduct of the study and the writing of the book. I am aware of my consuming interest in competence, incompetence, anxiety about one's incompetence, the development of increased competence, and the drama involved in development. I projected myself into this book just as executives project themselves into their roles. Rather than fight this reality, I chose to work with it by trying to be as objective as possible about my subjectivity.

I will even use myself occasionally as an example, I hope judiciously. This is not, I believe, exhibitionism but an outgrowth of the fact that I share some of the core characteristics of the executives we studied. I am not an executive (though I do manage a department), but it has become clear to me that, in part, I have been drawn to understand the personal makeup of executives as a way of understanding myself. As, in the course of the project, my self-understanding and development progressed, so did my grasp of the executive phenomenon. I reveal this on principle: No matter how hard we as researchers try to be detached and objective, the study of human nature has an irreducible element of subjectivity. We all do better to acknowledge it than to pretend it doesn't exist.

Indeed, the relationship that my colleagues and I had with participating executives was intentionally personal. We sat side by side with each person as he or she sorted through the high-impact information we had to offer and the feelings stirred up by it. We worked closely with executives as they struggled to put their insights to work. Under these circumstances, the work relationship quickly took on aspects of friendship. The warmth and caring that developed supported the service we offered, but it also supported the research. No knowledge of the sort we sought, no access to intrapsychic processes, would have been possible without a close, personal relationship.

These personal relationships have influenced even the writing of this book. In writing about individuals, I have taken the same stance as I did while working with them — constructive, critical, sympathetic. I have also tried to remain true to my commitment to them to keep their data private. To honor this commitment and to write about individuals revealingly put me on the horns of a dilemma: As a responsible social scientist, I wanted to report the data accurately; as a responsible practitioner, I wanted to avoid exposing and possibly hurting the executives. How could I be faithful at the same time to the interests of science and to the interests of the executives?

I resolved the dilemma by placing red herrings in the case studies of every executive featured in the book. I did not just disguise each person's circumstances, I also changed one or more characteristics, always being careful to make these changes in light of what I knew about the type that the executive represented. This strategem is aimed at those readers who think they can recognize the real executives behind my descriptions. I hope there are no readers who would try to use such information for ill, but if there are, let me remind them that there is no way to determine what is taken from a given executive and what is taken from someone else.

Some readers may fault me for tampering with the data. I sympathize. I would vastly prefer to present the executive exactly as he or she is. But if I did, I would be liable to the charge that I acted irresponsibly towards the executives. Given these conflicting interests, I chose, in effect, to create partial composites. In doing so, I followed an established practice in clinical research, one adopted, for example, by George Vaillant in his book, *Adaptation to Life,* which analyzes the character and lives of 100 Harvard graduates.[8] As a final precaution, each executive featured at any length in the book read and signed off on the description of him or her.

Thus, without jeopardizing these individuals, I have been able to make use of their examples to construct a theory of how personal character influences senior leadership and how senior managers can lead (and live) more effectively through personal growth.

Part One

Gaining Awareness

Upon my word, I think the truth is the
hardest missile one can be pelted with.
— George Eliot, *Middlemarch*

Unreviewable power is the most likely to self-
indulge itself and the least likely to engage
in dispassionate self-analysis.
— Warren E. Burger,
former chief justice of the
Supreme Court

Chapter Two

Barriers to Self-Awareness: The Bill Flechette Story

This entire book is an assertion that the way executives are as people matters greatly to the leadership they offer. Further, it is an assertion that executives generally have a particular sort of character — something I call expansive. What this is and what significance it has will remain hopelessly abstract unless we get down to cases. For this reason the book begins with a case study.

In this part of the book, I am concerned with how character influences the ability of executives to take realistic account of their strengths and weaknesses. In general, the effect of what I call expansive character is to make executives resistant, at least at first, to facing up to their failings. To understand concretely how resistance to realistic self-appraisal can inhere in character, we turn now to the case of Bill Flechette. When he was presented with constructive, if quite negative, criticism, Bill had a hard time coming to terms with it, and the difficulty he had seemed clearly to inhere in his personal makeup. (Like the other major cases in this book, this one is based to a large extent on a single individual, but with data and quotes drawn from several different people; thus the reader who thinks he or she knows who this person is should reserve judgment.)

In addition, the case of Bill Flechette illustrates one type of expansive executive, what I call the "striver-builder." It is important to note at this early junction that not all expansive executives are alike. Of the several readily identifiable types of expansive executive, two others — the "self-vindicator/fix-it specialist" and the "perfectionist-systematizer" — will be featured in chapter-length case studies.

In the case of Bill Flechette, we cannot appreciate fully why his character type interferes with self-awareness unless we first understand what it is that he resists becoming aware of: his weaknesses. And to put those in context, we must first appreciate his very real strengths.

Bill's Strengths

The head of an important worldwide function in his company, Bill Flechette possesses very considerable managerial strengths, which are manifested clearly in the results he gets. A superior told us he picked Bill because "he is a smart, no-nonsense guy who gets things done." This comment is representative of what several other people said. Bill himself takes pleasure in his ability to get results: "I've been amazed that when you get an organization to work, just how well the things works. You put it together right, and you get it rolling. It just exceeds your wildest expectations, and you know we've done it so many times now that it just isn't an accident."

Bill's special capability as an executive is building organizations. A subordinate captured it best: "He's a builder. For example, his plans for his organization's development — making it function better, improving the quality. . . . He has built up his organization. That's his greatest strength in this context."

Bill's skill in building organizations is also a passion, which may explain why he developed the skill in the first place. A peer remarked, "He wants to make this the top company of its kind in the country with the best people and the best service. He wants people to say that this company has no peer in the industry." A superior saw the same compelling need: "That's his objective for our organization — to make it one of the premier organizations of its kind anywhere. That kind of thing kicks up his competitive instincts."

In Bill's own words, the reward is "seeing the organization take shape as a high-powered function, seeing the professionalism be on the forefront. It vindicates the hard work and preparation. God, we've got one of the best staffs [of its kind] in the world." He described himself as being "on a crusade for the last several years to make his organization world-class." In his crusade he has joined forces with a change-oriented top executive in an all-out effort to rouse their slumbering organization.

So his specialty as a leader is making organizations first-rate. But *how* does he do it? Three capabilities stand out: strategic planning, staffing, and driving toward implementation.

First, Bill Flechette excels at planning, at setting strategy. He works hard at sorting through the possibilities before choosing the way to go. One of his peers spoke for a number of people in saying, "Setting strategy is one of William's biggest strengths. He's a builder, which requires the ability to see down the road and identify what's needed, have a good assessment of internal resources, and know what has to be parachuted in. He understands the big picture, knows the right direction to go in." Bill credited himself with "insight into strategy as well as tactics. I can immediately see the issues." His wife also saw him as a planner: "He never does anything impetuously. He sets priorities, weeds out the incidentals, ends up with what he's aiming for."

Second, he excels at staffing, which may be his strongest point. Practically everyone we talked with mentioned it. Excellent performers attract him as much as the prospect of a high-performing organization. A few years ago, he deliberately set about the task of recruiting talented engineers with managerial ability, and he invested heavily in their development. He said, "We put together an extremely impressive cadre of technical managers here. I regard that as about our best achievement. . . . After a few years here I got out there and aggressively started hiring the best. My strategy was to get a group of good people in and build on that." He was enthusiastic about hiring the cream of the crop: "If you come out of an Ivy League [school] with a Phi Beta Kappa, that pretty much puts the thumbprint on you. I knew when I hired [blank] I got the real McCoy."

A number of other people share Bill's high opinion of his staffing ability. A human resources person told us, "He's amazingly good at putting together teams. He recognizes good talent and develops it." A peer echoed this praise: "He has an almost uncanny ability to find the right person for the job, internally and externally." Further confirmation came from ratings by co-workers. All but one indicated that he assesses people well and has a nose for talent.

Third, his leadership is distinguished by an exceptional drive toward implementation. Whatever it takes, he'll find a way. Bill Flechette told us, "I tend to move heaven and earth on vital issues to get things to happen." A peer spoke graphically of his never-say-die approach: "He likes to get his way. He puts on the football pads and charges. He'll write long memos. He'll send you memos on a number of occasions. Unless he's told he's way out of line, he'll continue banging. He doesn't sulk quietly." There is no doubt that he is aggressive. He was described by subordinates as a mover and shaker, a fighter, a good person to have on your side, someone who doesn't readily back off.

Bill Flechette's own picture of himself as an implementer conformed to that of others except that he portrayed himself as employing a higher ratio of finesse to force. "Once I have a clear idea of how or what we ought to do—which I think out carefully beforehand—then I have to operate all the necessary plans, people, training, etc., while building a support base for the moves with senior management. Sometimes it's possible to go at something head on, but rarely. I have learned to patiently and obliquely move my planning into place until I get an operation moving. I always try to establish several champions and give them support and neutralize the likely objectors. I've learned to be patient and do only about two major initiatives every year."

Unfortunately, his very considerable strengths are offset by some glaring weaknesses. In addition, his enthusiastically high overall estimate of himself isn't matched by many of the people around him, especially among his peers and subordinates.

Bill's Weaknesses

We have seen that Bill Flechette is extremely concerned to do well by recruiting the best people so that his organization can do the best job. But if we boil down his weaknesses to the essence, it is that he is too concerned about being the best personally. He is too ambitious for himself. This driving ambition seems to account for the major weaknesses that came out in the data: Bill is overly concerned with impressing higher-ups; he neglects his peers and takes advantage of his subordinates.

Bill was widely viewed as too upward-oriented. The heavy investment he makes in relationships with superiors pays off organizationally in that it helps him win support for his initiatives. However, some of this investment seems designed purely to meet his need for recognition. From the way he talked about higher-ups, it was evident that he very much wants their approval and that he relishes it when he gets it. For example, he said, "I think [a certain superior] was favorably impressed with the technique I used." In fact, he confessed that "my superior's opinion of me matters most." It comes as no surprise that he received the highest scores on the managerial ratings for relationships with superiors. He was so identified with his superiors that his subordinates suspected that his ulterior motive for adopting his program of change for the organization was to ingratiate himself with the change-oriented CEO.

While Bill acts as if superiors are his primary source of gratification, he treats peers as if they have little importance to him. Superiors, peers, and subordinates alike—everyone but Bill himself—indicated that his peer relationships were very much in need of improvement. From a superior came the comment that Bill is "excessively upward-oriented at the expense of his peers." His interest in "looking good," his "personal agenda that overrides organizational goals," the "too high priority on career," and his "turf orientation" all arouse his peers' mistrust and resentment and costs him their support.

If he is overeager to please his superiors and neglectful of his peers for his superior's favor, he is prone to taking advantage of his subordinates. They faulted him for having "more of an I-orientation, than a we-orientation." This I-orientation shows up, for example, in his taking more credit for his subordinates' accomplishments than he deserves. Subordinates wished he would understand that "taking credit is the biggest turnoff for people around him." In general, he was regarded as being too concerned with getting recognition for himself rather than for his people, even though he does talk up his subordinates, especially the rising stars, and gets them promoted.

A sense has developed among Bill's subordinates that they are being pressed into service to meet his objectives. They feel that they are somehow "serving his master plan." Bill's subordinates end up in a diminished role because of how intensely he wants certain outcomes. He becomes so preoccupied with his own agenda that everyone else's pales by comparison. The human resources director told him, "You're focused on your agenda and not receptive to input unless the input relates to your agenda." The fact that his subordinates have trouble getting through to him further prevents them from playing their proper roles. Their frustration was palpable. One said, "For his sake he needs to cultivate the art of listening, of accepting other points of view. . . . I sometimes feel the need to gag his mouth and tie him up so he'll listen." A superior made the telling statement that Bill's chief developmental problem and the thing that will most affect his future is that "he's not sensitive enough to the needs of the people he's talking to. He's more interested in telling people what he wants them to know than hearing what they have to say."

The only time Bill does pay full attention to his subordinates is when he feels they have made him look bad. In fact, he occasionally loses his cool completely when subordinates inform him of a problem. It was said about him that "he takes problems personally." That is, when something goes wrong in his organization, he feels it reflects on him.

Bill's Difficulty with Self-Awareness

In fairness to Bill, he has become aware over the years of certain of his faults and taken some steps to correct them. Of the several subordinates and peers who gave him credit for this, one said, "He recognizes he has some weaknesses, and he wants to improve. He's making a real effort to change." Some of the people who have worked with him for several years had seen a change in him even before our program. A representative comment came from a subordinate: "The changes that are taking place in Bill now are greater than any in the past fifteen years. He's definitely trying to change his style." He was reported to be "less dictatorial and more willing to be influenced." And whereas in the old days he was looked upon as "an ogre, not a prince," he was now seen as using a lighter touch.

And yet, if some people felt Bill had smoothed his rough edges, at the time of our assessment, he remained an intensely problematic figure for others. A few skeptics even doubted that he had truly changed. The evidence does indeed suggest that his adjustments had fallen short of a genuine breakthrough. The reason seems to be that he had not fully accepted the need for change.

Unflinching awareness of his impact does not come easily to Bill. His defensiveness shows up in a number of ways. According to the results of one psychological test, he is "somewhat defensive" and attempts to place himself in a favorable light; he puts his best foot forward; he is reluctant to admit his faults; he tends to deny problems. The fact that he often gave himself higher marks on the managerial ratings than his co-workers did is consistent with this interpretation. On one out of every six items, he saw himself as having a strength in an area where at least four co-workers indicated he needed definite improvement. To his credit, he was not without some sense of his own defensiveness. On the managerial rating form, he marked himself as needing to improve at listening and accepting criticism. He admitted that he had a problem with "not listening as attentively and sympathetically as I should/could."

Yet he did not admit the full extent of these faults. Because he denies problems that another person firmly believes exist, he was described as "a bit of a rationalizer. When things go wrong, he isn't self-critical." A subordinate (one of many who felt this way) commented, "Bill doesn't involve subordinates in decision making well. He thinks he does it well, but he doesn't." This attitude carries over into his personal life. One summer recently he got it into his head that the family should take up sailing, and he went out and bought a thirty-foot sailboat with minimal consultation with his wife. Yet he told us that, although it was his idea, he had included his wife in the decision. Her side of the story was, "Yes, I stated my objections, but it didn't do any good."

Bill seems unable to bring himself to take his full share of blame, which appears to be the converse of his tendency to take more than his share of the credit. Being a persuasive fellow, he tries to squirm out of tight spots by arguing that certain problems don't exist or that he's in better shape than he actually is. As a result, he has a reputation for creating self-serving myths. A peer remarked, "He's so articulate, he almost creates reality. He would almost take reality beyond what was real."

Characteristically, he exaggerates his own part in a successful outcome or someone else's part in an unfavorable outcome. When he is in real pain, he might go so far as to blame someone else for causing it, as he did his wife when a cross-town move led to adjustment problems for one of the children. His wife complained, "When we moved here, our son was very unhappy. I was the obvious person to blame for insisting that we change houses, which I never did. I resented being blamed."

If Bill doesn't see himself the way others see him, it is not entirely his fault. He has received minimal constructive criticism of his leadership style from his superiors—or from anyone else, for that matter. According to a human resources professional in a position to know, he is not alone. Senior managers like him get very little feedback or coaching in this company—as is true of many organizations. The refrain—repeated over and over—was that he had received very little direct feedback from any quarter.

If Bill did not know his problems because no one really told him, the assessment we did was a golden opportunity because suddenly everyone spoke to him at one time. But for the most part, he passed up the opportunity. Although he accepted some of the data, he disputed much of it. Admittedly, the report was difficult to accept all at once. Along with clear endorsements of his strengths, there were sharp critiques of his weak points. In reporting on his defensive reaction during the feedback session, we must also make allowances for how we might have aroused his defensiveness — by, for example, pressing him to acknowledge the data. Nevertheless, he responded with unusual vehemence to the bad news. He objected strenuously to the low marks he received on openness to influence on the managerial rating form, and rather than give the data any credence, he attempted to explain it away: "I vehemently disagree. My subordinates have had lots of influence, but their expectations are too high. I have a problem with this conversation because it's out of context. The CEO is so autocratic that this pales out of significance!" Similarly, the ratings indicating problems with his relationships prompted him to say combatively, "I reject the data base. I think we might have to redo the data base because things have settled down since the survey was administered." Thus he stoutly resisted the clear indications in the report that people found it hard to get through to him.

We are not the only ones who have had trouble conversing with Bill about himself. A co-worker once tried to talk through a rough spot in their relationship but says Bill "couldn't sit and talk objectively."

In a subsequent session with us, Bill was no longer vehement, but he was hardly more receptive. If we give him the benefit of the doubt, we should allow for the possibility that he had accepted some of the data even if he couldn't openly acknowledge its validity. He may have discounted the criticisms because the culture places a value on many of his qualities. The other situational influence likely to weaken the impact of any criticism is that top management, especially his sponsor, basically accepts him as he is. As a human resources professional noted, "Bill's style has worked for him up to this point, and the reason that it has worked is that [Bill's sponsor] has liked his style. He likes gutsy fist fighters who don't go away." Or as a subordinate put it, "Top management here is less concerned with how he gets results, just that he gets them."

Bill's Difficulty with Owning Up

One direct subordinate, who took his share of responsibility for what hampered his relationship with Bill, made a particularly insightful point: "He doesn't believe he has a problem." Then, as if speaking to Bill, he said, "Bill, you've got a problem, too. Can you accept that? It's up to you." That, of course, is precisely the problem: Bill simply cannot bear to admit to a failing. He is a classic case of ego needs getting in the way of accepting criticism. But what is it about his ego needs that stops him?

Quite simply, his whole reason for being is to be good at what he does — in fact, not just good, but exceptionally good. He is *driven* to be exceptional. It is an absolute imperative. Following the same logic, he is equally motivated by the need to avoid failing, because to fail is to violate this imperative. Since he expects so much of himself — really, more than it is reasonable to expect of anyone, even a gifted person — he is always in danger of *failing* to live up to those expectations. Because failure is intolerable to him, he will go so far as to deny its reality, should it occur.

Bill's ego needs hang out for all to see. Even the members of his inner circle recognize his ambition for what it is. We asked his co-workers: What motivates Bill? A subordinate commented, "He is egotistical and self-centered. He likes to win. Of course, that's the description of most people who rise to the top of their company." A peer spoke for a number of people in observing that "he's very I-oriented in his speech and in his description of events." Another subordinate made a point of Bill's competitive instincts: "People are conscious of Bill's tendency to want to be at the head of the class. Bill has a need to feel that he holds the edge, that he knows more, that he has better insights or ideas than the person he's dealing with. He has a *need to impress others*" (emphasis added). Others spoke of the way Bill gets caught up in the "aura of omniscience" surrounding senior managers, how he needs to be "an important personage," and how he has been "a little strident about the fact that he's made it." Several people attributed to him a need to be "on top." This phrase aptly connotes both his competitiveness and his need to be in a superior position.

Bill does see some aspects of his drive to succeed. How high are his standards? "Just short of perfection." What motivates him? "Most of my life it's been to be well thought of professionally. To be included in that group of people that had value. High standards are something I've clung to—to distinguish myself." Some considerable time after the feedback session, he became able to see his competitive nature playing out even in conversations. "I just argue my point to a fault. . . . Being in a win-lose situation is fine as long as I'm not the loser. During my postcollege days, I even had great debates with my family when I wanted to show them how smart I was. It was fun to feel important. I had no idea it was devastating to people." Having risen to a senior level, he is now surrounded by other exceptional people, who "give their support on the condition that you live up to their superhuman image. It's intimidating, exhausting." In a phrase, this describes the self-imposed pressure Bill Flechette lives under—to live up to a superhuman image.

For him to be the best, his organization must be the best, as it usually is. The problem is that his ambitions for himself get too tied up in his ambitions for the organization. Some weeks after the feedback session, Bill admitted, "The data said: He's selfishly motivated. *He wants the organization to look good so he can look good*" (emphasis added).

Bill Flechette's high aspirations for himself seem to have their roots in his childhood. He was the firstborn child in his family. "As a first son and so on, you accumulate a lot of stuff that people hang on you; . . . certainly you get an imprint in the early years that 'my hopes are resting on you.'" Growing up he took the role expected of him. He was always a top student, and he starred as a bruising hockey player, becoming the captain in his senior year. He played other leadership roles, including president of his high school class.

So the pattern was set early on: He met the high expectations of people in authority, and they rewarded him accordingly. "I took responsibilities very early . . . . I was hardly a child. I couldn't understand others who didn't do what their parents or other authorities wanted." As a father, in cooperation with his wife, he has passed on the same orientation to his children. One of his children spoke for both in saying, "I want to please him and make him proud . . . . Our parents' opinion means so much to us. We want to try so hard to please them, and I also like to try hard for myself." A friend of the family observed that "his children are serious children, and Bill has reinforced that. Bill has impressed upon them the weight of their capabilities and the seriousness of their careers." (Bill's mother said of him, "He was always a serious child, always mature.")

There is ample evidence, then, of his driving ambition to excel. Directly relevant to his difficulty with self-awareness are the clear indications of an equally strong need not to fail. He said that what drives him is "the natural professional pride and the fear of failure." What really gets under Bill's skin? "The worst thing is embarrassment. *I hate being made to look bad* and that's something I really react to" (emphasis added). Privately, he worries that he is an imposter who someday will be "found out." As a teenager, despite his favored position in the family and his success in school and on the playing field, he was painfully insecure. "I had a strong sense of insecurity. . . . I strived for perfection." It is striking that other people see the duality of his motivation as clearly. A peer said, "He's a complex guy. He gives you the impression that he's confident. Deep down, I don't know if he is. Maybe fear of failure is pushing him to some degree, but that's too simple." Another subordinate: "He struggled like hell to get where he is, and his self-doubt comes along like luggage."

His wife has been both exposed to his arrogance and privy to his doubts about himself. When we entered the scene, she was critical of him — fresh from Harvard's Advanced Management Program — for being "arrogant, for acting as if he is smarter than everybody else." She also recalled bouts of self-doubt during his career. When, for example, he was considering moving out of his professional specialty and into the management track — a decision that would require a relocation — he went through a prolonged period of indecision that his wife attributed to lack of confidence. "He had a period of self-doubt. He didn't know if he could make it on the fast track." Although he made the changeover in the end, he told us that he very much likes to feel secure in his position and is acutely conscious of the challenge and danger in what he calls "moving his ground."

Bill's need to do extremely well and to avoid falling short of this mark are acute. The power this two-edged sword has over him is so complete that it impels him to great effort to turn his aspirations for himself into reality. More than that, he will go so far as to tamper with reality so that it will conform more nearly to his desired image of himself. This explains why he plays up his part in what his subordinates have achieved and why he plays down his part in problems he has created.

This double-edged need also keeps him from recognizing the lengths to which he goes to fulfill his destiny. The need is such that he must deny its consequences. He cannot, as Ernest Becker says, acknowledge what he does to purchase his self-esteem.[1] In fact, he must deny the need itself or, more accurately, deny its full extent. The reason is starkly simple: Being someone who wants to be admired, he recognizes all too clearly that there is nothing admirable about being afraid to fail. Sensing this about Bill, one of his subordinates volunteered, "Bill has to come to terms with his motives." It will not be easy for him. He resisted comments in the feedback report that touched on his egotism. The fact that he has "arrived" may give him the sense of security he needs to come to terms with himself. At least he thinks so: "Confidence grows with high position. I'm more secure; . . . there's a hell of a lot you can do to adapt. Confidence helps." One hopes that, for his sake, this isn't his usual overoptimism about himself.

Bill Flechette is a brilliant strategist and a passionately determined mobilizer of people. Yet his gifts are tarnished by a pattern of adaptation that sometimes emphasizes his emotional needs at the expense of the needs of his organization and his people. Tied up in his pattern of adaptation is a defense against clearly seeing the pattern for what it is. The developmental question then becomes: Will his egotism prevent him from recognizing his egotism?

The Striver-Builder

Bill Flechette is a prime example of one type of expansive executive, the "striver-builder."[2] This type of person strives to impress other people; for example, Bill said that as a teenager he liked impressing people and having them think he was "sharp and capable." This type has a need to be esteemed, even admired, by others. For people of this type, their own personal value may come not so much from how they view themselves as from the prestige or status that other people assign to them.

As a manager, this type specializes in building up organizations into objects worthy of the high praise and admiration that they want for themselves. As children, striver-builders often had lavish attention and admiration from their parents, and as adults they expect this same high regard from the world. Their parents expected a great deal of them, and they internalized those high expectations. As adults, they repeat this upward orientation with their organizational superiors.

There are better and worse versions of the striver-builder. In the worst cases this type is competitive to a fault. People of this type may have an overwhelming need to be number one in all spheres of their lives. Nearly every activity is turned into a contest, regardless of whether that is appropriate. They often lose friends and alienate colleagues in their competitive frenzy. They are also unduly concerned with impressing their superiors and tend to flaunt what favored standing they achieve. They put so much energy into upward relationships that they neglect relationships with peers and subordinates. They further aggravate this situation by using exploitative tactics to get what they want. To top it all off, they have a penchant for viewing themselves in a favorable light despite evidence to the contrary. Executives like this have been labeled "self-deceptive narcissists" because of their tendency to think well of themselves even if it means deceiving themselves.[3]

In the best cases, striver-builders are able to get beyond the heavy dependence on external recognition and come to a personal acceptance of themselves, including their limitations. They no longer need the applause of an audience so much, and they learn to get satisfaction out of committing themselves fully to something or someone outside of themselves. Most importantly, they transcend the compelling need to look good through deceitful means. They overcome the tendency to take credit not due them or to withhold credit due others. They are less prone to envy the accomplishments of other people. Instead, they win people's respect by investing heavily in self-improvement as a way of gaining mastery.

Epilogue

In the months following the feedback session we made only halting progress in helping Bill Flechette lower his defenses. Our work with him waned, and we fell out of touch.

Several years later he called to say that he had been moved sideways in a reorganization. This major setback followed a slow decline in which he had lost several of his prize staff to resignations and transfers out of his unit. He said he could now see better how he got himself "in hot water." The phone call was followed by a letter in which he began to acknowledge what years earlier he had been virtually unable to acknowledge: "Overall I am a strong leader who demands success and is willing to drive hard for success. Sometimes my desire is seen as excessive ambition, especially when combined with a desire to work closely with my superiors.

"The risk is that the people who work for me will see my actions not as doing what is best for the company but what is best for me. Unfortunately, people do not see me disagree with my superior because I do that in private.

"The solution is not to alter my desire for success or to reduce my drive, nor is it to stop working closely with my superiors. Instead it is to spend more time genuinely listening to my people and helping them to pull their ideas and needs together in a way that meets the goals of the company and that gives them their place in the sun.

"I think if I could improve my self-confidence it would reduce my need for approval from my superiors. This in turn would allow me to focus more of my efforts on supporting the people who work for me and with me. In the absence of raising my self-confidence, I can still focus more of my efforts on those who work for me." This statement is a start in recognizing the deep sources of his weaknesses as a manager.

What can be done with executives like Bill Flechette who are extremely resistant to self-awareness and change? Even as we make a case for working hard to help executives develop, we must admit that Bill represents a class of executives who, for practical purposes, can be beyond reach. For these individuals to stand a chance of developing further, they require an infusion of time and energy that exceeds what many organizations are prepared to invest. Even with a heavy investment over a long time, the prognosis is uncertain. One's best choice may be to reconcile oneself to the flawed striver-builder by calling upon an extra measure of empathy. Although it may be difficult, the Bills of this world can actually be seen as more or less sympathetic figures when one realizes the poignant vulnerability that lies behind their vigorous defenses.

It is a loss when an organization writes off an executive who is in fact salvageable. But it is no less a loss when the organization persists in throwing resources at an executive who is impenetrable. The trouble is, it can be devilishly difficult to tell the difference. Executives who seem like extremely doubtful candidates for a turnaround can surprise you. So don't persist in trying to do the impossible, but at least give flawed and talented people a fair chance to come to terms with themselves.

Chapter Three

Why Some Managers Don't Get the Message

Of all the challenges that executives face, one of the most difficult, as we saw in Bill Flechette's case, is knowing where they stand. So much about their high position — and even their psychological makeup — deprives them of good information about how they are doing. Organizations being what they are, executives have enough trouble simply finding out what people think of their plans and decisions. Yet even this is much easier than getting reactions to *how* they make decisions.

To appreciate the value of this kind of personal information, it may help to think of the executive as a kind of musical instrument, and the executive's job as making the best use of this instrument. This may seem mechanistic, but it illustrates the notion that, to be effective, executives must be able to call upon all the resources available to them — their knowledge, expertise, experiences, interests, and drives. To learn to play better, executives need information about how well they currently perform.

The actor Jack Nicholson says he "tunes" himself by attending to "what's actually happening inside . . . [by] locating

29

the tensions, the tiny tensions, the problems with your instrument that can get in the way of getting into the role."[1] Executives face an analogous challenge of identifying and dispelling the problems that can interfere with performing their roles. Can they tap into the precise capability required in a given situation? Or, knowing their limitations, can they marshal that capability in someone else?

Knowing what their instrument can do enables executives to capitalize on their strengths, just as knowing what it cannot do makes it possible to limit the damage done by their weaknesses. Self-aware and reflective executives do not simply accumulate knowledge and expertise; rather, they call upon the right capabilities at the right time.[2] Such executives perform more effectively because they adapt better to the particular situation; they are more flexible. The more aware they are of what they can and can't do, the better able they are to deploy themselves in an enlightened way.[3]

Because such self-awareness is so important, the key question that executives must ask themselves about their instrument is: "Am I kidding myself about how well I play?" It is easy for executives, with their high aspirations for themselves, to imagine that they are better than they are. This in turn makes it easy for them to rationalize the criticisms they do get. Thus, as important as it is for executives to "know their instrument," there are many obstacles to such knowledge.

The chief factor blocking helpful feedback to anyone in an organization is the near universal norm that inhibits people from telling other people what they really think of them. The norm functions as a defense against the anxiety practically everyone feels about "getting personal" with someone else, especially when the message is critical and when much is riding on the judgment being rendered.

To this condition affecting everyone is added the executive-specific condition of holding a highly placed position. As much as the executive needs positional power to meet the challenge of the job, the difference in power and status between the executive and his or her subordinates can easily inhibit the flow of feedback. The more sharply this difference is drawn, the greater the inhibition.

How Power Inhibits Criticism

The perceptions, critical or otherwise, that others may have of an executive are based on their relationship with the executive, their own personality, their organizational interests, and their view of the world. It is up to the executive to sort through such personal input to determine its validity, just as he or she would do with input of a business-related nature. But even allowing for the judgments the executive must make about such characterizations, we are left with the question: Will the executive put him or herself in a position to discover a need for change? Several factors related to elevation and power bear on the executive's chances of getting useful personal criticism. They are: isolation, exemption from feedback mechanisms, and the executive's use of power and pressure to support an image.*

Isolation. Executives no doubt need to stand somewhat apart from the organization to keep from being besieged by requests, demands, and interruptions and to develop a sense of the whole. But the organization does executives a disservice if it sets them too far apart in rank, privilege, and location. This is because structure and physical setting exert a profound influence on patterns of interaction.[4] Yet just when the need to build and maintain a network of contacts becomes critically important, executives are placed in settings that militate against this networking function. In this way, they can lose touch with potential sources of personal feedback. As one human resources executive remarked, "When you're a manager, you develop a set of people you can get feedback from — a web, a grapevine. But as you rise in the hierarchy, it withers, and by the time you get to the top, it's dead." An experienced director of human resources development observed, somewhat cynically, "Most executives have very few people they have contact with — twenty or thirty people in a 20,000-person organization, and those people tend to be high-level executives who also tend to be isolated."

*The following section of this chapter draws heavily on R. E. Kaplan, W. H. Drath, and J. R. Kofodimos, *High Hurdles: The Challenge of Executive Self-Development* (report no. 135). (Greensboro, N.C.: Center for Creative Leadership, 1985).

When executives do have contact with people outside this small sphere, the meeting often takes place in the executive suite, with its trappings of power. This makes it virtually certain that subordinates will feel too uncomfortable to deliver critical messages to the boss.[5]

Isolation is not a condition entirely of the executive's making, but executives are responsible for the managerial life they choose to lead within that environment. One human resources director faulted senior executives for cutting themselves off: "Too many top executives stay cloistered and sequestered."

Exemptions from Feedback. Performance appraisal is a formal mechanism designed by many organizations to make it easier for boss-subordinate pairs to give and receive feedback on performance. This mechanism is not well used at any managerial level, but it is especially neglected at senior levels.[6] I continually work with executives who claim that over the course of a twenty- or thirty-year career they have never had a complete appraisal. A senior human resources manager noted that in his highly respected company there is "an inverse relationship between the quality of the [appraisal process] and organizational level. We do it better at lower levels than at higher levels." An executive said, "You rarely if ever get a performance review at this level or anywhere near this level." Another human resources professional, speaking of an executive in our study, told us that executives in his company got no feedback from above: "Top managers in this company don't confront; never in this world would that happen at this level."

Executives don't tend to receive performance appraisals because the organization seems to grant them immunity from being subjected to this sort of close scrutiny. Or if they are scrutinized, they are not told about it in detail or to their face. A consultant articulated the prejudicial attitude of some executives toward appraisal: "You talk about performance appraisal at the executive level! Unh-uh. That's for 'you folks' down there."

A top executive may set the tone for the whole company by ducking the requirement or by meeting it in such a way that the process is subverted. One executive described how his superior, the CEO, responded to the requirement: "We have a pretty good performance appraisal system, but there aren't appraisals for the top people. And, come to think of it, it's because of the chairman—he doesn't like to do them. He *thinks* he does them. I've had performance reviews, but they've always been at bars after a game of tennis. And the next day neither one of us remembers what was said."

If top executives excuse themselves from giving bona fide appraisals, who in the organization has the clout to enforce the system? Those in charge of the appraisals are usually the human resources managers, who are at least one level (and often several levels) below the CEO, and whose interest lies in staying on the good side of senior managers.

Some other formal feedback mechanisms are available in the typical large organization. Surveys for soliciting feedback from a manager's co-workers are more and more widely used. Co-workers respond anonymously to open-ended questions such as: What should the individual stop doing? Start doing? Continue doing? Or co-workers rate the manager on an elaborate set of dimensions. But these mechanisms only work for those executives who actually use them. A human resources executive told us that the entire management team of a major insurance company decided to go through an intensive feedback process run by an outside consultant. But the chairman, who did not solicit feedback on his style, elected not to participate. No one on the team was about to go to the mat with him over his decision. Ultimately, it was his prerogative.

Use of Power and Pressure. Naturally, position and status make a difference. The senior executive must recognize the fact that "all responses to his actions and to himself are filtered through the knowledge that he is in supreme command and in a position to control careers and occupational lives, [so subordinates are] circumspect in their dealings with him."[7] How such power is used makes a big difference. Many executives use power in their direct dealings with people in a way that discourages feedback. They push too hard, control the interaction too much, or simply abuse their power by attacking, insulting, or humiliating their subordinates.

Executives who intimidate people by what they say or simply by the way they carry themselves can stamp out direct feedback completely. One extremely successful participant in our study had a power-oriented and somewhat forbidding leadership style; few subordinates would take him on. A direct subordinate in good standing said, "It's easy to back off from telling him anything because his manner can scare you." Another participant in the study also tended to react against criticism of his ideas, to say nothing of his behavior. A peer said about him, "Getting feedback to him is hard for people to do. Very few people would feel comfortable criticizing him." A subordinate added, "The message is: 'I'm your boss. I criticize you, but you're sure not going to do it to me.'"

Executives may use power, sometimes unconsciously, to create an idealized myth of themselves and to get subordinates to believe it. And subordinates may be all too willing to believe. They are dependent on the executive and want to be in his good graces and are therefore well disposed to join their boss in a "delusionary system"[8] in which their illusions about him come to match his illusions about himself. This is the kind of collusion portrayed in the fairy tale "The Emperor's New Clothes." In one interview we got a brief real-life example of collusion: "There is a kind of pact of admiration. . . . You only say good things about this guy. . . . It's kind of like being in a king's court. . . . There's kind of a conspiracy that way."

Collusion to support an unrealistically favorable image is not always the executive's doing. Out of a desire to ingratiate themselves with their superior or because they want to reassure themselves that their boss can handle anything, subordinates can take the lead in mythologizing the boss. This can easily tempt the executive into believing he has virtually no faults. The subordinates of one executive in our sample admired him so much that they saw almost no weaknesses in him. One subordinate said, "I wouldn't feel right criticizing him." The executive himself saw through some of this: "My biggest problem with [a particular subordinate] is that he takes my suggestions too seriously."

Not all subordinates are so innocent and appreciative. Although they give their superior what he so badly wants, they do so from their own ulterior motives. In Shakespeare's *King*

Lear, two of Lear's daughters, Goneril and Regan, manipulated their father by pretending to be devoted to him when he was about to settle the issue of how to divide his kingdom among his three daughters. When his third daughter professed her genuine love for him but with equal honesty told him that she could not be *more* devoted to him than to the man she was about to marry, Lear disinherited her. The Duke of Kent, an early version of an organizational development consultant, warned Lear of the danger "when power to flattery bows."[9] For his trouble Kent was banished from the kingdom. As soon as Lear surrendered power, Goneril and Regan turned on him and in the end even refused him shelter. One of these daughters later explained why Lear had succumbed to flattery: "He hath ever but slenderly known himself."[10]

Similarly, executives can use their power to hire and fire to get uncritical support from their people and avoid being challenged. They may hire people who are too much like themselves. Such mirror-image subordinates are less likely to question the executive's basic assumptions and preferred ways of operating. Executives can ensure that they will be spared real or frequent challenges by hiring dependent individuals, loyalists, cronies, or people who are so beholden to them that dissent is out of the question.

In all, we have identified five ways that power can prevent executives from getting valid, constructive feedback: isolation, exemption from feedback, position in the organization, misuse of power, and collusion with the executive's desired image of him or herself (see Table 1). In these ways executives may end up deprived of input indicating a need for them to change and grow. Nevertheless, even under the generally adverse conditions affecting feedback to the executive, criticism can manage to reach the executive. In the next section we offer some ways to make it happen.

Getting the Message to Executives

The first step is to avoid overemphasizing power differences. Organizations can reduce the gap between executives and other people by locating the executive offices closer to those of other

Table 1. Power and Its Impact on Criticism.

Elements of power	Impact on getting criticism
1. Isolation at the top of the hierarchy	• Network may shrink • Executives cloister themselves
2. Executives' prerogatives	• Executives may be exempted from feedback practices
3. Position	• Subordinates defer because of executives' high position
4. Misuse of power	• Subordinates are reluctant to confront • Subordinates may be actively intimidated
5. Executives' need to be flattered	• Subordinates ingratiate themselves through conscious flattery • Subordinates collude unconsciously • Subordinates put executive on a pedestal • Executives hire in their own image • Executives hire yes-men

managers.[11] Intel, for example, avoids separating senior and junior people by eliminating private dining rooms and other perks.[12] If organizations segregate their top tier less and make sparse use of the trappings of power, then executives become more accessible.

Another approach is to create mechanisms for channeling feedback to executives. Performance appraisal is a prime example. In many organizations it may be simply a matter of applying an existing system to executives. But the key is whether the top executive takes the system seriously and uses it personally. For example, Jean Riboud, who has been CEO of the French corporation Schlumberger for almost twenty years, meets once a year with each of his top executives to assess their performance. One of these men, Carl Buchholz, described one such meeting: "[The CEO] said, 'Let's talk about the Buchholz problem.' He talked about my relations with other people and how I ought to improve them. He talked about what he wanted done that wasn't being done. He was quite specific."[13]

There are many feedback mechanisms available to organizations. Attitude surveys are increasingly common. Management development programs with a feedback component are an obvious option, although executives have historically been reluctant to participate. Organizations can even invent their own methods. One international financial organization, for example, conducts inspections of each major unit of the organization. A member of the board of directors heads a team of three, which goes into a division and conducts confidential interviews, the results of which are channeled to the division's top management. The report includes perceptions of the CEO and the top management team. Another corporation uses an outside consultant who knows the organization and has the respect of many people in it as a kind of ombudsman. He keeps his ears open and regularly reports criticisms of top management back to those concerned.

The people surrounding a given executive can also play an important role in providing feedback. Although in a distinct minority, certain individuals in the executive's world do have the courage to tell the executive about his or her shortcomings. A subset of these have the skill to pull it off. One executive talked about "the constructive critics who care enough about the organization and the person to help him and tell that person how his behavior is impacting on the organization. Those [people] helped me to understand myself better." In addition to associates at work, spouses are in a position to know and advise the executive on a personal basis, if the individual is willing to sit tight for this kind of counsel.

Perhaps the crucial factor is the executives themselves. Are they willing to have their behavior and motives characterized or criticized? If they want this kind of input, then the first step is to avoid isolating themselves. There is evidence, for example, that more effective general managers have a more extensive set of contacts—and make more adroit use of those contacts—than their less effective counterparts.[14] An observer of the corporate scene commented that "the less secure [executives] really hide, but the more secure ones will step out of their offices or go down to the departments, make it a point to stay in touch." The second step is to avoid assuming that one knows where one stands. Superiors at any organizational level consistently rate themselves more highly than do their subordinates.[15] Management professor Chris Argyris plays a little game to show executives how likely they are to be laboring under an illusion. First he asks them whether they know what their subordinates think of them. Generally they say yes, they do know. Then he asks them whether their own superiors know what they, the executives, think of *them*. This time the executives answer no, their superiors don't know. The point is made.[16]

Finally, if executives want input of this kind, they must actively seek it. It is a serious error to assume that no news is good news. One tactic is to attend to subtle cues. One CEO said, "You've got to learn to read very subtle complaints." If executives want more than signals, they must actively solicit reactions. In doing so, they must convince others of their sincerity in asking for it. Having invited input, they must manage to be receptive to it when they get it, even if it isn't what they wanted to hear. As a CEO said, "People have to be sure they're being asked honestly and that what they are going to get back is not a Louisville Slugger." If an executive kills the first messenger, he or she will have a difficult time finding others.

Ego and Resistance to Criticism

Executives must believe in themselves. They must have confidence in their capabilities because so much is riding on the judgments they must make day after day. A measure of humility is desirable in executives, but they can't afford to be plagued by doubts about how to handle a challenge. Referring to political and military leaders, Peter Drucker went so far as to say: "To be more [than mediocre] requires a man who is conceited enough to believe that the world . . . really needs him and depends on his getting into power."[17]

So a conviction of one's value is an occupational requirement for managers in highly responsible positions. A modicum of conceit or a modest narcissistic streak may be helpful (or even necessary) if senior managers are to face down the critics around them, as well as the critic within, when it comes time to step into the breach. But when does robust self-confidence laced with a certain cockiness cross the line and become arrogance? When does a strong sense of the rightness of one's way turn into self-righteousness? Where, in short, does one draw the line?

However fine the line, when a manager goes from having self-confidence to having a big ego, there are serious consequences, not only for that person's performance but also for his or her ability to learn from experience. Indeed, the size of an executive's ego is perhaps the biggest determinant of whether he or she can benefit from criticism. Executives who "believe their own press releases," as the saying goes, tend to be unreceptive to criticism. One senior person made the sweeping comment that "executives are susceptible to believing in their own infallibility. They think they can do no wrong." The power and status of high position, together with the knowledge of the steep ascent to that position, no doubt feeds the sense of self-importance. Along this line an executive commented, "As you grow in authority and responsibility, your confidence increases, and that can be good or bad. You can become fatuous and think you don't make mistakes."

Information about the way they behave as managers can benefit executives only if they accept it. Obviously, they don't swallow such input whole, nor should they. As with information of any kind, they should discriminate, consider the source, and make allowances for the kind of relationship they have with the person giving the criticism. But if they do not come to see the need for change that others see, then the input has gone for naught.

There are two especially important ego defenses that can prompt executives to reject potentially useful criticism: the need for self-justification and the need to appear competent. Both of these are characteristic, to one degree or another, of expansive character.

The Need for Self-Justification. Executives justify themselves and their actions out of their strong belief in their capabilities and their particular approach to leading and living. The expansive executive behaves pragmatically—to get the job done—but also, in a sense, ideologically—out of a conviction that his or her way is the right way. Actions and beliefs interact. Basic assumptions about oneself and the world give rise to actions, and, conversely, the way one chooses to act gives rise to rationales for those actions. In some cases where the line between rationales and rationalization becomes blurred, the individual adheres to his or her beliefs rigidly and may even regard them as the only right ones. This self-protective moral absolutism makes it difficult for the individual to give credence to criticism that challenges these bedrock beliefs.

A newly appointed and young general manager in our study, when confronted with the view that he made decisions too slowly, said, in effect, that he wasn't slow but deliberate and thorough. He argued that his way was really the only way to make decisions effectively. A superior said to us, "I told him that his division had analysis paralysis. He was defensive—said they had a lot to do."

Another manager also made liberal use of self-justification. On one occasion he told us belligerently, "I'm very difficult, and I feel it's justified." At another point he said, "Yeah, I am hard to influence. Maybe I've got a problem and I can't recognize it, but when a guy won't give me what he's supposed to, I'm going to be hard to influence." This manager's inability to accept criticism was captured by one of his peers: "It would be to his advantage if he were more willing to be open-minded and consider criticism. I've been there when he's had discussions about a problem with his people or his peers. A peer would say something like, 'Your attitude is too abrasive with customers. You drive them away.' And he would answer, 'I disagree with that concept. I am what I am; my way is the best way.'"

In both these cases, the executives became aware of what other people defined as a problem but denied its seriousness because they were so invested in their preferred ways of operating.

The Need to Appear Competent. For an executive to be presented with a legitimate criticism has a two-edged quality: It simultaneously offers the individual a chance to learn, and it takes the individual down a notch. To the extent that an executive is driven by a need to be competent, and to become more so, he experiences well-intentioned criticism largely as a benefit. A colleague of one executive in our study said that the executive's ability to accept feedback was "excellent" and that he was "always willing to examine his cherished beliefs [about how to run the business]." The colleague took this to be "an indication of a secure ego." Another executive was seen as largely open to feedback because of his "humbleness." According to a peer, "He has a less than normal ego [for an executive]. He doesn't spend a lot of his time trying to make himself look good."

But the need to *be* competent is quite different in effect from the need to *appear* competent. The need to appear competent is not just a property of the executive's ego; it is also a response to the pressures placed on the individual. The people around the executive — perhaps especially subordinates — have a stake in the executive's competence. The more realistic among them won't expect the executive to be infallible, but there is always a segment of the organizational population that expects the executive to be perfect or close to it. As someone close to the executive scene said, "Executives in general are not supposed to have problems. They're supposed to be strong and adequate to most situations."

And these expectations occur in a context of high visibility — people are watching. One recently appointed general manager confessed his discomfort with this exposure: "The spotlight is always on you . . . . I'm uncomfortable being the center of attention. I escape to the men's room." Life in a fishbowl heightens the normal human need to save face. Furthermore, because their highly visible position continually draws fire, executives often become thick-skinned. They learn to shrug off a lot of the disparaging comments made about their decisions and about them.

To the extent that an executive is driven by a need merely to appear competent, he or she experiences criticism as a threat. Rather than putting energy into seeking improvement and greater effectiveness, the executive takes a defensive position. The threat to the person's esteem prompts him or her to disown responsibility for problems and to project that responsibility onto others. Bill Flechette is a prime example of this tendency.

In reality, all executives (as well as all human beings) possess a mix of the two motives — the need to attain mastery and the need to project an image of mastery. For that reason they greet criticism with some ambivalence. Whether executives typically come down on the negative or positive side of their ambivalence depends on their inner lives.

When they come down on the positive side, they *actualize* their ambitions for themselves. They continually build up the expertise necessary to perform their increasingly challenging jobs. In this case, their ideals for themselves serve as a kind of beacon of efficacy and success that they approach but never quite reach. By contrast, executives who come down on the negative side of their ambivalence *idealize* themselves — they succumb to the temptation to act as if they are what they wish to be. Self-idealization is a shortcut to the fulfillment of one's ambitions for oneself — a substitute for the hard and sometimes painful business of getting there step by step.

So, should an executive receive useful criticism, various ego needs characteristic of expansive executives can interfere with his or her ability to give credence to it. These include the need to be perfect, the need to justify the value of what one does, and the need to appear competent (see Table 2). The question of what problems executives typically need to face and what can be done to help them overcome their resistance to change is the subject of much of the rest of the book.

Table 2. Ego and the Inability to Accept Criticism.

Ego Needs	*Impact on Accepting Criticism*
1. Need to be perfect (reinforced by others' high expectations of the executive)	• Criticism resisted because the executive feels it's not okay to admit flaws.
2. Need to justify oneself and one's methods	• Executive explains away performance problems. • Executive acknowledges a problem but dismisses its importance.
3. Need to appear competent (exacerbated by the executive's high visibility)	• Criticism is deflected as a threat to the executive's desired image. • The chance to become more competent is sacrificed to preserving one's image as already competent.

Part Two

Getting to the Root
of Performance Problems

Human beings have always employed an
enormous amount of clever devices for
running away from themselves . . . we can
keep ourselves so busy, fill our lives with so
many diversions, stuff our heads with so much
knowledge, involve ourselves with so many
people and cover so much ground that we
never have time to probe the fearful and
wonderful world within. . . . By middle life,
most of us are accomplished fugitives from
ourselves.
                                        —John Gardner

Chapter Four

Character and the Expansive Temperament: Accounting for Performance Problems

Having shown in Part One how difficult it can be for executives to know when and how they are not performing well, we turn now to the sorts of performance problems executives have and why they have them. The why has principally to do with their expansive character. The character type is inherent in upwardly mobile managers but is accentuated by the culture of the organization and the conditions surrounding executives.

What typically goes wrong at senior levels? Another way to ask this is: In what ways can senior people stand to grow and improve? The list of ways executives can get themselves into trouble is a long and varied one:

- Overreaching strategically
- Being risk-averse
- Running roughshod over subordinates
- Being cold and aloof
- Focusing on empire building and other kinds of self-aggrandizement
- Being inordinately concerned with getting ahead

- Not distinguishing clearly enough between high- and low-priority items
- Pushing themselves too hard and burning out
- Pushing their people too hard and burning them out
- Being rigid or difficult to influence
- Being too concerned with status symbols, trappings of power, and the like
- Not delegating enough (especially right after moving up to an executive job)
- Having an inflated sense of their own importance
- Distorting reality to create a favorable impression
- Generally lacking integrity

I could go on. But rather than compile an exhaustive list, let's try to account for performance problems such as these. Each of them can be — and usually is — dealt with separately. Instead of attacking them in piecemeal fashion, however, we prefer to take a unified approach — one that defines them in terms of the basic character and motivations of typical executives. To be sure, these performance problems reflect various individual skills and skills deficits, but even these we see as resulting, in the long run, from powerful underlying drives.

Let's look at the inability of executives to empower their subordinates, for example. More and more people are getting on the empowerment bandwagon, and rightly so. The argument is that if today's institutions want commitment and creativity from their people, it is vital to give employees their own heads. The manager's job is to "lead others to lead themselves."[1] Increasingly, we hear of employee involvement, autonomous work teams, fewer layers of supervision, high-performance work systems, and the like. Few senior managers argue with this trend philosophically. Quite a few, however, have trouble playing their part in empowering their own people. Bill Flechette, as we saw, is one such individual. While there was no single thing he did to diminish his subordinates' autonomy, there was a steady stream of ostensibly little things he did or said that reminded everyone: "I'm in charge around here."

When senior managers prove to be unable to turn over

the appropriate amount of control to their people, it is tempting to try to remedy the problem by honing the offending manager's skills. But skill deficiencies are often merely a symptom and should not be confused with the cause, which is reluctance, rooted in the person's character, to give up control. Bill Flechette talked a good game about sharing power, and no doubt believed in his own stated principles, but his emotional need to be the top dog kept him from consistently acting on his good intentions. Worse yet, his deeply felt beliefs on the subject led him to take offense when anyone suggested that, in a given instance, he had taken inordinate control. As with many other executives, character, not skills, lay at the bottom of Bill's difficulty with empowerment.

In fact, the difficulties executives cause *and* the good they do spring in large part from the same source: their highly specialized natures as human beings, which are further shaped by their present situations. It may go without saying for some readers that character is a potent influence on the way a senior manager runs an organization. However, this idea is not well established in the field of management development, and some scholars have recently challenged the assumption that a manager's disposition makes much, if any, difference to the organization. Their argument is that external factors, most notably the environment, swamp any impact that personal characteristics might have.[2] Yet people in top jobs are the type who go to great lengths to ensure that their organization will accomplish its objectives. Such individuals are also quite capable of going too far.

For better and for worse, executives play a highly specialized part in our society. To understand their character better, it is instructive to first consider briefly what the specialized role consists of. Just what is the executive job?

The Executive Job

No executive job exists apart from its incumbent, but we can abstract the functions an executive must perform and the capabilities he or she needs to perform those functions. The thing that stands out most about a senior job is how much responsibility the incumbent bears. Broadly speaking, this heavy responsibility comes down to two basic functions — setting the organization's aspirations and mobilizing the organization to meet them. We don't mean that senior managers perform either function single-handed, but the very fact that they must, in some sophisticated way, call upon both their own resources and those of the organization's members is some measure of the challenge inherent in the job.

To set an organization's aspirations is to chart its course. This executive function has to do with looking for opportunities and positioning the organization to seize them. It has equally to do with recognizing diminishing opportunities and taking the necessary and often unwelcome steps to cut back. It often involves not so much maintaining the organization — a full-time job in its own right in a big organization — as making new departures that change the way the organization relates to the outside world.

We use the word "aspirations" purposely, because to set direction for an organization is not simply a cognitive exercise in which brain power is applied to information to reveal a promising way to go. Setting direction also has a strong component of emotion. The end point, the destination, becomes something people in the organization *want* to reach.

Having participated in a process of setting aspirations, the executive faces the very considerable task of mobilizing the organization to meet those aspirations. In practical terms, executives must not only set strategy but implement it. The strategy could be to fix the organization, build it, systematize it, milk it, start it from scratch, revitalize it, and so on. Implementation is a matter of making the strategic idea operational by finding ways to move the organization in the desired direction.

Executives put strategies into operation by reducing them to projects and activities of various kinds. They also practice an admirable kind of opportunism by taking advantage of impromptu day-to-day events to push their long-term agendas.[3] In addition, they communicate strategy up and down the line in such a way that it excites imaginations. The best institutional leaders have an almost magical ability to turn a phrase and articulate their agenda for the organization graphically, compellingly, memorably.

The sheer numbers of people, running into the hundreds, thousands, and even tens of thousands — coupled with the never-ending stream of problems and opportunities — make it a daunting task to move a large, established organization. A lively intelligence combined with a command of the organization's business is required to condense the myriad of problems, large and small, into something manageable. An extensive network of contacts inside and outside the organization and a facility for influencing individuals and groups are required to reach people's hearts and minds. Because of the large scale and broad scope of many executives' domains, it is easier to *conceive* of a strategy, however shrewd and imaginative, than to maneuver an organization to adopt and act in concert with that strategy. Bright ideas and even grand plans come to naught without founts of energy, persistence, conviction, confidence, and resourcefulness to make them come alive. As John Kotter concluded from his research on senior managers, "Effective leadership in senior management jobs . . . seems to require a tremendous energy level and a deep desire to use that energy for supplying leadership."[4]

Executive Character

If this is the stiff challenge posed by the senior management job, then what sort of individuals are we likely to find holding, and aspiring to hold, this type of job?

Industrial psychologists have come up with answers to this question using psychological tests and assessment center exercises. Jon Bentz, for example, did a longitudinal study of those individuals at Sears who reached executive levels.[5] Comparing these individuals' scores on a battery of tests taken at the start of their careers at Sears with performance evaluations twenty-one years later, Bentz concluded that "executive performance is predicted by a series of personality variables: sociability, social ascendancy, and self-confidence."[6] Bentz called this constellation of traits, which he considered necessary for someone to be effective in an executive job, "competitive leadership." Individuals exhibiting competitive leadership were "persuasive and self-assured, aggressive in moving into a central role, confident, catching on rapidly, moving into action with energy, flexible, having a heightened concern for status, power, and money, and working hard to achieve positions that yield those rewards."[7]

Another longitudinal, predictive study (the Management Progress Study at AT&T) reported, among other things, the impact of personality on career success.[8] The data on personality was collected in 1956 on young AT&T managers participating in an assessment center that administered paper-and-pencil tests but also rated behavior displayed in simulations. Twenty years later, managers who had reached executive levels in the company differed from those who had not in having "better cognitive ability, better organization and planning skills, higher inner work standards, higher need for dominance and ascendance."[9] In addition they "expected more from their careers" and had "greater motivation for advancement."[10] In the process of taking leadership positions, they had become less nurturant, supportive, and empathic.[11] From these findings one gets a sense that the main elements of the senior manager's personality — ambition, dominance, cognitive ability, certain interpersonal skills — are certainly compatible with the demands of the senior manager's job. Our research simply adds to this picture by rounding it out and giving it depth.

I prefer not to try to understand executive makeup in terms of a person's traits, that is, by looking at whether the person is gregarious, talkative, private, industrious, impatient, strict, self-deprecating, and so on. Instead, I prefer to take a holistic view, one that reveals the coherent pattern that predominates in a person. To describe this unity and the basic motives underlying it, I use the term *character*. Character, then, is the fundamental pattern that unites what might otherwise appear to be a set of disparate traits. It suggests not surface characteristics but a deep unifying structure that encompasses the individual's nature. An individual's character can more readily be reduced to its essence if one hunts for the individual's crowning purpose in life, his or her life plan and life goal.[12] This life goal is typically implicit — something that needs to be carefully inferred by consulting the person's actions and emotional life.

The political scientist Harold Lasswell spoke of a leader's "ruling characteristic."[13] Judging from what seems to matter most to Bill Flechette, we can define his ruling purpose as making himself into a person to be respected and admired — a purpose he pursues by working hard to impress people with his achievements, his rapid career progress, and his superior gifts in general. Thus the array of discrete motivations that play upon the individual — for example, the need to belong, to provide for one's family, to be loved, to maintain one's health and vitality, and so on — can be arranged in a hierarchy, with the ruling drive placed at the top, where it prompts a panoply of lower-order needs.

The Expansive Temperament

Over and over again in our research, my colleagues and I have encountered executives with the type of character I term *expansive*. As I noted in Chapter One, I am using this concept in a special sense as it applies to executives. Expansiveness, in this sense, is all about the drive to mastery — the ambition for it, the willingness to expend great energy in its pursuit, the willingness to push other people hard to attain it, and the hunger for the rewards that come with it. There is also a concomitant resistance to seeing oneself as lacking mastery. The notion of expansiveness is, fundamentally, a theory of motivation. The field of organizational psychology is crowded with theories of motivation, most of which assume that people are rational beings who calculate what is worth investing themselves in. Expectancy theory, for example, points out that the motivation of managers to do their jobs is a function of (a) the outcomes, intrinsic and extrinsic, that they expect from their work and (b) the value they place on those outcomes. This theory seems accurate as far as it goes, but — like with other objectivist theories of motivation — it also seems bloodless.[14] It misses the passion or obsession that expansive individuals bring to their jobs.

The Czechoslovakian novelist Milan Kundera put forth the notion in *The Unbearable Lightness of Being* that for everyone there is an "Es muss sein!"—an "It must be!"—an "overriding necessity" that governs the person's life. "Insofar as it's possible to divide people into categories, the surest criterion is the deep-seated desires that orient them to one or another lifelong activity."[15] Intense drive is exemplified in D. Wayne Lucas, who for the last several years has run the most successful U.S. stable for thoroughbred horses. He has driven himself as hard as a jockey rides a horse in the Kentucky Derby. "He would do without sleep, if he could. For six or seven years, he said, when he switched over to thoroughbreds from quarter horses, he got by on three to four hours a night. He would work out his schedule on a yellow legal pad, budgeting his time for twenty hours a day, seven days a week, allowing thirty minutes for lunch and forty-five minutes for dinner."[16] Lucas has made an informal study of success and discovered that what makes the difference is the "intensity factor." "These people who are extremely successful, whether an Olympic athlete, a baseball coach, or the head of a large corporation, they've got a fire burning in them that the average person doesn't have . . . . The successful person can reach down and get a little extra, and win when the chips are down."[17]

Aggression is inherent in expansive character, a "moving against," as Karen Horney called it.[18] Margaret Thatcher is an excellent example of an aggressive leader. Gail Sheehy's study of her life and leadership revealed how Thatcher's frantically upwardly mobile father propelled her out of her lower-middle-class origins to the position of prime minister, a position that she held for eleven and a half years beginning in 1979. Thatcher's trademarks are phenomenal energy, a strong drive for superiority, an indomitable will, and a fierce, combative instinct. The epitome of the self-made man or woman, she was quoted recently as saying, "I have to fight every day still." She must win, she must prevail, even at the cost of antagonizing others. The attitude toward her, according to Sheehy, seems to be: "You can't help but admire the energy of the engine, but you can do nothing to change its direction."[20]

Expansive individuals like Margaret Thatcher climb to high institutional positions because they thrive on challenge and because they strive mightily to prepare themselves to meet challenges. This leads to the next challenge, and the next organizational level, and so on. Interestingly, in a study of the managers in the AT&T Management Progress Study eight years after the original assessment, another researcher identified a personality type comparable to the expansive type and with a similar label — the "enlarger."[21] The enlarger is the sort of manager who "extended his scope" by seeking out challenges at work and "expanded" himself intellectually by attending courses and getting involved in the community.[22] The enlarger emphasizes "the extension of influence outward."[23] Consistent with their attraction to challenge, enlargers were more upwardly mobile than the rest of the managers in the research sample.

The Absence of Expansiveness

An understanding of what expansiveness is becomes clearer by understanding what it is *not*. For example, Dennis Hassett, one of the characters in Peter Carey's recent novel *Oscar and Lucinda,* lacked the expansive temperament: "His greatest weakness . . . was an excess of detachment from his own life." Although this detachment was something of an asset because it gave him perspective on himself, it ruled him out from consideration as the manager of a glass works. Despite the extensive knowledge about glass Hassett had built up as a hobby, "glass was his enthusiasm but not his passion; . . . he did not care sufficiently. There was something missing from his engine. It could not sustain the uphill grades."[24] James Barber, a political scientist who studied the effects of personality on the way U.S. presidents carried out their jobs, called such a type "withdrawn."[25] (Karen Horney used the word "resigned.")[26] Barber used Calvin Coolidge as a classic example of the withdrawn personality. Coolidge spent much of his time as president staring out of his office window and managed to find time for eleven hours of sleep a day not counting a nap. Unlike expansive individuals, he made a habit of *not* exerting or asserting himself but believed instead in the virtue of patience and leaving well enough alone. Rather than rise to the considerable demands placed on him as president, he shrank from them.

Ronald Reagan seems to provide another counterexample to the expansive type, at least according to the investigative journalist Frances Fitzgerald.[27] While embracing an expansive ideology and vision for the United States, he employed an essentially withdrawn managerial style. He and Margaret Thatcher embraced similar conservative views but differed drastically in how they applied themselves to their jobs. Like Coolidge, Reagan got a full night's sleep supplemented by a daily nap. His pace was leisurely. The memoirs of his close advisers and cabinet members testify to a distinctly disengaged way of relating to people and problems.

Frances Fitzgerald captured Reagan's laid-back style in an article based on those memoirs. According to Donald Regan, first Reagan's secretary of the treasury and then his chief of staff in the White House, "Reagan chose his aides and then followed their advice almost without question. He listened, acquiesced, played his role, and waited for the next act to be written. Rarely did he ask searching questions and demand to know why someone had or had not done something. He just sat back in a supremely calm, relaxed manner and waited until important things were brought to him."[28]

Reagan's passivity was striking in a role that has scope for untold engagement and action. Fitzgerald wrote that "according to Martin Anderson (an election campaign aide and White House staff member), all Reagan's close associates knew about his passivity but they talked about it only rarely among themselves, and never to outsiders . . . . Yet Reagan apparently did not suffer from any sense of inadequacy. According to Regan, he loved his job; he seemed to enjoy everything about it."[29] His passivity also expressed itself in a hands-off posture toward conflict among members of his staff and cabinet. Socially, the pattern was the same: He and Nancy Reagan spent most weekends by themselves. He was, reportedly, close to no one, family members included, except Nancy.

In general, it seems as if Reagan's unwritten psychological code was to have pleasant experiences and avoid the unpleasant. His aides and his wife joined in arranging things so that this need could be met. "His aides did everything possible

to make life easy for the Reagans . . . creating a pleasant, up-
beat atmosphere, and generally insulating them from the hub-
bub of life."[30] Likewise, Nancy Reagan's "main goal in life was
to maintain a charmed circle of peace and security about him."[31]

The same penchant for pleasantness manifested itself in
Reagan's approach to the nation's problems. According to an
article in the *Economist* as he left office, "One secret of Mr. Reagan's popularity—the essence of his magic—was his penchant
for the good news: he told few difficult truths, made few painful demands."[32] Likewise, Elizabeth Drew, writing in the *New
Yorker* at the same point, noted that when Reagan left office "his
disengagement was becoming tiresome as well as worrisome. There
were big problems to get on with confronting" (emphasis added).[33]
His wish to live his own life in a rose-colored bubble was paralleled, it seems, by his attempt to surround the country with an
aura of optimism and prosperity.

To be sure, Reagan had high aspirations for the country,
but the way he went about his job—even considering that he
took a policy-oriented rather than operation-oriented approach—
stands in sharp contrast to the expansive approach. His passivity and relatively lax work ethic represent the absence of
expansiveness.

Elevation: How High Position
Brings Out Expansiveness

The expansive personality can be brought out or intensified by
the senior manager's environment. Every executive is located
in certain settings at work and outside of work, and these settings serve to support or challenge the individual's behavior and
character. For executives a major aspect of this *embeddedness*[34]
is their elevated situation, consisting of high position, high socioeconomic status, substantial power and prestige, and prerogatives and special treatment.[35] Executives sit in the upper reaches
of their organizations and are accorded special treatment that
can amplify already well-developed expansive tendencies or bring
out latent ones. Of course, organizations differ in how much
deference they give their senior people, how many privileges
they bestow, how sharply they draw hierarchical lines, and

whether they treat their executives as a corporate aristocracy. Yet every organization has its own reasonably clear dividing line beyond which the executive enters this special preserve. The line varies from one organization to the next, but generally there is some invisible cutoff point beyond which upper-level managers take their place in the corporate aristocracy. One executive described his passage into the upper echelon this way: "When I joined a subsidiary company of ours in 1979, I was made a vice-president and became an officer. I had been a plant manager. It was obvious to me that in this organization the officer group had an exalted status. They could do no wrong. I found that people down in the organization just didn't feel comfortable to sit down and talk."

Another executive noted the different response — generally, a better response — that he now received: "I get more attentiveness from superiors. I'm listened to more — I also get more respect from industry outsiders. And there is more expectation from subordinates regarding competence."

The executive can easily internalize this sense of being special. Individuals vary a great deal in how susceptible they are to letting special status go to their heads — to developing an exaggerated sense of their own importance, and even of infallibility. One executive described a peer with this kind of arrogance: "He assumed a holier-than-thou attitude, an air of royalty. He was really strong on that 'I'm the boss; don't question me.' Matter of fact, if you questioned him twice, he'd tell you to go look for another job."

In the last example, we don't know how much of the arrogance is attributable to the man's inherent personality and how much to his elevated standing, but we do know that elevation has an influence on character. Some of this influence is good in that it supports executives in their tough jobs. There is no doubt that the power, prestige, and prerogatives of high position — what we call elevation — fortify executives and enable them to meet the leadership challenges thrust upon them. Yet elevation can easily blow expansive tendencies out of proportion.

The social scientist David Kipnis spoke of the "metamorphoses of power" — the transformations that leaders undergo as a result of attaining and holding power.[36] This change can also occur in people on their way up if the organization anoints them as likely eventual executives; this is sometimes referred to as the "crown prince syndrome." The transformation can, for example, take the form of an exalted sense of self-worth. Teddy Kollek, the mayor of Jerusalem for twenty-five years, was said to have changed in this respect over time. According to a long-time associate, "In the old days . . . Teddy didn't have such a big opinion of himself and saw his shortcomings. Since then he has learned to accept that people regard him as something special, something elevated."[37] Elizabeth Drew observed the phenomenon of elevation in presidential candidates: "Despite the strain, campaigning for the presidency, if one has enough success, is intoxicating, and it's difficult to walk away from the crowds, the cheers, the acclaim, and even the comforts of limousines and Secret Service protection. Like addicts, candidates come to need a regular shot of adulation. Candidates don't have to get airline tickets, or wait at gates; they don't even stop at stoplights."[38]

Kipnis's major argument is that "the continual exercise of *successful* influence changes the powerholder's views of others and himself" — a transformation that is most dramatic in the holders of very high position.[39] As Kipnis pointed out, the Greek tragedians portrayed vividly how heads of state could be swept away by a sense of their own importance and could, simultaneously, devalue the opinions of others and become impatient with disagreement.[40] The result in modern organizational life is that if the manager already has bad habits, they may get worse; or if the manager had been relatively free of such habits, he may suddenly develop them. On the other hand, a manager who before had lacked a commanding presence might emerge with the extra measure of expansive thrust needed to carry off the senior job.

Thus, the executive job and the career track leading to the executive job carry with them expectations for the very sort of expansiveness that no doubt leads individuals to seek high positions in the first place. The executive subculture (along with the culture of the institution itself) reinforces expansive tendencies by encouraging and rewarding people for being hard workers and high achievers.[41]

Another factor that bears on expansiveness is stage of adult life. As Daniel Levinson and his colleagues have shown in their study of forty men in four different occupations, the drive to establish oneself in the world is especially pressing in the first half of adulthood.[42] One's twenties, thirties, and forties can be a period of nearly ceaseless striving to enter a chosen field, master it, and achieve a measure of success in it. It is only later (typically in one's forties), when one has either realized one's dream or seen that one never will do so, that one begins to pull back on the heavy investment in achievement, mastery, and career success in favor of other aspects of life.

The Value of Expansiveness for Executives

It makes sense that the expansive temperament is strongly represented in the executive population. To be expansive is to possess a very considerable drive to achieve and to advance. The executive job requires someone who can move an organization forward by overcoming the inertia inherent in any institution. Expansive people and executive jobs are made for each other. To propel an organization, executives need more than the power that comes with their high position. They need personal power. This is where the expansive temperament comes in: It provides the raw energy and thrust needed to have an impact.

All the talk in recent years of the need for true leaders as opposed to mere managers underlines the premium now placed on people who can bring about major change in organizations. The distinction between leadership and management is artificial because leadership — the ability to effect change — is required, to one degree or another, in all managers. However construed, though, the new priority on making change means that expansive executives are indispensable as prime movers.

Expansive executives are a valuable resource because of the way they pour themselves into their work. The main character in Saul Bellow's novel *Henderson the Rain King* explains himself at one point by saying, "If I don't get carried away I never accomplish anything."[43] *Leaders must get carried away.* Even in the best case, to be expansive is to go too far in some way or at some time. It is too much to expect high-powered individuals to be finely calibrated at all times. Some price has to be paid for consequential acts of leadership. Something is sacrificed, whether leisure, or health, or organizational stability.

But there is an important line to be drawn between largely effective expansive executives who go to productive extremes and significantly flawed expansive executives who go to destructive extremes. In the one instance, there are certain *necessary* losses occasioned by the exercise of leadership by high-powered human beings. In the other instance, there are *unnecessary* losses, serious ones, caused by excessive ambition. The sorts of performance problems itemized at the beginning of this chapter and those we saw in Bill Flechette issue, to some considerable degree, from excessive self-concern. This connection between distorted leadership and excessive self-concern may be more apparent if we turn to the case of another executive, Rich Bauer.

Chapter Five

The Impact of Character
on Leadership:
The Rich Bauer Story

Everyone knows that the way a supervisor supervises is, in part, a reflection of his or her personality. What is less well understood is how the makeup of a particular executive is reflected in the way he or she leads the organization. To further develop the idea of expansive character and how it is expressed in executive leadership, we include here a chapter-length case study of a senior manager. The case is useful in conveying concretely the general nature of expansive character and in defining another type of expansive executive. In Chapter Two we had an example of the striver-builder. Here is an instance of the self-vindicator/fix-it leader.

Rich Bauer is a high-ranking manager whose assets and liabilities clearly seem to be tied to his character as a human being. Rich is, in general, an expansive executive — ambitious, hardworking, influential — but he is also, in particular, a self-vindicating individual who specializes in turnaround leadership. In this way he represents another variation on the theme of expansiveness. In contrast to the striver-builder, whose reason for being is to live up to high expectations placed upon him or her, the self-vindicator/fix-it leader's reason for being is to *live down* a poor reputation foisted upon him or her early in life. Both types are driven individuals, but they differ fundamentally in how their basic drive is shaped and how it, in turn, gives a distinctive contour to their leadership specialties.

We met Rich Bauer through his company's human resources vice-president, who thought that Rich was ready — at midlife and midcareer — to do the sort of sweeping stock-taking that our action research offered. Having recently been elevated to a key executive slot, Rich Bauer's star shone brightly in the organization. No hint of career trouble led him to consider the program. After years of concentrating on the "hard" (performance-oriented) variables, he felt it might be time to take a greater interest in the "soft" (people-oriented) variables.

For a year after his feedback session, my colleague (a clinical psychologist) and I stayed actively involved with Rich in a coaching capacity, during which time our relationship with him went from stiff and businesslike to comfortable and relatively warm.

Rich's Leadership

Richard Bauer is senior vice-president and general manager of the most vital and fastest-growing division of his corporation, a long-established company that started out as a supplier to other companies and later also entered the consumer market. Over the course of his career, which has consisted of a series of assignments on the manufacturing end with a couple of broadening jobs thrown in, Bauer has consistently produced good business results. On the strength of his track record and his good relations with the CEO, the chairman, and the vice-president of human resources, he is, at the age of forty-two, a candidate to become CEO within the next ten years, provided that he continues to grow as a corporate leader.

What is the secret to his success? How has he achieved good business results and become an executive whose stock is currently so high? The answer is his special talent for the turnaround.

Rich's specialty is shaping up poorly performing organizations. He is gifted at quickly understanding what ails an organization and doing whatever is necessary to restore its health. The CEO speaks for a lot of people in saying, "What gets to Rich is an organization that *falls short* of standards of excellence, businesswise. He energizes a *'This-isn't-good-enough'* approach. In the business he's running now, Rich is bringing leadership under the banner: 'We have to do better'" (emphasis added). It's almost as if he is offended personally by inadequate work. In the view of his other superior, "What galls Rich the most is subpar performance."

Rich has built his career on the strength of eye-catching turnarounds. As one peer said, "The turning point in his career, when he first came to the full attention of top management, was an assignment as plant manager of the worst problem plant." Several people telling Rich's story recall this job as pivotal in his rise to the top. He was able, as one person said, to "rebuild the morale of the plant" in timely fashion. By demonstrating to his superiors that he was a guy who could save the day, he greatly increased his value to the organization.

Beyond the inherent value of turning around a failing organization, Bauer seems to be personally energized by what's gone wrong in an organization. He is acutely sensitive to dysfunction and has a visceral need to rectify it. His oldest child, a daughter in her first year of college, described revealingly this core aspect of her father's leadership style: "He's always gone in and *found out what's wrong* and turned the plant upside down. He leads by *attacking what's wrong*. When he goes into a plant, he finds out *what isn't working* and puts a lot of energy into *putting it right*" (emphasis added).

If attacking what's wrong is the secret to Rich's success, it is also inevitably the source of the difficulties he creates for the organization. His daughter provided a clue to his problematic side in the telling phrase "turned the plant upside down." While management may welcome the outcome, those people *inside* the plant being upended feel the disruptive effects of his actions.

As Rich Bauer goes about the job of fixing an organization, his use of power stands out above all. Power is written all over him. His physical presence radiates power. It emanates from his big, muscular frame—he played defensive tackle on his college football team. His voice booms. His facial expression is usually impassive. A former subordinate reeled off a series of phrases to describe Rich's power-oriented style: "Rich is a very assertive person. He sells in the extreme. He's authoritative and commanding. You hear lots of 'I want this.'" Another subordinate said, "He can be gruff and direct, and he's not afraid to use his position." His daughter saw the same quality in him both at work and at home: "He lets people know in no uncertain terms what he expects of them. He's demanding."

Intent on rooting out problems, Rich can be severe with people. He is quickly angered by problems and by any delay or incompetence in solving them. A subordinate said about him that "if things aren't done right, he gets upset." He will "pound the desk with an element of intimidation." His wife had seen the same approach with the children: "He plays hardball with the kids when they displease him or when they don't measure up. He means business. He's so authoritative as to be frightening." The way his son put it: "He doesn't play games [when it comes to addressing misbehavior]." Rich's brother teases him by calling him "the cosmic ass kicker" and by telling him that he "kicks ass, takes no prisoners, and shoots the wounded." In a bit of self-mockery that was in character, his choice of costume for a Halloween party was—Darth Vader!

But let us not overdraw the dark aspect of his leadership. His severity is tempered for many people by the fact that "he's a good, decent guy." People trust him. What someone called his "impeccable character" showed up dramatically on one item in his managerial ratings: Every single one of the twenty-three people rating him indicated that he definitely had integrity and was trustworthy. His use of power is also tempered by the underlying warmth and goodwill that people close to him can detect. A peer said, "He gets mad, but he gets over it quickly. It's his father image, he gets mad but he still loves you." A number of people who know him reasonably well commented on the contrast between his outward behavior and his inner warmth. A typical comment was: "He's an authoritative executive type, but there's a pussycat inside that tempers the authoritative demeanor."

   Still, his approach takes a certain toll on people not able
to see past his gruff exterior. These include individuals who feel
insecure organizationally, such as those just starting their careers
in this highly competitive culture, who have only occasional contact with him and therefore haven't accommodated to his style.
The problem is compounded because now that his office is on
the top floor his shyness combines with the physical separation to
make him a remote figure. A superior aware of Rich's impact
said, "There are people in his organization who are scared to
death of him . . . . He can be quite intimidating." It is not hard
to imagine feeling intimidated at the prospect of walking into
his office to present a proposal. It was well known that "he gets
angry if recommendations are not carefully thought through,
so recommendations are presented in an atmosphere of fear."
The trick is to stand up to him, as he prides himself in standing
up to his own superiors, but some people cannot do it.

   One subordinate summed up his style: "Rich Bauer rules
by fear and not by love." This pithy statement pinpoints the
missing piece in Rich's style. He isn't supportive. Another subordinate put his finger on it: "There's a gap in his leadership. He
leads negatively. *He points the way but he doesn't support people as
they try to follow his lead*" (emphasis added). In the organization's
parlance, he "sets the bar high—but it was their job to jump
over it." He makes demands, but he doesn't coach or encourage
people as they struggle to meet his demands. Someone several
levels below him complained that "the problem is his negative
leadership. He only knows how to make demands. He doesn't
know to express faith in people."

   How does this negative leadership hurt him? In a word,
people become demoralized or don't give their best effort. Two
items on the managerial ratings were especially telling: Rich
got low scores on "bringing out the best in others" and on being
able "to inspire and motivate people." The several people who
indicated a need for improvement on both items included his
direct subordinates. Unaware of his impact, he rated himself
as doing well at these things. After seeing the scores he acknowledged that "the only way I know how to build morale is to drive
the individual and organization towards high accomplishment.

I don't know how to build morale by giving incremental approval . . . . I take pride in doing it with substance as opposed to superficiality. *People feel good because they've done good, not because they've been told they are good"* (emphasis added).

In fairness to him, let's recognize that his leadership is effective for many people. His outstanding track record is evidence of that. A subordinate explained, "He's distant and negative, yet lots of folks have felt challenged to put out. The good thing is that in a macho company like this, most folks respond by taking the extra step. The evidence is progress in results."

Subordinates like this one, whom he respects and who have access to him, learn to accommodate to Rich's approach. They read between the lines for signs of his esteem and support. The trouble comes with subordinates lower down in the organization who are not in regular contact, and especially with those whose competence he questions. Rich disapproves of faulty work to be sure, but he also tends to discredit people whom he perceives as inadequate in any way, including those who have an unaggressive style. He showed some awareness of his elitism in talking about how he rewards subordinates: "I reward the top performers — the top 10 percent. I need to do better with the 30–40 percent below the top tier."

A subordinate two levels down saw clearly how Rich discriminated between people: "He judges people as having it or not, and if you don't have it, he'll be less likely than usual to support you, and he might well relieve you of your job." He can at times actually contribute to the inadequate performance of marginal people. A relatively timid subordinate whom he inherited "set up his files and positioned his department defensively against Rich," which distracted him from his job and contributed to his failure. Another subordinate described Rich as a "good people manager, especially with middle-class overachievers" — but not, the implication was, with underachievers. Other people, including his boss, saw him as not doing as well with "the average performer."

When Rich Bauer turns into an inquisitor who discredits people unfairly, he stops helping and starts hurting his cause. A subordinate who replaced a failed predecessor commented that "he's got high standards, and if others don't meet them, he'll clean house, even if it gets him a reputation as an SOB." To the extent that, as many people believe, he gets rid of dead-wood, he performs a service to himself and the organization. To the extent that, as a few others believe, he gives up prematurely on potentially good people whose performance withers under his negative judgments, he performs a disservice.

Further evidence of Rich's elitist discrimination came from the following contrasting comments. A protégé three levels below Rich said, "He cares about people who work for him. He has made a point of keeping up with my progress." Yet a former subordinate who performed well (but was not a protégé) complained, "I sensed a low interest in training or tutoring me and in me personally. He loaded projects on me, but I didn't get any help from him."

Rich's motive for exercising power is one shared by Bill Flechette and expansive executives generally. A peer made this perceptive comment about why Bauer prefers to take a hands-on approach to the decisions that matter to him: "He needs to be in control. He doesn't like the uneasy feeling of not knowing how it will turn out. He knows where he wants an issue to go, though he's willing to change his mind if major information comes out. . . . But he's not willing to go in and not know which way he wants to go and just shoot an idea around." Rich acknowledged in the feedback session that he frequently goes to meetings with his mind made up.

The same thing happens in his relationship with his children. He is so keen on having them turn out right that he over-controls them, even to the point of interfering in their choice of careers. In the process, he jeopardizes their development as independent people. His daughter: "He wants us not to make what he considers the mistakes he made. I consider it all a growing experience." Ironically, he takes great pride in the fact that he did things his own way, but he is so concerned about his children measuring up that he may deprive them of the same opportunity.

A key fact about Rich Bauer's use of power is that, as was the case with Bill Flechette, he is not fully aware either of his need for power or of its impact on other people. This point is perhaps clearest in relation to his family. He does not fully recognize his tendency to control the lives of his two children. He said, "We try to arrive at decisions democratically." People both inside and outside the family, however, saw him as "clearly father," as "calling the shots," and even as "rigid." His second child, a sixteen-year-old girl, saw his controlling style with her better than he does: "I don't work well when I'm forced to do things."

While he recognized he has more influence than his wife, he sees the two of them as being more or less on a par. She says, "He's the stronger one. Decisions tend to go in his favor." As a matter of fact, they were recently separated for six months because his dominance made it difficult for her to establish her own identity: "I married him because he was strong and he would take care of me. . . . Rich didn't see his power, and I abdicated." Rich got some insight into his need for control in the feedback session: "I feel that I need to be in control. I wonder why . . . . Is there no confidence that things will turn out right?"

In summary, Rich Bauer's leadership has a distinctive signature. He is at his best when an organization is at its worst. Turning around a poorly performing organization requires a strong hand, and Rich has it. What he *doesn't* have is a soft touch. As a result, his leadership comes across as negative. What's missing from his approach is an ability to provide moral support to people under pressure to meet his expectations. Many people perform well under these conditions because they basically trust him and find a way to accommodate to him. But there is an attrition. Some people who might have excelled working for someone else give less than their best or give up altogether.

Power in the service of rectifying what's wrong is Rich Bauer's trademark. Where did this approach come from?

Rich's Upbringing

A stint in the army between high school and college could have contributed to Rich's hard-nosed style. Coming up through the organization in the tough environment of the manufacturing function no doubt also left its mark. Yet a far more powerful influence on the formation of his character, it seems, was his upbringing.

Rich Bauer's childhood was tragic in some respects. His father was an abusive alcoholic whose problem got much worse when Rich, the youngest, was little. Rich described him as "a go-and-binge alcoholic" who was "gone for months at a time." He died when Rich was twelve, but not before he had done a lot of damage: "He beat my mother, and he beat me," says Rich, adding, "To this day, when my mother and sisters talk about him, I find myself on edge."

Rich's mother, along with his two older sisters, alleviated things some, but because she had to support the family, she spent long hours working as a waitress. Rich says, "I have a tremendous amount of respect for the compromises she made in her life for her children." He describes her as "a pillar of strength." But with this strength came "an inability to share emotions"— an inability that he sees himself as inheriting from her. She also expected a lot of her children. According to Rich, he didn't get much praise as a child; "perfect was the only acceptable thing." While not cruel, his mother was critical of him, often about little things such as the way he did his chores. His father was, of course, much worse: "I could never please my father. I can't remember a word of encouragement or praise. It was always supercritical, depreciating of my self-worth." His father's wanton mean streak is evident in Rich's statement: "If I was pleased with something—on the dinner table or on the TV—that was immediately changed." His father would explode at him, way out of proportion to the seriousness of the offense. Note the phrase "depreciating of my self-worth." In words and actions, Rich's father demeaned him. The violence, whether verbal or physical, seared into Rich's consciousness a message of low worth.

To contend with what must have been extraordinary pain, Rich evidently repressed much of this traumatic experience. He reported that "there are only four things I can tell you about [my father], and none of them are good." He downplays the horrific nature of his relationship to his father as well as its destructive effects on him. His posture contrasts with that of one of his sisters, who saw it all happen and who has educated herself on the subject of alcoholism and abuse. "She attributes more things to my upbringing and my relationship to my parents than I do. I may be missing things, but during the time I was with my parents, I didn't feel low self-worth. I just felt unreasonably treated."

Rich went so far as to *credit* his father's rough treatment with helping to make him a success. "I'm not angry with my father. I feel sorry for him and not for me. In a way I'm grateful to him because without him I wouldn't be where I am. It's like the Johnny Cash song, 'A Boy Named Sue.' The boy's father gave him a girl's name to toughen him because he [the father] wouldn't be around." The reference to the song is an indirect acknowledgment of an emotional handicap, which Rich has turned into an asset. It may also be an unconscious admission of anger, even rage, toward his father, since at the end of the song the boy beats his father.

Rich's makeup would seem to be compensatory; that is, he has been moved by his father's treatment to compensate for feelings of low worth. Speaking of her brother, Rich's sister offered this interpretation: "In an abusive home a kid is powerless. So it's common for kids from abusive homes to be power-oriented." As a child Rich was powerless, in general, to do anything about his father's behavior. And, in particular, he was rendered acutely powerless at those moments when his father was violent with him. If, on a continuum of power, physical violence is at the high-power end, then to be victimized by a violent person is at the extreme opposite end. The power that Rich Bauer exudes as a manager and as a man could very well have developed in reaction to his early experience.

Rich's Career

On the surface, Rich Bauer's career tells the usual story of an ambitious and talented young man's rapid rise to the top echelons. On closer scrutiny, his upward mobility also has a significance particular to his character. In a sense, his career has been a setting in which he has, so to speak, whipped himself into shape — just as he has specialized as a leader in whipping organizations into shape. Of course, the parallel extends to his childhood experience of being subjected to abuse from someone who purported to be beating him, by some stretch of the imagination, for his own good.

His very choice of organization set the stage for a drama of self-vindication. A graduate of a little-known local college, he applied for a job at a top company that normally attracted graduates of top-flight universities. He chose a situation that immediately placed him at a disadvantage.

His native ability and record in college got him on the fast track, but he was clearly a dark horse at best. Staying on that track was virtually a matter of life and death psychologically. He bore down: "In my first job I was not doing well. I kept trying to work harder and harder." After a series of rotations through several training assignments, he was intent on getting promoted to foreman. "Three of us who were close friends outside of work had a real sensitivity about being promoted to foreman. It's the first promotion you get. One of my peers got it. It tensed me up. I pushed harder. Then the second one got it. I didn't know if I was going to go or if I just had more to learn. One day my boss called to say, 'You're getting promoted.' I was high as a kite."

This intense regimen was the story of his life for his first half decade with the company. "The first six years I was focused on *survival*. That's how long the extreme pressure lasted" (emphasis added). It was a matter of survival, not just in a career sense, but probably also in a deeper personal sense. After narrowly surviving an assignment with a difficult boss, he went to work for someone who made it possible for him to excel. "I worked day and night . . . . He basically saved my life." "Saved my life" seemingly has significance beyond the casual use of the phrase. His mother, in recalling the early period of his career, also uses a phrase with special significance for Rich: "He was afraid he wouldn't *shape up*" (emphasis added). Note the sense that there was something wrong with him that needed correcting.

Throughout his career he has worked punishingly long hours for extended periods. Upon taking a promotion, he had been known to work ninety hours a week until, a year or two later, he got on top of the situation. When he made plant manager for the first time, he took over a plant that was in bad shape. "I spent the first six months working eighty to ninety hours a week. It just about killed me." He has worked as if his life depended on it. Summing up at one point, he speaks what seems to be the essential truth: "My evolution has been a kind of personal salvation." Note the language of self-vindication and redemption: "survival," "saved my life," "shape up," "personal salvation." (On the same theme, a professor who took an interest in Rich in college described himself as someone who "salvages character." Throughout his career Rich has sent this professor, apparently serving as a surrogate supportive father, press clippings of his promotions.)

The objective reality of Rich's unlikely climb to the top has vindicated him within the organization. Fortunately for him, the subjective reality is also one of having proved himself. "Now I know I'm good." His deliverance came only with stunning success. Speaking of an earlier time, he said that "it wasn't clear I was going to be a superstar." However, he isn't free — nor would one expect him to be — of the old feeling about himself. When he made general manager "faster than anybody had ever gotten to that level," he found himself — as soon as the triumphant feeling faded — feeling "humbled, unprepared, unworthy." So again he placed himself in a position of having to prove himself to erase a feeling of inadequacy.

The Self-Vindicator/Fix-It Specialist

As we have seen in Rich Bauer's case, people of this type are motivated fundamentally by the need to dispel a sense of personal inadequacy. More than anything, they seek to vindicate themselves in their own eyes and in the eyes of others. Their orientation to life attracts them to things that are not working well and motivates them to take corrective action. As managers they make excellent turnaround artists, adept at taking the tough actions necessary to correct failing organizations.

As children, people of this type typically had a parent or parents who actively diminished or mistreated them. They may even have been abused physically. From this mistreatment (or from being at a disadvantage or handicapped in some other way) they developed a sense of themselves as unworthy. As adults they may turn their work and careers into campaigns to dispel the sense of themselves as unworthy.

At their worst, their quest for vindication makes them tough, unrelenting taskmasters who are long on making demands and short on offering support and praise. They tend to be intolerant of anything but the highest performance and focus almost exclusively on what is wrong, even in people and organizations that perform well. Even a smile is a rare occurrence. They never stop pushing, fearing that if they let up, they and others will lose their motivation.

In the better cases, expansive people of this type possess or gain a measure of self-acceptance that allows them to temper their tough, demanding natures with a measure of supportiveness. They develop a better appreciation of what is valuable about people, even those unlike themselves, and reduce the compulsion to root out anything and everything substandard. At the same time, they learn how to channel this drive into selectively improving things that genuinely need improvement.

Having been mistreated or victimized as children, the self-vindicators may compensate for their remembered sense of powerlessness by becoming powerful, even dominant, as adults. But well-adapted individuals of this type overcome their need to dominate and learn how to empower others.

Epilogue

The danger in becoming a skilled specialist is that one may never escape the specialty. Once Rich Bauer established himself as a wizard at his special brand of leadership, management handed him one fix-it assignment after another. In the process he honed his skills and no doubt reinforced his personal predispositions. Yet he may be trapped in his specialty; his superiors are concerned about whether he is well-rounded enough to advance to a top job. What it would mean for him to grow and develop is an interesting issue. It would be more than a matter of changing the script the organization has expected him to follow. It would also be a matter of revising his internal script. It would mean taking a close look at the particular heroic role he has chosen for himself. It is a heroic role that has no doubt served as an antidote to feelings of worthlessness and powerlessness. If he buys the role completely and equates himself totally with it, then from one perspective he has no need to learn, no reason to look behind his superb adaptation to the hurt and defenselessness he experienced as a child. Yet one of his protégés saw things another way: "If he could come out from behind his wall, he would be dynamite." To change the metaphor a bit: For Rich Bauer to grow, the wall between himself and other people — and between himself and his own emotions, particularly his pain — would have to come down, at least partially. No trivial matter.

We will return later to the issue of Rich Bauer's development. In the meantime, we will delve further into the causes and effects of the exceptional drive found in many executives.

Chapter Six

Where Expansiveness Comes From and How It Affects Performance

To make a difference in an organization, executives must be highly motivated — even driven. However, this irrepressible drive is rarely an unalloyed blessing. With the single-minded determination to succeed frequently comes a willingness to sacrifice other considerations — personal, physical, even moral or legal. The temptation to dispense with considerations not directly related to one's objective is related to the intensity of one's drive: With extreme intensity, the price paid for success, in whatever terms, goes way up. I will not pretend that it is an easy matter to distinguish, in high-powered executives, between acceptably high levels of intensity and unacceptably high levels. For one thing, what is acceptable depends in part on what an organization's various constituencies want most and what they are willing to give up.

In this book the concept of expansiveness is defined on two dimensions — *type* of expansive character and leadership and *degree* of expansive intensity. So far we have covered two major types of expansive executive, the striver-builder in Chapter Two and the self-vindicator/fix-it leader in Chapter Five. A third major type will appear in Chapter Eleven. This chapter pivots

74

on the distinction between generally desirable and generally un-
desirable levels of intensity. The two dimensions of expansiveness are related in the fact that each type of expansive executive can operate at varying degrees of intensity. At the end of
the last chapter, for example, we saw that the self-vindicator/fix-it
specialist at his worst operates at excessive intensity and at his
best keeps his intensity within bounds.

The difference between extreme and moderate expansiveness is something practicing managers readily understand. Lee
Iacocca, an expansive executive in his own right, made a parallel distinction in his autobiography between a strong ego and
a big ego: "There's a world of difference between a strong ego,
which is essential, and a large ego — which can be destructive.
The guy with a strong ego knows his own strengths. He's confident. He has a realistic idea of what he can accomplish, and
he moves purposefully towards his goals. But the guy with a
large ego is always looking for recognition. He constantly needs
to be patted on the back. He thinks he's a cut above everybody
else. And he talks down to the people who work for him."[1]

A moderately strong expansive drive reflects a more or
less healthy appetite for mastery. Individuals in this category
could be described as mature. An extremely strong expansive
drive reflects a ravenous appetite for mastery. Individuals in
this category could be described as immature.

Expansive executives vary in how driven they are. Within
a given *type* of expansive executive there is the same variation.
It is the extent of the drive that seems to determine whether
a striver/builder like Bill Flechette or self-vindicator/fix-it specialist like Rich Bauer is at his or her best or worst.

Managers with extreme drives to mastery are responding to an underlying insecurity. Fundamentally, they do not
have a secure feeling of their own worth. For this reason they
are inordinately concerned with performing well and with otherwise demonstrating their value as managers and people. Karen
Horney, in speaking of the "expansive solution" to the problem
of living, showed how incessant striving for mastery indicates
doubt as to one's own worth and is designed to shore up self-
worth.[2] Existentially speaking, the pressing need to amount to

something owes some of its strength to the fear of, in some sense, amounting to nothing. It was said about Lyndon Johnson that "he couldn't stand not being somebody—just could not stand it."[3] In adults, the dread of nothingness may stem from their fear of not fulfilling the destiny thrust upon them as children by loving parents whose feelings for them were always warmest when they did their very best. Or it may stem from the need to avoid feeling worthless and contemptible, as a child can come to feel at the hands of uncaring or punishing parents. It may also be related to what Ernest Becker identified as an understandable rebellion against the human condition—the condition, no matter how celebrated or powerful a person becomes, of being subject to forces much larger than oneself and utterly beyond one's control, especially the condition of being mortal.

In extremely expansive individuals, anxiety about self and self-worth runs so high that the executive has trouble seeing beyond it or caring much about anything or anyone else. Under the sway of this strong self-preoccupation, these executives are prone to overdo things in some respects—and therefore necessarily to underdo them in others. They are very much out of balance. In addition to going to extremes, they tend to be rigid, clinging to what they believe to be the right way to do things and the right way to be.

In his laboratory research on the need for achievement, David McClelland found some evidence to suggest that too much motivation to achieve is detrimental to performance, just as a shortage of motivation also hurts performance. "Neither the subjects with the highest or lowest motivation performed as well as those with moderate motivation."[4] This is the classic "inverted U" relationship between motivation (on the horizontal axis) and performance (on the vertical axis). Managers who reach senior levels rarely have too little achievement motivation, but some have so much that they undercut their performance.

The remainder of this chapter is divided into two sections. The first briefly examines *origins:* Where does expansive character originate, and how, in particular, does it become exaggerated? The second section turns to the *effects* of expansive character, with particular attention to how extreme expansiveness gives rise to the performance problems often found in executives.

Origins of Expansiveness

All human beings are born with an instinct whose function is to ensure their survival — by spurring them to master their small corner of the world well enough to get what they need. This inborn urge is then heightened or dampened by the individual's experience as a child.

Inherited Expansiveness

What we are calling expansiveness starts out at birth as a bundle of drives that is the rough equivalent of the instinct to self-preservation. The way a newborn survives is by making known in no certain terms its needs for nourishment and nurturance. Born into this world in a peculiarly human state of extreme dependence, the infant rapidly increases its capacity to do for itself. The vigor with which a baby shakes a rattle reveals its satisfaction in gaining control of its environment. It has been well established that human beings, like other animals, have built-in aggressive instincts, built-in needs for dominance.[5] Witness the often-repeated episode in which one child yanks a toy away from another. Human beings are also programmed to learn and develop. The child's biological need to gain the skills required to meet its needs — what Robert White termed "competence motivation" — is evident in every young child learning to walk or talk or climb stairs or eat with a spoon.[6]

The basic needs to learn, to accomplish, to dominate can be viewed as components of the still more basic expansive need to develop the capacities necessary to make one's way in the world. The psychologist Kurt Goldstein argued, for example, that "the tendency to actualize [oneself] as fully as possible is the basic drive."[7] Similarly, Ernest Becker has posited a fundamental innate drive that he called "expansive organismic striving."[8] This is not simply the young child's need to become effective but its primitive narcissistic assumption that it is the center of the universe. Its needs come first; its claims supersede those of rivals such as siblings, playmates, or the parent that would presume to interfere with the child's primacy with the other parent. This "natural narcissism," as Becker called it, is vividly familiar to anyone who has spent time with young children and knows their insistent need to be the center of attention and their "prerogatives of limitless self-extension."[9] Children partake of "the pleasures of incorporation and expansion"—that is, of consuming the world and expanding into it.[10] Becker's writing is full of expansive imagery: The child is an organism that strives to *expand* into the world. It gives itself the prerogative to *extend* itself without limit.

Just as children reach out into the world, they defend themselves against it. In particular, the instinct for self-preservation leads the child, once it reaches a certain age, to defend against the knowledge of its own eventual demise. So expansive organismic striving, according to Becker, serves in part to quell fears of being diminished or destroyed: "On the most elemental level the organism works actively against its own fragility by seeking to expand and perpetuate itself in living experience; instead of shrinking, it moves toward more life . . . in this way, it would seem, fear of death can be carefully ignored or actually absorbed in life-expanding processes."[11]

Rather than *shrink* in the face of its dawning sense of its smallness or fragility or mortality, the child follows the principle that the best defense is an effective offense: It renews its efforts to create an efficacious, potent presence in the world.

The sense of smallness and vulnerability that the child contends with is due, in part, to its biological inheritance. Inevitably, even as the child passes from the helplessness of infancy to the advancing skillfulness of early and middle childhood, it is smaller, weaker, less smart, and less skillful than the adults and older children around it. The pioneering psychologist Alfred Adler built his theories on the assumption that childhood places every human being in an inferior position. As Adler put it: "Throughout the whole period of development, a child perceives a feeling of inferiority in both its relationships with the parents and the world at large. Because of the immaturity of his organs, his uncertainty, and lack of independence, because of his need for dependence upon stronger natures and his frequent and painful feelings of subordination to others, a sensation of inadequacy develops that betrays itself throughout life."[12]

The human animal's dependency in childhood is the secret to its exceptional educability. But dependency also poses a developmental challenge, one response to which — according to Adler, the most common — is to compensate by adopting a style of life that puts the individual in a superior position. Influenced by Adler, Becker saw the child's character "as a modus vivendi achieved after the most unequal struggle any animal has to go through,"[13] a style of life that is the individual's effort "to banish the actual fact of his natural impotence."[14] Again, to combat the experience of being made to feel small and weak, the child reacts expansively and becomes motivated to replace its early inferior position with a superior position.[15] Thus, expansiveness would seem to be the product of a biological double imperative — the original expansive striving to ensure one's survival is later augmented by the drive to compensate for the childhood experience of inferiority and the developing fear of annihilation.

Present in everyone, the expansive propensity varies from individual to individual. To illustrate, I will cite the cases of two young children I know well. One, a little girl, has from birth been a live wire. As a newborn her screams were ear-piercing to the point that her grandfather predicted she would grow up to be an opera singer. Now, as a six-year-old, when she wants something, she will not be denied; persistence should be her middle name. If her parents criticize or discipline her, she often fights back, meeting redoubled parental efforts with increasing noise and defiance. If a member of the family laughs at something she does, even if that person is clearly laughing affectionately with her, not at her, she immediately takes offense. This child is the living embodiment of expansive organismic striving, the energetic appetite to learn and grow, the vigorous demand for attention, the aggressive defense of prerogatives. When crossed, she is given to calling the offending member of the family "dumb" or "stupid," which translated seems to mean "you don't understand: I am the center of the universe and my needs come first." She turns simple activities like taking a walk into a contest as to who will be first, which she does her best to be. This child's expansiveness may in part be a rebellion against limitations; some family members comment that she seems to be frustrated by the limits on her ability to do things.

Beneath this child's sometimes tough exterior lies a keen sensitivity, which, if her parents respond to her with compassion, sometimes prompts not anger but tears. In fact, the combative instinct no doubt protects the vulnerability that lies within. The fact that this strongly expansive child is a girl reminds us, if we need reminding, that females too are born with aggressive, competitive tendencies. So as not to overdraw the portrait, I should note that she also regularly exhibits the softer side of her nature. Her parents owe it to her to accept her aggressiveness, even though it is not traditionally considered feminine, to channel her abundant energies, and to avoid fighting fire with fire so that she does not become thick-skinned. In this way her expansive nature will have the chance to develop in a balanced way.

Her younger brother entered the world a gentle presence whose cries from the next room could almost be ignored, who rarely clamors, who is much more willing to take no for an answer. His joie de vivre is understated; his is a quiet strength. He fights for his rights, but he has always been much more likely than his sister to go along with what other people want. He is not without a desire to win, but he also has a habit of ending board games by arranging for both people, his opponent and himself, to win. He makes his needs known, but he often is touchingly solicitous of other people. Once his mother gave him one of her favorite cookies, the type with a jellied center. He ate the cookie except for the center, which he offered to her, saying, "You have this, mommy, because I love you." This little boy has the sort of accommodating nature often stereotypically associated with females in this society. His nature is predominantly relational. He is typically a mild child, whose parents owe it to him to reinforce, rather than disregard, his claims for centrality and to take seriously, rather than lightly, his efforts at self-assertion. In this way the expansive side of his nature will have a chance to develop.

If, allowing for differences among individuals, all human beings are endowed with expansiveness, then how is this universal condition influenced by the particular circumstances of a given individual's upbringing? My attempt to answer this question is merely suggestive, not conclusive. I find no basis in our data or the literature for ascertaining what part of a grown man's or woman's makeup is attributable to genetic factors versus environmental factors. It is entirely possible that any given highly expansive adult owes his or her boundless energy almost entirely to biological inheritance.

Acquired Expansiveness

The socialization of the child is, in part, a domestication of raw, inbred self-expansion. As one psychologist wrote, "One goes from archaic and untamed grandiosity and exhibitionism to a tamed and modulated grandiosity, which is expressed in realistic ambition and pursuits."[16] The child graduates to a socialized, yet still ample expansiveness when, according to the psychoanalyst Heinz Kohut, its outsized self-oriented needs are frustrated in an "optimal" way.[17] By optimal frustration, Kohut has in mind a middle course in which the parents neither break the child's spirit nor fail altogether to frustrate the child's overblown ambition for itself.

A solid, yet not grandiose, sense of self takes shape in the child, according to Kohut, if two basic psychological functions are performed in the early years. One function, called mirroring, is the reflecting back to the child of its own sense of itself as worthy of praise and appreciation. The other function, idealization, is the child's internalizing of role models.

The parent's involvement in the child's free play is one indication of how these two functions are performed. Play is an activity that the child can control and therefore is one in which it can assert its own need for mastery. When the child wishes, will the parent join in the play and do so on the child's terms? Does the parent serve as a positive model for how to cooperate, how to solve problems, how to handle frustration? Does the parent assign importance to the play and therefore to the child itself? Or do adult priorities always take precedence over the child's activities?[18]

When these mirroring and idealizing functions are not performed satisfactorily, the result is a shaky sense of self. One reaction to this can be an extreme drive to mastery, because there is, at bottom, a fragility that the child and later the adult tries to make up for by forever striving to succeed, forever taking a posture of power and invincibility, forever warding off slights, real or imagined.[19]

Childhood circumstances that deprive the child of a sense of security are hardly limited to the family circle. Wars, economic depressions and booms, natural disasters, and societal culture are all larger forces that can influence a child's fate at a given time and place. In the same way, socioeconomic status, race, religion, and ethnic background locate the family in society and indirectly affect the child's standing, whether favored or disfavored. This discussion is confined, however, to the psychological impact of the family, even as that reflects outside influences. For the sake of simplicity, we will consider just two of the several ways that families affect the development of expansive character. Each of these ways corresponds to one of the two types of expansive character already treated in depth—the striver-builder and the self-vindicator/fix-it specialist.

The striver-builder. The striving child is frequently the first born and therefore the repository of its parents' high expectations and anxieties. The child is typically treated as special and feels special, but that select place in the family is something the child must also earn by continuing to fulfill its parents' expectations. Executives in our sample recall being expected to "do your best," "go all out," or even "become president of the United States." They will tell us that they never felt pressured, but, if one consults their record in school or on the playing field, little pressure was necessary since from an early age they took the role assigned to them. Our data indicate that parental pressure, subtle or otherwise, was present, even if it is not experienced or recalled.

A midlevel manager with executive potential told us that he, an only child, knew from the age of seven that he would go to Harvard, though no one pushed him to do it. Consider, however, the pressure implicit in the fact that three generations before him had attended Harvard. Recall that Bill Flechette felt, as a firstborn child and grandchild, that his family's "hopes were resting on him." The extent of the burden placed on Bill is reflected in the extremes to which he later went to fulfill his destiny.

John Sculley, CEO of Apple Computer and formerly the president of Pepsi, had parents who modeled the accomplishments they expected of him. A firstborn, he described his parents in the following way in his autobiography: "A senior partner at Jackson, Nash, Bruphy, Barringer & Brooks, my father was devoted to his three sons. . . . He was willing to sacrifice anything in his own life to ensure we had the opportunity to become successful. . . . He was satisfied in the fact that I had been president of my class, captain of the soccer team, and head monitor at Broadway School. . . . He instilled in us high expectations for success. . . . My mother, Margaret, an eternal optimist whose guiding principle in life was 'doing right' had a far greater influence on me in many ways. . . . [She was] a renowned horticulturist and a prize-winning flower arranger."[20] Needless to say, Sculley turned into an extraordinarily hardworking overachiever.

The mirroring function can be *overdone,* as in the case of the striving type, so that the child becomes overburdened and, as an adult and executive, cannot tolerate failure or anything that doesn't conform to his or her highly favorable self-image. In such cases the parents act out of their own considerable expansive needs and overwhelm the child by paying too much attention to him or her. Out of a need for reflected glory, the parents put too much psychic energy into encouraging the child to look good in one way or another.

Do the parents regularly take over the unstructured play of the child and turn it into a lesson in how to perform better? The father of one striver-builder type, for example, sat down with his six-year-old boy to help the child put his collection of baseball cards in order. The boy was interested up to a point but soon lost interest. When he went outside to play, his father finished the job. Whose need was it? To redefine playing with baseball cards into a responsibility to keep the collection organized not only takes the fun out of it for a six-year-old but reveals him as lacking in a skill prematurely expected of him.[21]

To expect a lot of one's children, to want them to do their best, can be seen as a form of abuse if the children are loved and valued only for performing well.[22] Favored children can become extremely expansive adults if, praised lavishly and admired as children, they come to overrely on praise and admiration of what they accomplish and lose touch with parts of themselves that were not rewarded or that were actively discouraged.[23] They may disallow feelings of fear, hurt, vulnerability, or anger. They may feel undeserving of nurturance or support except as a reward for exceptional accomplishment. As an adult, the individual's overwhelming need to succeed and his or her sensitivity to failure in any form can be so acute as to disturb the way he or she performs roles at work and at home, as we shall see later.

Executives raised under these conditions are likely to become flawed versions of the striver-builder such as Bill Flechette. Under more healthful versions of these same conditions, the result is likely to be a better-adapted version of the striver-builder.

The Self-Vindicator. If one pathway for developing an expansive personality is to be a favored child, then another, the compensating path, is to be a child who must overcome a handicap. I have in mind an emotional handicap resulting from a history of being consistently diminished or mistreated as a child. A victim of verbal or physical abuse has much to overcome, and for some such children the self-vindicating expansive way is the means of salvation.

Similarly, the child of an alcoholic, who as a child was spared direct abuse, nevertheless becomes saddled with the family's collective helplessness and as an adult may assume the role of hero to make up for the deficit in self-worth from which his or her parents as individuals and the family as a whole suffered.[24] Rich Bauer, a child of abuse, went the compensatory route. His career, which took him to the highest reaches of a major company, became, in part, a campaign to prove his disparaging parents wrong: "Underlying all my achievement was wanting to show them I could do it."

It is interesting that in another intensive study of managers, Robert Ochberg found that five of the seven ambitious men in his sample "felt bullied, frightened and humiliated by their fathers."[25] In response, each of them turned to work and career to find the appreciation and recognition that they missed as children, but each remained fearful of "diminishment, a loss of pride and power."[26]

Self-vindicating individuals may be the result of a failed idealization function. In Kohut's words, "The child's search for an admirable figure to identify with is blocked."[27] An abusive or alcoholic parent is hardly someone the child will look up to. The child's search for someone to admire may also be blocked because those who are potentially available spurn the child. They refuse "to permit a merger" with what for the child is their "greatness and power."[28]

A child may also turn to self-vindication as a result of a failed mirroring function. The child's parents are not empathic. They do not, in all the small ways possible every day, confirm the child's value; they do not validate the child's existence.[29] Worse yet, the child may have been the target of what might be termed "negative mirroring." Instead of gratifying the child's natural narcissistic need to be applauded, the parent perversely thwarts that need and instead reflects back to the child a picture of inadequacy.

Whether for lack of a positive role model or positive reinforcement or both, the result can be an adult who works overtime to dispel any hint of inadequacy — that is, if the person doesn't succumb completely to a devalued self-definition.[30] The productive self-vindicating executive manages to avoid a defeatist attitude on the one hand and extreme overcompensation on the other if he or she was lucky enough to have some kind of offsetting source of support in his or her early life.

Consequences for Leadership Style

Having taken a look at how childhood experience can exaggerate the natural expansive tendencies in human beings, we now turn to how exaggerated expansiveness can cause problems in

the way an executive leads. This section covers four characteristics of expansiveness: high ambition for mastery, extraordinary effort and self-assertion in quest of mastery, hunger for
the rewards that come with attaining mastery, and resistance
to experiencing oneself as lacking mastery (see Table 3).

**Table 3. Comparison of Extremely and
Moderately Expansive Executives.**

Characteristic	Extremely expansive	Moderately expansive
1. *High ambition for mastery*		
a. Ambition for self	Has to win, succeed, be right, even when counterproductive. Feels morally superior. Self-oriented ambition.	Driven to get on top of tough jobs, to take on bigger challenges. Task-oriented ambition.
	Competitive with others.	Competitive against own high standards.
	Makes exaggerated claims for own value as manager. Arrogant. Offsets feeling inferior by acting superior.	Conveys strong sense of self-confidence. Makes realistic claims for own value. Offsets feeling inferior by doing a superior job.
	Places high value on own way of doing things. Lacks perspective: "My way is the only way."	Has conviction about own way but also perspective on it. Has learned humility.
	Polarizes self and therefore also others into good or bad.	Able to see shades of gray.
b. Ambition for organization	Makes overly ambitious plans for the organization. Causes the organization to attempt impossible objectives or sets too many otherwise attainable objectives.	Sets ambitious objectives but keeps them within the organization's reach.

Table 3. Comparison of Extremely and
Moderately Expansive Executives, Cont'd.

Characteristic	Extremely expansive	Moderately expansive
	Unwilling to accept limits on what organization can do. Unrealistic about what it takes to get big jobs done.	Reconciled to the limits on the organization's capacity. Accepting of the gradual progress toward distant goals.
2. *Extraordinary effort in quest of mastery*		
a. Pushes self hard	Compulsive in the extreme; almost totally absorbed in work. Prone to burnout.	Exceptionally hardworking but knows how to turn it off when necessary.
b. Pushes others hard	Capable of burning out others.	Expects hard work but cognizant of people's limits.
	Too quick to exercise control and take over. Abrasive, in some cases.	Able to take charge but receptive to subordinates' influence and needs for autonomy. May be dominant, charismatic.
	Wants power too much for its own sake.	Uses power primarily to get things done.
	Unilateral: too concerned with pushing own agenda and not responsive to others' agendas. Can be exploitive.	Reciprocal: absorbed in own agenda yet able to invest in others' agenda.
3. *Hunger for the rewards of mastery*		
a. Strong need for recognition	Addicted to ego reinforcement. Can be an exhibitionist.	Needs ego reinforcement but delays gratification and allows recognition to flow from accomplishment.
	Intent on making one splash after another; not thorough.	Does the homework and follow-through necessary to fully earn kudos.

Table 3. Comparison of Extremely and
Moderately Expansive Executives, Cont'd.

Characteristic	Extremely expansive	Moderately expansive
b. Need for heroic standing	Wrapped up in looking good. Overly concerned with image, the trappings of status, power.	Bases reputation on solid record of accomplishment. Expects to look good as result of doing good.
4. *Resistance to experiencing self as lacking mastery*	Highly resistant to criticism. Reacts by withdrawing or by becoming enraged. Has trouble admitting mistakes; projects failure onto others.	Has a hard time with criticism but accepts it out of a need to *be,* rather than *appear,* masterful.
	Self-protective, rigid resistance to change. A poor prospect for self-awareness and self-improvement.	Relatively nondefensive, flexible. A good prospect for self-awareness and self-improvement.

A caveat: The distinction between moderate and exaggerated expansiveness is not an either/or proposition. It is the rare executive who approximates the paragon of complete moderation in expansiveness, because this requires a rare combination of qualities—the ability to go to extremes yet do so in moderation. At the other end of the continuum it is the equally rare executive who embodies *all* of the negative attributes of exaggerated expansiveness. The several characteristics of the expansive executive are somewhat independent of each other, so that an extremely expansive executive who is negative in one respect is not necessarily negative in other respects. Yet the more intensely expansive an executive is, the greater the number of negative attributes he or she is likely to have. Let me hasten to add, however, that extreme does not necessarily mean unproductive—a point we will return to in the next chapter.

High Ambition for Mastery

Most executives crave mastery. They strive mightily to master the challenges chosen by them or for them; they strive to master the skills needed to meet these challenges; they strive to master themselves as instruments of their ambitions. They put themselves to the test and then do everything in their power to prevail. Referring to the appetite for mastery in another field, the British mountain climber Chris Bonnington wrote of "the complete control of mind and body on steep, near-holdless, sun-warmed rock."[31] Likewise, expansive executives are irresistibly drawn to getting to the top of organizational mountains by gaining mastery over themselves.

This desire to place themselves on top of situations often has a driven quality. The title character in *Henderson the Rain King* explained at one point what prompted him, an outsider, to perform a near-impossible feat in an African tribal ceremony: "I have a voice within me repeating *I want,* raving and demanding, making a chaos, desiring, and disappointed continually, which drove me forth as beaters drive game."[32] At the moment that Henderson volunteered to attempt this improbable feat, he noted that "in my breast there was a flow—no, that's too limited—there opened up an estuary, a huge bay of hope and ambition. . . . [I was] craving to show what was in me."[33] Let's not dismiss this as the temporary insanity of a fictional character: Many people in leadership positions possess ambition of similar extent.

Expansive executives are ambitious for themselves and ambitious for their organizations. Whether these parallel ambitions are healthy and productive depends on the intensity of the drive.

Ambition for Themselves. Expansive executives want to establish themselves as masterful, whatever route they may take. A colleague of Rich Bauer said that "for Rich everything is a test of mettle." John Sculley, who at the age of thirty-eight was the youngest president in Pepsi history before he left to become CEO of Apple Computer, had a similar need to prove himself masterful. As we saw earlier in this chapter, his particular expansive nature, different in tone and emphasis from that of Rich Bauer, evidently derived from his parents' high expectations, both spoken and conveyed through their own impressive examples.

The drive to establish one's mastery can manifest itself in executives positively or negatively. On the negative side, it takes the form of needing to win, to succeed, to be "number 1," to be right, even when that need defeats the purposes supposedly being served. Executives of this type cannot stand to lose an argument. They lock into a sort of mortal combat with other candidates for the next promotion. Ironically, by being — and by seeming to others to be — inordinately ambitious for themselves, they may actually hurt their chances for promotion.

In the positive cases, the ambition for mastery is far more task-oriented. These individuals put most of their energy into proving themselves worthy by tackling rough jobs, taking on ever-increasing responsibility, and consistently increasing their managerial capability. They, too, have a sharp edge on their ambition, but they are more selective about what they take on. As much as it matters to them to succeed, they compete against their own standards of excellence and not so much against real or imagined rivals: They focus their competitive instincts on making the organization a success. John Sculley's competitive zeal, even allowing for the influence of Pepsi's competitive culture and the competitiveness of the soft drink industry, vibrated off the pages of his book. He evidently took great pride in coming out of nowhere at Pepsi: "I went from a nonentity to the youngest vice-president of marketing in Pepsi's history by racking up one accomplishment after another."[34] Yet his goal as a Pepsi executive was more organizational than personal: to make the company number one in the industry. Referring to an advertising campaign that he masterminded, Sculley wrote with considerable pride about overtaking the market leader: "The Pepsi Challenge had pushed us over the top, allowing us to unseat Coke as the number-one soft drink in supermarkets."[35] While he obviously felt that the company's success was his success, he gives the impression in his book of managing to keep a fairly good balance between his ambitions for himself and his ambitions for the organization.

Extremely and moderately expansive executives are also different in how they *express* their ambitions — in the claims they make for their value as managers. Exaggeratedly expansive individuals make inordinate claims; they are overly ambitious for respect and standing and predictably overevaluate their contributions and capability. This is true in what they advertise to other people, and it tends to be true of how they look upon themselves, at least at a certain level. This attitude makes for self-confidence that gives way to arrogance. Carl Jung referred to this exaltation of the self as "inflation" or the "*expansion* of the personality beyond its proper limits" (emphasis added).[36] To satisfy their ambition for superiority they play one-upsmanship with other people. They are constantly on the lookout for ways to elevate themselves. For the same reason, they are slow to feel or show appreciation of other people's success and are in fact quick to envy it. In a nutshell, exaggeratedly expansive executives have considerable self-doubt, but they repress it and convey instead a sense of themselves as extremely self-assured. An executive reflecting back on the time when he had been this way offered: "It's easy to repress when you have to achieve. If the achievement is there and there are goals that you have to reach, you don't have a choice, in essence, *not* to repress."

Executives who are moderately expansive, on the other hand, convey a strong sense of self-confidence that is both palpable and welcome to the people around them. As much as they desire to establish themselves as masterful, they lay claim to a sense of importance that matches what other people are prepared to grant them. These executives may not, however, feel as confident as they seem. Over and over in our work with executives, they confess to, or give indications of, some sense of inadequacy. This applies even to widely admired and apparently self-assured individuals in the top positions of well-known and highly successful companies. One such individual, when asked what drives him, declared, "Insecurity." He went on to say, "But if you ask 100 senior managers in this company the same question about me, no one would give you that answer."

He had recently become more aware of his insecurity in counseling (not with us) but preferred to keep it a secret. Of the best executives I have worked with, the more self-aware of them wrestle with their self-doubt and their reactions to it, which helps them keep from developing an overblown sense of self. Having less doubt about themselves than their extremely expansive peers, it is naturally easier for them to wrestle with it.

With a strong belief about oneself comes ideology. Each person makes an ideal out of the particular path through life he or she has chosen.[37] The tendency is to make a virtue out of a psychological necessity. Extremely expansive executives place a high value not just on their managerial ability but also on their particular way of doing things. From these individuals one hears, in so many words, "My way is the right way." They apply a righteous overlay to the methods they have adopted to meet their own needs. Because they believe so fervently in their way of being and doing, they become inflexible in applying their beliefs and practices to themselves and to others. The superior of one such executive described him as "too dogmatic sometimes in believing that his way is the only way. It's his way or forget it!" Similarly, one of his peers observed that "you either do it his way or you don't do it at all." Another peer said about him, "He has supreme confidence in himself and his judgment. Once he comes to a judgment, even if others see it as flawed, it doesn't deter him. This may appear as arrogance, but I'm not sure it is. I think that he gets such a strong belief in an issue that he can't be shaken. He has no regard for input from others, and this impedes his relationships."

Executives who are only moderately expansive also commonly believe in what they do, just as they do what they believe is right. But somewhere along the way, they have gained some perspective on their deeply held beliefs with regard to their particular expansive mode. Displaying this humility, one executive said, "I now recognize there's more than one right way, and my way may not be one of them."

Expansive executives, because of their ambition to be highly valued, are susceptible to experiencing themselves as either good or bad. In other words, they tend to polarize their experience of themselves, often alternating between the two. Inevitably, this self-polarization is mirrored in their experience of others, who become split into the very good and the very bad.[38] One manager called this "the halo effect and the bum effect." Bill Flechette and Rich Bauer both had this tendency. These individuals strongly favor some subordinates and disparage others, or they oscillate between one day feeling that their key people are terrific and the next day feeling they are awful. They see things and people in black and white.

One executive polarized people in this way to such an extent that both he and the people around him recognized it. He said self-reflectively, "I put people in two categories — they're in or they're out. If they're in, it means I like or believe in them. I cater to their style and support their weaknesses. If I don't have respect for them, I write them off." His subordinates confirmed this: "With him, you're either a superperformer or a lousy performer." Another subordinate observed that being a favorite is no guarantee of remaining a favorite: "He falls in love or out of love with people. He goes to the extreme, and you go from one to the other quickly."

This tendency to polarize looks like the flaw that contributed to one of the few losing seasons that Bobby Knight, the long-term and highly successful basketball coach at Indiana University, has had. Knight, a leader if not an executive, despised substandard performance. He made a habit of relegating players, even his star players, to the bench. During practices he regularly kicked players off the court and banished them to the locker room. During the 1984–1985 season he became so disgusted with the team in midseason that for a game against another Big Ten opponent he benched four starters in favor of four freshmen. Predictably, Indiana lost, and, unfortunately, Knight and the team never recovered. In general, Knight's compulsion to project a highly favorable image and his aversion to an unfavorable image put him and his team on "an emotional yo-yo."[39]

Ambition for the Organization. Executives' ambitions for themselves become especially important and consequential when they

are expressed as ambitions for their organizations. Harold Lasswell phrased it as "the displacement of private motives . . . onto
public objects."[40] The word "displacement" is significant because
it refers to a mechanism by which top executives covertly fashion
their organizations to suit their personal needs. The action is
covert not because executives are deceitful but because they and
those around them, thanks partly to the code of impersonality
that operates in most organizations, take the public agendas at
face value and disregard, except in the most superficial sense,
the deep personal needs that lie behind those agendas. It is widely
recognized that self-respecting leaders must have a vision of their
organization's future.[41] What is not so well recognized is that
the genesis of the vision lies in part in the personal makeup of
the leader.

Nonetheless, executives give profound expression to their
personal ambitions through the ambitions they develop for their
organizations. Treating their businesses as extensions of themselves, executives want their organizations to become the same
sort of objects—masterful entities—that they themselves seek
to become. Just as executives expand into their organizations,
they want their organizations to expand into their environments.
This is done by inspiring the organization to rise to the challenge,
to equip itself to meet those challenges, to contribute something
of value, to do well relative to the competition, and to emerge
in the end victorious.

In Rich Bauer's case, projecting his own needs onto the
organization has paid off handsomely so far for him and the organization. A high-integrity individual, he was characterized
as a "business builder," not a "career builder." But the relationship
between personal ambitions and ambitions for the organization
is often an uneasy one.[42] If, in the exaggerated, negative case,
executives are grandiose in their assessments of themselves and
their huge need to have an impact, they can set an overly ambitious agenda for the organization. They can cause the organization to overreach by setting what prove to be unattainable
objectives or by taking on too many major projects and making it difficult for the organization to do any of them well. A
study of executive teams produced the finding that team per-

formance is hindered by "leaders who put constant pressure on the team to perform on a never-ending line of objectives, each of which is described as 'critical,' and who apply this pressure out of a concern for their own present or future well-being rather than out of a concern for the quality of significance of the performance objective itself."[43] In an article on Jim Bakker and his PTL television ministry, the journalist Frances Fitzgerald compared Bakker's empire to "a vast balloon, which expanded on the breath of faith until [it] overextended itself and burst."[44]

The tendency to overreach is frequently born of an unwillingness to accept limits on what either the executives themselves or their organizations can do. Paraphrasing Horney, no obstacle is too big to be overcome by their superior abilities and dedication and those of their organization.[45] The refusal to accept reality includes a habit of seriously underestimating the actual work involved in attaining a major objective. This is because, as Karen Horney points out, these individuals are frequently interested less in climbing a mountain than in quickly placing themselves on the peak.

James Robinson, chairman and CEO of American Express, and Peter Cohen, the head of its subsidary Shearson Lehman, combined to fashion a take-over-the-world plan for Shearson in the 1980s. According to investigative reporter Connie Bruck, Shearson's strategy — expansionism — under Robinson and Cohen was "not mindless empire building." "Behind the vast majority of initiatives lay a strategic rationale . . . [but] what appeared to impel the whole enterprise — its generative force — was an *ethos of limitlessness:* that there was, and should be, no limit to resources, no limit to businesses in which to invest, no limit to the sublime business conditions of the mid-eighties" (emphasis added).[46] In the late 1980s, Cohen and Robinson collided with the hard limits on Shearson's expansion, resulting in a series of disasters topped by Shearson's failed attempt to finance the leveraged buyout of RJR Nabisco in 1988. An insider later said about Jim Robinson, "You didn't have to be a genius to know you were talking to a guy who wanted to own the biggest brokerage firm in the world. Jim, I think, was blindsided by his ambition."[47]

On the other side, some executives, equally ambitious for the organization yet sharply concerned about having everything come out right, regularly shoot *too low*. They are overly cautious. A variation on the theme: In the interest of increasing the chances of success, they prolong the decision process and run the risk of missing opportunities.

Executives who keep their expansive drive in some kind of moderation press high ambitions upon their organizations but, through their handling of their personal needs and the decision process, manage to keep objectives within reach. Less prone to grandiosity, they can think big but retain a sense of their own limits and the limits on what their organization can do. They couple their drive to make things happen with an adequate appreciation for *what it takes* to make things happen.[48] They wax euphoric over visions of what the organization can become yet remain in touch with the gradual, step-by-step process of growth and evaluation that the organization must undergo to get there. They have "both the vision of possibilities, the perspective of infinitude, and the realization of limitations, of necessities, of the concrete."[49]

Extraordinary Effort in Quest of Mastery

With the fire of ambition for themselves and their organizations burning hot, it's no wonder executives work so hard and do their best to get subordinates to do the same. Pushing themselves hard, they also push other people hard, using a wide repertoire of tactics that may include force and the threat of force. (Those executives who resort to force in any way but sparingly are, except in the most dire organizational circumstances, the exaggerated, negative cases.)

Pushing Oneself Hard. Long hours and intense concentration usually come easy to expansive executives because so much of their sense of self is tied to high performance, because they have placed themselves in situations that require intensity of them, and because, if they are fortunate, they take real pleasure in their work. Recall the Herculean efforts that Rich Bauer made to get himself on the fast track. Eighty hours a week was the norm when he started out, and this norm was reinvoked whenever a promotion jumped him a level or two in scope.

Executives who are only moderately expansive are hard-driving and exceptionally hard-working people in whom the work ethic is especially intense. Yet as dedicated as they are, they can still distinguish between those times when they need to go all out and those when they should moderate their efforts. They have some ability to retreat from work and replenish themselves.

Executives of the exaggeratedly expansive variety are compulsive; they absorb themselves almost totally in work. They throw their lives so far out of balance that family relationships and health are adversely affected.[50] Their overinvolvement in work, as much as the executives themselves may claim they enjoy it, has a way of turning back on itself and impairing their effectiveness. Overly dedicated executives eventually burn themselves out — consumed in the hot flame of their ambition and intense exertion.

Extremely expansive executives waste effort by trying to do everything, have trouble distinguishing clearly between high and low priorities, and, as we will soon see, disrupt the reciprocity between their priorities and those of others. They lack sufficient flexibility to choose when to exert themselves and when to take breaks, so they fail to regenerate themselves during the course of a day, a week, or a year. They are susceptible to losing their edge.

An executive in our sample, driven by an acute sense of responsibility, had risen to a top job in his company and had continued to maintain time-consuming voluntary leadership positions in his church and in a national service organization. He had virtually no time for himself or his marriage, which suffered. His performance at work also suffered because he regularly felt overloaded and worn out, and on occasion he showed up at meetings ill-prepared for important decisions. He burdened himself. In person he gave off a tired, joyless feeling that subtly undercut his efforts to inspire and motivate his people.

Extremely hard work, while detrimental in the sense that it costs the individual in other spheres of his life, is commonly valued by the organization and by the expansive individual. John Sculley made repeated proud references to his "obsession with work," his being "willing to work relentlessly," and to the strenuous schedule he kept at various points.[51] For example, he boasted, "I worked through the weekend, long into each night [to prepare for a presentation to the board]."[52] Total dedication to work may be necessary during crises or challenging transitions such as the one Sculley made in crossing industries in the move from Pepsi to Apple. Whether Sculley's continual sky-high levels of activity took a toll, he did not reveal in his book.

Pushing Others Hard. In the pursuit of mastery, expansive executives assert themselves strongly with others; they make their presence felt. To be masterful is to gain control. As the psychologist David McClelland has discovered, effective managers are motivated not just by a high need for achievement but also by a considerable need for power. How can managers achieve anything in an organizational setting except by being willing to exert influence over other people? Let us correct any impression, however, that to want influence is necessarily the same as to act aggressively toward others. Actually, quite powerful managers can be potent without being pushy interpersonally; instead, they exercise influence through what they stand for — their values.

One way that executives assert themselves is through their expectations of how hard their subordinates should work. Usually, though not always, their expectations of themselves correlate closely with their expectations of their people. Moderately expansive executives expect a lot in this regard and may expect punishingly hard work at times, but at the same time they are cognizant of the limits on people's capacities for work and alert to indications of overwork. Extremely expansive executives, whose own strenuous efforts know virtually no bounds, tend to require the same boundless dedication of their subordinates and thereby put them at risk of burnout. This symmetry between what one demands of oneself and what one demands of others applied to Lyndon Johnson, whose career in politics was "a story of intense physical and spiritual striving that was utterly unsparing; he would sacrifice himself to his ambition as ruthlessly as he sacrificed others."[53] One top executive described an executive-level subordinate as "too hard a worker, probably the hardest in his organization. This can burn people out because of the tone he sets." A peer of this hard worker said, "I think there's some feeling on the part of his subordinates that they can never do enough."

In exercising influence, executives are perpetually faced with the choice of how much power to take personally and how much power to allow and encourage their people to take. Moderately expansive executives strike a balance between empowering themselves (direct power) and empowering others (indirect power). They are willing to take charge but don't always have to be in the dominant role or do the job themselves—even a high-priority job. They use "loose-tight" controls, which combine tight control over direction and core values with loose control over execution.[54] To capture this optimal mix of control and autonomy, Robert Waterman came up with the phrase "directed autonomy."[55] The academics Charles Manz and Henry Sims feel so strongly about managers sharing control that they define "superleaders" as those who "lead others to lead themselves."[56]

At nearly all times, moderately expansive executives exercise control only to get things done. They use what McClelland called socialized power, power used for the benefit of the collectivity: "The positive or socialized face of power is characterized by a concern for group goals . . . and for giving group members the feeling of competence they need to work hard for them. . . . It functions in a way that makes members of a group feel like initiators of action rather than pawns."[57]

In contrast, the extremely expansive executives in our sample convey a sense that the exercise of power attracts them for its own sake. They seem to want power not so much to pursue organizational ends as to gratify their need to assume a large presence—larger than what their role in the situation requires. These executives know too well how to assert themselves and not nearly as well how to make it possible for others to assert themselves. As one young executive said, "I make up my mind;

then I lean on people until I hear them saying my words." Excessively expansive executives may often make a practice of crossing the line between being appropriately assertive and unnecessarily aggressive, to the point of being abrasive—one of the leading causes of executive derailment.[58] It is important to note that these managers don't tend to be indiscriminately abrasive but reserve their mistreatment for those people who seem to block them or those whom they do not respect.

Rich Bauer employed a negative sort of power that stood out all the more because of the lack of much counterbalancing softness in his style. But Steven Jobs, the cofounder of Apple Computer, easily outdid Bauer in his consistently heavy-handed or destructive use of power. Jobs was described by his co-workers as tyrannical, dominant, a megalomaniac, overbearing, intimidating, sadistic, someone who ran over people. This is a clear case of a personality characteristic being compounded by the person's situation. While still in his twenties, Jobs, with little experience in management, became chairman of a $2 billion corporation and held $436 million in stock. One associate was quoted as saying, "The money turned Steve into a kind of monster."[59] The greater his power, wealth, and reputation, the more arrogant, exploitative, and destructive he apparently became. Former President Lyndon Johnson may have outdone Steve Jobs in his need to dominate other people for the pure pleasure of personal ascendancy. "The hunger that gnawed at him most deeply [was for] power in its most naked form—to bend others to his own will. . . . What he sought was not merely power but the acknowledgment of it by others—the deferential face-to-face, subservient acknowledgement that he possessed it."[60]

Overcontrol is often accompanied by righteousness. An exaggeratedly expansive executive in our study had such strong beliefs about *how* things should be done that he tried to dictate to the experienced managers below him how to go about their jobs. One subordinate said it was a case of "do it his way or else." Another subordinate described him as a "follow-up maniac, who would follow up on picayune things. It was constant harassment." Predictably, he irritated even his best performers and made enemies of many of his subordinates. In large part because of the overassertion of "his way," his career stopped short of where his business acumen and drive could have taken him.

A moderately expansive executive strikes an appropriate balance between being a force to reckon with and allowing other people their potency, not for the sake of egalitarianism but on the basis of everyone's ability to contribute. Hanging in the balance here is the question: Whose agenda should prevail, yours or mine? If executives are to be effective, they must find a way to mingle their own agendas, springing from their deep ambitions for themselves, with the agendas of the people around them. They must set up a reciprocity by which they and the people around them take turns working on their respective issues. Moderately expansive executives can do this: They can reciprocate. They are intensely absorbed in their own objectives, and this intensity attracts other people. However, they don't rely exclusively on this personal magnetism to lead. They also absorb themselves in what other people are trying to do — people whose interest and cooperation they need. And they actually find ways to merge their interests and those of others.

Extremely expansive executives let their objectives become the sun that obscures all lesser lights. Ultimately, their inability to invest in other people's projects hinders their ability to attract investment in their own. Predictably, they run into a lack of enthusiasm for, or even resistance to, their initiatives. Their relationship with their subordinates becomes unilateral. The terms of the relationship, dictated by the executive, are that his or her ideas matter most and that they are automatically the ones that deserve to be nurtured.

For the exaggeratedly expansive executive, other people exist primarily to serve the executive in his or her campaign to attain mastery. Bill Flechette's subordinates felt at times that they were simply part of his master plan. Such "servants" can all too easily become dispensable. As a thirty-year-old marketing vice-president, John Sculley was so intent on realizing his ambitions that he treated people like a consumable supply. Recognizing retrospectively that he didn't understand "how important it was to build an organization," he reported, "No one could do his work well enough to meet my standards. Other than the six-man team settled around me, I was just going through people, chewing them up. I went through four marketing research vice-presidents in two years. I didn't care: I was convinced that what I was doing was right, that I had to get my marketing ideas out, and I wasn't going to let anything get in the way.[61]

Hunger for the Rewards of Mastery

Expansive executives may be strongly attracted by the sheer satisfaction of using and increasing their capabilities. Mastery is its own reward. Chris Bonnington, the mountain climber, identified "this combination of the thrill of risk and the mastery of mind and muscle that brings the feeling of intense exhilaration that makes rock climbing so addictive."[62] This thrill and exhilaration are available to executives who set out on high-stakes institutional adventures. But in addition to intrinsic satisfaction, expansive executives also generally want recognition of their capabilities and attainments and a certain heroic status.

Need for Recognition. Moderately expansive executives are motivated both by the intrinsic satisfaction of accomplishment and by the pleasure of having others recognize and appreciate their accomplishments. They feel keenly the need for ego reinforcement, yet they are usually able to delay gratification and can work hard for long stretches on the promise of ego-reinforcing "supplies."[63] They are reminiscent of Mark Twain, who said he could live for months on the strength of one good compliment.

The difference in this respect between moderately expansive executives and their extreme counterparts hinges on the strength of the need for recognition. Moderate ones need recognition, but they operate on the principle that work and achievement come first and recognition follows. Executives like this are described by people around them as desiring personal success as a byproduct of the success of the organizations they lead. They also have a sufficiently strong sense of self-worth that their need for external reinforcement stays within bounds.

Extremely expansive executives, on the other hand, have

an infirm sense of self that necessitates a large and constant supply of reinforcement from the outside.[64] Bill Flechette was labeled "credit-hungry." Some executives are exhibitionists, constantly calling attention to themselves and turning other people into an admiring audience.[65] One clinical psychologist put it this way: "The craving personality must be fed. He is devastated if supplies are not forthcoming . . . [for] while he is unfed, his self-esteem suffers; where is his specialness and where are the nourishing objects?"[66] One young high-potential manager told us that he was susceptible to bouts of depression at any point at which his performance or career did not bring him the high regard he needed. There is a strong connection between the need for external ratification of worth, gained by excelling or being special in some way, and depression.[67] With recognition, this type feels terrific; without it, he or she feels downright lousy.

The search for recognition can possess executives to the point that they become exploitative. There is a sense in which they use others, or they take credit due others. Steven Jobs was nicknamed the "reality distortion field" because of his penchant for pooh-poohing someone's idea and then later making it his own.[68]

The tragic irony is that executives who overrely on external signs of success for a sense of self-worth only prop up their self-esteem temporarily. They may think that the next promotion or jump in income will make them feel truly good about themselves, but their problem is that external compensation does not genuinely strengthen an insecure sense of self.[69]

Need to Attain Heroic Status. Closely associated with the need for external reinforcement is the wish, perhaps unconscious, to take a heroic role that confers the admiration the expansive executive seeks. Privately, the individual longs to become a legendary figure in his or her organization. Becker makes this point in relation to all human beings, but it pertains particularly to expansive types: "[Man] must desperately justify himself as an object of primary value in the universe. He must stand out, be a hero, make the biggest possible contribution to world life, show that he counts more than anything or anyone else."[70]

The heroic impulse is discernible in the comment an executive made about his appetite for winning against the odds: "I like it best when the odds are against me. It's a chance to show I've accomplished something—the chance for a triumphant moment." Another executive confessed, "I set high standards to be heroic. I am attracted to doing the impossible." The heroic impulse is also evident in the difficulty CEOs have in stepping down when they retire or *try* to retire, as Jeffrey Sonnenfeld recently found.[71] They want the heroic stature to continue, and they want to stay on some immortalizing mission.

As with their need for recognition, moderately expansive executives do not sacrifice the requirements of the work to their need to be a hero. Ego needs remain in proper proportion to the need to perform a role and to contribute. In other words, this kind of person operates on the principle, enunciated in all the management texts, that looking good is contingent upon doing good. Again, owing to a reasonably strong sense of self and appropriate internal controls, these executives do not alternate sharply between high self-regard and feelings of worthlessness. Their ego strength allows them to respond to victory and defeat without falling prey to extreme mood swings. Because they avoid this bouncing back and forth, they are able to discriminate gradations of competence both in themselves and in others.

John Sculley, evidently in an effort to recapture his childhood experience of being especially esteemed, coveted the chance to strike a heroic pose but seemed to harness this impulse to his efforts to advance his organization's cause. He strove to improve Pepsi's image as a way to burnish his own. Having decided that Pepsi would never be able to gain market share unless its image could be improved, he and his team hit on the idea of the Pepsi Generation advertising campaign. "Working late at night, almost every night, our six-man team developed and implemented these upstart plans," Sculley wrote. "It immediately clicked, winning awards and becoming the longest-running campaign ever to run on television; . . . within Pepsi, we were heroes."[72]

Excessively expansive executives are unduly concerned with the trappings of status, power, and success.[73] Also, whereas moderately expansive executives are by and large what they claim to be, extremely expansive executives are given to making false claims. They are willing to deal in illusion and may try to deceive themselves and others. Lyndon Johnson bragged about having fought in the Pacific theater during World War II; in fact, he was strictly an observer, in which capacity he went on a single, admittedly dangerous bombing mission. A contemporary of his said about him, "He could convince himself of anything, even something that wasn't true" if it served his ambition.[74]

Even without resorting to outright lies, extremely expansive executives may be self-aggrandizing in the sense that they pretend to be more important than they actually are. Bill Flechette, who confessed to being intimidated by his co-workers' expectations that he "live up to a superhuman image" was, in fact, viewed by some of those co-workers as needing to be "an important personage" and having a tendency to get caught up in the "aura of omniscience" with which senior managers in his company sometimes surrounded themselves. Senior managers may build an empire for what it represents rather than as an instrument of the organization's purposes. They wish to be admired for organizational standing or personal attractiveness rather than inherently useful or mature human qualities.[75]

A strong desire for heroism can lead the executive astray, as John Sculley admitted had happened to him on occasion. His need to win big and thereby stand out showed up when he tried unsuccessfully to land a major eye-catching deal with the French government: "We . . . invested weeks hoping for a deal that would dazzle the world."[76] Referring to this and other misadventures, he commented, "Instead of chasing miracles, I should have been tightening down the business."[77]

The heroic impulse can lead executives to cut corners in the quest to create a good impression. They may not do their homework or follow through conscientiously enough because they want to emerge victorious from one arena after another. An executive who was faulted for not attending to detail and for leaving a trail of little problems traced this managerial sloppiness to his motivation to make one splash after another: "I get bored. I am always looking for the next windmill to tilt at."

Despite his high position and excellent reputation, he was greatly concerned about creating a good impression, even with his wife. Worried that his wife might learn something unflattering about him, he told her nothing about work — to "keep her from thinking poorly of me."

Resistance to Indications of a Lack of Mastery

Expansive executives, at least initially, resist criticism and have trouble with self-correction and self-development. Given the need for mastery and the associated need for acclaim and admiration, expansive individuals instinctively have trouble, to one degree or another, with evidence of their inadequacy and with calls for improvement. The question becomes: Which need wins out — the need to *be* masterful or the need to *appear* masterful? Becker wrote of the "terror of admitting what one is doing to earn his self-esteem."[78] Those who overcome their reluctance move closer to healthy, moderate expansiveness. They avoid some of the distortions of which expansive people are capable. As Becker put it, "To become conscious of what one is doing to earn his feeling of heroism is the main self-analytic problem of life."[79]

Those executives who were moderately expansive overcome their reflex reaction against indications of their faults because the need to grow and to become more competent prevails. They may feel deflated for a time, but they can recover and move on. They are governed chiefly by the drive to fulfill realistically their ambitions for efficacy. Although mistakes rankle, they manage to be emotionally and intellectually honest. They are able to admit ignorance. Or, as one executive did, they admit to themselves the difficulty they have in saying "I don't know" and are on the alert for the temptation to act as if they understand something they do not. The need to know their strengths and weaknesses overcomes their fear of knowing and therefore makes continuing self-development possible.[80]

In the case of extremely expansive individuals, image-consciousness and the craving for ego-reinforcement make it difficult or impossible for the expansive person to accept criticism or other evidence that he or she isn't masterful. The criticism or mistake or failure is experienced as a "narcissistic wound." The unwanted input or event is experienced as a violation, and the person reacts by withdrawing and sulking or by becoming enraged. In this vein, one clinician referred to an attitude of "entitlement," the sense that one deserves to be treated well and therefore should be spared bad news about oneself.[81] People who are extremely expansive characteristically have great trouble admitting mistakes or failures or owning up to failings and may instead project them onto others. In unconsciously and aggressively protecting their reputation or image, such highly resistant managers sacrifice the chance to remedy problems, and ultimately they put their effectiveness and careers in jeopardy.

Summary

All expansive individuals are alike in their highly developed drive to accomplish and to be accomplished. Yet there are important differences in how compulsive that already above-average drive is. In what I have called extreme or exaggerated expansiveness, the drive to mastery is acutely personal and emotionally charged because the person's self-esteem is fundamentally at risk. So much is on the line psychologically that this type's ambition to attain mastery and to be recognized as having done so interferes with work. It may interfere by depriving them of flexibility, creating a driving personality that causes them to hold on rigidly to their ideas and their ways of doing things. The interference may mean that they care too much about career progress and too little about the organization's welfare. In pushing for dramatic success, they are quite capable of overextending both themselves and their organizations. They may be so concerned about projecting an image of efficacy and success that they become preoccupied with appearances and trappings and may even, in effect, cheat to create the desired impression. They bend or break the rules to get what they feel they must have for themselves. In this and other ways, they lack integrity and, being experienced as such, damage their reputation as well as their effectiveness. In addition, extremely expansive individuals tend either to misuse or to abuse power. We can understand better what Ernest Becker meant by "the terror of admitting what one is doing to earn his self-esteem" when we put ourselves in the place of someone who is willing to do practically anything to succeed.

In contrast, executives who are moderately expansive manage to harness their intense drive for mastery and their need for control for the benefit of the organization; they subordinate their ego needs to the organization's needs. There is an essential honesty about these managers: They make sure to *earn* the credit given them; they support whatever claims to mastery they make; they are able to acknowledge their mistakes and failings. While they are capable of expending and expecting extreme effort, they observe and respect their own limits and those of the organization. They manage to mobilize the organization to attain its objectives without weakening or destroying it in the process.

To hit this happy medium of being driven but not too driven is socially desirable, and one might guess it would also be good for the organization. Yet the relationship between expansiveness and effectiveness is not a simple, linear one, as we shall see.

Chapter Seven

The Expansive Manager, the Bottom Line, and the Human Cost

In the last chapter, we saw clearly the connection between the character of an executive and the way he or she behaves. Executives who are extremely expansive have a way of going too far in the effort to distinguish themselves and their organizations. Moderate executives generally stop short of these destructive extremes.

In this chapter, we take the next step and link managerial behavior to organizational outcomes. We revisit extremely expansive executives and see that, while we may deplore their methods, such managers are by no means always ineffective. Though their drive to mastery may be exaggerated, they can often deliver outstanding results. In this chapter we also revisit moderately expansive executives and see that, while some are exemplary across the board, others get less than optimal results.

Before explaining further, let us identify two criteria against which to measure an executive's impact on the organization: the bottom-line results that the organization is able to produce and the state of the organization after those results are obtained. Depending on the type of organization, bottom-line results mean quantity and quality of products made or services rendered, profitability, market share, return on equity, and the like. The state of the organization refers to the condition of the *means* by which the organization produces results—its physical plant, its finances, and its staff. We'll focus on the organization's human aspect: employee morale and commitment, the state of relationships up and down the line, the stock of talent at all levels, and so forth.

Destructive Productivity

While, as we will soon see, some extremely expansive executives can produce good outcomes, others fail miserably; under their direction the organization performs poorly and deteriorates. For example, Bill Millard, the founder and CEO of Computer-Land, helped create a highly successful franchising operation only to contribute just as actively to bringing it to the brink of disaster.[1] ComputerLand rode the crest of the personal computer revolution to become a major distributor, but it only succeeded to the extent that former IBM executive Ed Faber ran the company and Millard stayed in the background. When after several years Millard reinserted himself into an active role by creating an officious, overstaffed, and overzealous office of the chairman, he drove management crazy and drove Faber into quasi-retirement. In addition to demoralizing employees, he alienated store owners by introducing a highly restrictive and inequitable new franchise agreement. He saw himself as merely acting on his high-minded principles, and he could get away with that view because of his top position and his 95 percent ownership of this privately held company. But his longstanding practice of taking the maximum for himself and giving the minimum to others caught up with him in two dramatic and devastating ways. One, he lost a suit that cost him 20 percent of the value of the company plus $140 million in punitive damages. Two, the association of franchises staged a revolt that ousted him from his chairman's role and made Ed Faber, whom Millard had recently reinstated as CEO, the chairman.

How is it possible that a top manager can stay in charge while bringing down an organization? A simple answer is: Under certain circumstances the individual is able to build a power base so solid that the institution is powerless, or acts as if it is powerless, to unseat him or her, and during that time the individual runs the organization into the ground.

How can someone who fails on both counts get to be an executive in the first place? One of many possible explanations might be the so-called Peter Principle, which states that a person will rise to his or her highest level of incompetence in an organization. Although effective at lower levels, at least in terms of the bottom line, the person fails to make the grade at higher levels. The strategic ability just isn't there, the individual loses his or her sponsor, success goes to his or her head, and so on.[2]

As long as the most destructive executives are subject to a responsible higher authority, they're relatively easy to deal with: They can be moved aside or let go because they fail to get good results on any count. It's the extremely expansive executive who gets great results who poses the greatest dilemma. Take the case of a general manager, later a division president, who, according to a peer, "in five years single-handedly evolved a strategy for [commercializing and marketing a new product], brought it into commercial development, and made it into a big money-maker . . . . He was an irascible bastard, pompous, domineering. There were just two ways to do things — his way and the wrong way." In the eyes of a subordinate: "His flaw was his kick-in-the-ass approach. People were afraid of him and his impact on their careers. He would shower abuse on people — in public. It wasn't a bed of roses. There were people who wanted him dead."[3] (He may have been as self-destructive as he was destructive: He died in an accident that he brought on himself.)

Thus, although extremely expansive executives can be destructive, they also can be very productive, at least if managed appropriately. The principal drawback to the extremely expansive executive who obtains good bottom-line results is that he or she harms the organization in the process. These executives reduce the organization's talent pool by driving people away and demoralizing some of those who remain. For those subordinates who are chronically exhausted or demeaned in the mad dash for results, success proves to be an inadequate tonic. This class of leader is like Mac Michaelson, a senior manager whom a subordinate, speaking for many other people, described as "effective—but with a human cost." Michaelson said about himself, with the benefit of feedback, "My key strength as a leader is that I get the job done even though sometimes *the cost is very high*" (emphasis added). Michaelson's superiors gave him high marks for producing but a lower overall rating of leadership effectiveness because of the human toll. Using a 10-point scale to rate leadership effectiveness, one superior said: "From a results standpoint, a 9. But from an all-around standpoint, a 6." Another superior gave him an 8. Why not a 10? "His authoritative aspect detracts from it, and his overzealousness of goal achievement." His peers share this view of him. One remarked that "he's so goal-oriented that he's unable to compromise. He can only attack and win, win, win."

Clearly, Mac is excessively expansive. His feedback report was sprinkled liberally with comments to this effect. He "works too hard"; he "presses too hard"; he is "too demanding." Two different people say that he "goes overboard." Mac now knows this about himself: "I am personally driven to be the best that I can be and to run the best operation of this kind in the world. But the downside is that I get very upset when things don't go right." He simply pushes people too hard, to the point where he singles out for harassment those individuals who, to his way of thinking, don't put out enough. Because Mac goes too far, his boss, like the conscientious superior of any such manager, feels he has to keep Mac in check. "Mac Michaelson is someone you do have to manage. He's very aggressive. He charges. But I'd prefer to have a Mac Michaelson on my team than someone I'd have to motivate."

Thus we have in Mac Michaelson a highly intelligent and extremely intense executive who has made work the center of his existence and who has derived from that heavy investment a consistent ability to get outstanding results. But his drawback is serious enough, despite his superior's appreciation of what he can produce, to put his continued career progress in serious jeopardy.

Extremely expansive executives like Mac Michaelson dispel the naive idea that leaders should move mountains and also be nice guys. As management professor Jay Conger pointed out about charismatic leaders, to effect a major organizational change is inherently off-putting, at least to those people wedded to the status quo or jealous of the leader's magnetism and following.[4] But the energy, drive, and aggression of extremely expansive executives goes beyond what is required by the work of leadership, and the excesses rub other people the wrong way.

In deromanticizing leadership and giving up our innocence about the exercise of great power, must we take a fatalistic attitude toward the destructive side of this class of executives? I believe not. Although difficult to do, it *is* possible to contain this type of manager and shape his or her behavior.

Reining In Destructive Executives

Destructive executives partially redeem themselves by delivering results, but they pose a dilemma because of the toll taken. Anyone with a stake in both the organization's present success and its future well-being ends up on the horns of this dilemma. On the one hand, the executive may cause the organization to succeed beyond all expectations, even beyond everyone's wildest dreams. This was true of the personally destructive division president described earlier in the chapter — the one who died in an accident — who was credited with engineering a breakthrough that generated profits for many years. It is also true of Bobby Knight who, next to John Wooden, has won more national basketball championships — three — than any other college coach. At the same time, the way leaders of this kind conduct themselves and treat people disturbs their admirers and appalls their detractors. Knight, for example, is notorious for pushing his players around, throwing chairs across the court, punching a photographer during the Pan American games, and in an exhibition game against the Soviet Union, pulling his team off the court, supposedly in protest of the poor officiating but probably out of frustration with his team's poor play.[5]

The dilemma is no doubt most distressing for top management. Despite the damage the division president did, top management kept him on, presumably in full knowledge of his reputation as a destructive manager. In a blatant case like this, top management must address the question: Do the benefits outweigh the harm done to the organization and the individuals in it? If the answer is yes, what can top management do? Apart from demotion or dismissal, one thing is to keep productive-but-destructive executives on a short leash, as Mac Michaelson's superiors did. Speaking of such individuals, one executive told us, "At any time I like to have a couple of them in my organization, if they can adopt my agenda, because they'll charge ahead and get more done. But if you're not careful, they'll burn themselves out and the organization, too." Rather than turn a blind eye to the harm this type of executive is causing, it is clearly advisable to stay informed about the damage and do what one can to contain it. This is no mean task, because extremely expansive executives can be hard to manage and because the emotions kicked up in the supervising executive may be such that he or she prefers to avoid the trying subordinate.

A second thing top management can do, with the help of the human resources staff, is to recognize that the executive's offensive behaviors are probably drive-related. Rather than try simply to contain the individual's excesses, they may find it helpful to consider what it is inside the executive that prompts the excesses. The various complaints about the individual probably revolve around a drive to mastery taken to an extreme, and this extreme drive is probably a reaction to high anxiety about self-worth. To consider the inner drives of such an executive can result in greater empathy and therefore a more effective response to his or her provocations.

A third option is development. In reconciling ourselves to the fierce drive and sometimes naked aggression these executives display, must we — and they — accept those qualities as fixed and immutable? Or can we entertain the possibility that these powerhouses can ameliorate their negative style while retaining their high output? Is that another pipe dream? In fact, as we will show in Part Three, this sort of tempering is, under certain conditions, indeed possible — and desirable. All of Part Three is about development; in particular, the development of extremely expansive executives. Suffice it here to make one point.

In investing in the development of this sort of executive, one's first thought may be to help the individual learn to control his or her high-powered ambitions. If, the reasoning goes, the person could become a little less ambitious to excel, then he or she wouldn't treat other people so badly. Call this approach "ego management."

What this line of approach misses is that executives overinvest in mastery not just because it holds a magnetic attraction for them but because, if the truth were known, they despair of gratifying themselves through relationships per se. They obtain a sense of self-worth primarily through mastery and only secondarily through relationships. The colleagues of a derailed executive used hair-raising language to describe the ferocity with which he campaigned for results: "Sometimes he froze the skin off your face." "He could be very insensitive; he'd tear strips off people." In discussing disturbing comments like these with him, I began to see that his obsession with accomplishment correlated with his avoidance of close relationships. As congenial and charming as this person could be, in actual fact he had real difficulty forming close relationships. Sensing this, one co-worker said, "You can't be his buddy; he puts up a brick wall." His difficulty in this area came out when he squirmed at my suggestion that he confide in someone about the data in his feedback report. It was clear that he didn't have close friends, his wife included, and more than that, that he avoided having them. To the extent that he had given up on close relationships as a source of self-satisfaction, he had latched onto work that much harder. And of course this extreme lopsidedness led him regularly to make a mess of his relationships at home as well as at work, which must only have reinforced his unconscious assumptions and expectations.

Thus, if driven executives are to strive less ferociously for business objectives, two routes are open. The direct route is to tamp down somehow on their overweening ambition. The indirect route is for them to discover the intrinsic satisfactions of close relationships.

Constructive Productivity

Is it possible for an executive to get great bottom-line results and
at the same time be a constructive, people-oriented force in the
organization? This doesn't appear to be the norm in the executive population, but it does occur. To show it is possible, let us
turn to an executive whose data documented fully his well-
balanced approach to management. In his late forties, John Holland had an excellent track record. Superiors, peers, and subordinates were unanimous in seeing him as consistently delivering
the goods, even in adverse situations. They spoke almost with
one voice in attesting to John's exceptional ability to pursue business objectives. A superior said it succinctly: "He has a tremendous drive to get results." He was characterized by a subordinate
as "an aggressive charger" and by a peer as "a real charger —
'Let's build it, grow it, do it!'" Using similar language, another
superior complimented him by saying, "When he says, 'Let's
charge,' people charge." In general, he got high marks for his
ability to mobilize an organization. A peer who had worked with
him over their entire careers declared him "terrific!" in this
respect. "I've observed that he has strong animal leadership instincts, and people recognize that. He wins their loyalty and
people follow him." His performance in a recent assignment as
president of a major subsidiary was cited by a few people as an
example of his talent at improving an organization's effectiveness. He was applauded for doing a terrific job, a courageous
job. Subordinates also point out the force he exerts on an organization. He was described as "tough" and as "hauling people along with him when he makes changes." He takes firm hold
of an organization and aggressively pursues excellent outcomes.

John Holland's true achievement as an executive, however, is that he operates at full throttle *and* handles people well.
As a peer noted, "He builds very strong bonds with the people
who work for him." He builds strong bonds by trusting his people, giving them appropriate autonomy, staying involved without
interfering, sharing praise and rewards, and being open to their
influence. Apparently one reason why he and so many other
people use the word "balanced" to describe him is that he makes

full use of his formidable strengths, managerially and personally, while he welcomes and enhances his subordinates' strengths. One subordinate described his stance this way: "He trusts and listens and gives freedom to people—most unusual. He really turns people on." In addition to "giving trust," he listens, and thereby stays in touch with events unfolding in his organization. More than one person used the phrase "stays in touch."

John's success in handling people so positively is a function of his success in handling himself. Everyone was unanimous, for example, in stating that he does not steal credit, that he does not put his interests ahead of the organization's. His ego for the most part does not intrude. A superior put it this way: "Like all good leaders, he has a distinct sense of his own worth—he has confidence in what he can do—but he's well liked." Subordinates experience him the same way, which the following person found several ways to express: "He is easy to interact with. You are not talking with God. He is an ordinary guy. It means that people can level with him—he's not majestic. He's good at not being bigger than life."

How does one explain this effectiveness? Clearly, a generous measure of the expansive temperament is required to make things happen. Yet that restless energy must be channeled toward larger purposes and must not overwhelm other people. Moderately expansive executives avoid two extremes in exercising power: They neither give uninhibited—and therefore sometimes destructive—expression to that power nor restrict it to the point of limiting their ability to get things done. One way to understand the achievement of this happy medium is that as children they were successfully socialized but not oversocialized. Yet their training as children—along with whatever code of conduct they internalized—does not adequately account for the balance they later strike as adults. A considerable part of it must be attributable to the good fortune of developing a firm sense of self. James Baker, secretary of state under President George Bush, is widely viewed as an extremely capable executive who, according to one observer, has "no hang-ups or neuroses or ego problems." Although he has "plenty of energy" he is "unaggressive but nonetheless very tough." Baker's ability to be hard-driving but not aggressive or self-important seems to be associated with "the sense he conveyed of feeling secure within himself."[6]

Similarly, John Holland told us, "I had a lot of self-esteem built into my life at a young age. My mother made you feel good about yourself. So did my father. They were supportive. There was a sense in the household of a lack of criticism; there were good feelings. . . . I didn't get beat over the head when I didn't get A's. My parents concentrated on the A's I *did* get." His experience in the family of being valued (but not having to be perfect) was paralleled by his experience with peers: "I was always in the center of things, I was always in the [high-status] clique in high school."

John's self-confidence may also have derived from his parents' practice of placing him in a variety of challenging situations. His mother challenged him to speak and to write well. His father introduced him to a number of outdoor activities — sports, camping, fishing, hunting. His father also showed John how to investigate whatever subject — planets, engines, gardening — piqued John's interest. John felt "empowered" by his father and "took away the attitude: let's try a lot of things." This "generalist approach" bred in him a confidence that he could handle new situations.

The examples his parents set also seem to have influenced the formation of John's reasonably solid sense of self. His father preceded him as a successful executive. His mother rose to prominent leadership positions in the community. Both parents modeled a sense of self-efficacy.

Moderately expansive people like John Holland possess the enviable ability to manage people well and get great results. But balanced does not mean perfect. Having the big pieces in place doesn't mean that there aren't smaller pieces that could profitably be moved into place. John Holland felt, going into our program, that he didn't have many weaknesses, and the data confirmed that impression. But going in he did not regard himself as faultless, and the data also confirmed his view of himself in that respect. He told us immediately after going over the data, "I had a very high opinion of myself going into this process and expected it to be deflated. However the opposite has occurred.

On the other hand, the negatives, although understood before-hand, are articulated in a much clearer fashion — which should allow me to work on them more effectively." Of the few negatives, none of them serious enough to hurt his performance in the present job or to mar his suitability for a top job, one problem area grew out of his intense competitive instinct. There were times when being challenged angered him. Criticism of his organization or of his leadership of it could too easily make him react defensively. In exploring with him the roots of this over-sensitivity, we found that, as firm as his sense of self was, this hair-trigger readiness to jump reflected what self-doubt he did have.

Executives like John Holland are plainly "good enough" (Donald Winnicott's phrase for being as competent as we can reasonably expect to be without succumbing to perfectionism.)[7] So the question arises, as it can with any effective executive: Why not leave well enough alone? In fact, a peer of John's confessed to me his uneasiness about our program. He was sure that John's strengths far outweighed his weaknesses. He didn't want the feedback to "spook" his colleague, and he succeeded in transmitting some of his anxiety to me. In raising this particular concern, he also underlined Holland's sensitivity about being criticized. We will return later to the question of the risk run in attempting change.

What does one do about the development of the moderately expansive executive who appears to have it all? First, correct the misconception that any executive, in fact, has it all. As good as a senior manager may be, it does neither the individual nor the organization any good to glorify him or her. Second, what appear to be minor weaknesses can, in someone with great institutional power, turn into sizable problems down the line. Development for highly effective, well-balanced executives may not be absolutely essential, but it is desirable.

Insufficiently Expansive Executives

If some moderately expansive executives are virtually paragons, others are flawed by not being expansive enough. In our experience most executives err, if they err at all, on the side of being too expansive, but it would be a mistake to overlook this other type. These executives do not treat people roughly, do not generally exercise control unilaterally, and do not degrade the organization. Instead they are respectful and considerate of other people. They are skilled at forming strong interpersonal partnerships. However, they lack aggressiveness to the extent that they get less than optimal results. They are the inverse of the extremely expansive executive who excels in bottom-line terms, with opposite strengths and opposite weaknesses.

Because this variant among senior managers is relatively rare, we will give an example. Mark Tabor, in a senior line position, lacks expansiveness in certain respects and seems for this reason to impair his ability to get optimal results. But he is by no means a washout. Indeed, he has been a well-regarded executive for many years.

Mark possesses many of the moderately expansive type of virtues, which accounts for his sterling record in handling the human side. He is a person of impeccable integrity; he does not put his own ambitions ahead of the organization's interests; he does not hide his mistakes. He has exceptionally good relationships with the people he works with. On the ratings of his relationships (given by superiors, peers, and subordinates), his scores were unusually high for the executive population. The same was true of his scores on being open to influence and his capacity for give-and-take. Among the descriptors applied to him are the following: "delegates responsibility well, gives subordinates freedom, an excellent listener, trusts his people, builds a strong team, develops relationships, inspires loyalty in subordinates." From subordinates he received high praise. One said, "He uses power very constructively: delegates, trusts, supports subordinates extremely well." Another said, "He is a very smart guy who works hard and who is well liked and respected by everyone." Yet another said, "Mark is a natural leader. He generates strong support from subordinates without employing fear or threat." The opposite of Rich Bauer, who "led by fear, not by love," Mark Tabor epitomizes constructive, people-oriented leadership. On the strength of positive attributes he is a "natural leader."

How, then, can one account for the shortfall in the results he gets? It is not for lack of applying himself. Not only does he work hard, he works exceptionally hard. In this respect, he keeps company with those who are extremely expansive. He is driven to attain mastery. His wife called him a workaholic and said that "success is very important to him." For years he has made a habit of being the first one to arrive at the office and the last to leave. As a firstborn son he inherited a vigorous work ethic from both his parents. The drive to mastery also shows up in his private life. He worked thirty years before taking two back-to-back weeks of vacation. He is a runner who has for many years religiously covered several miles a day.

Thus there is no doubt that he pushes himself very hard. The shortfall comes from a reluctance to push other people hard. Mark's limitations as well as his strengths were captured by a subordinate's pithy characterization: "He's a leader, not a pusher." His limitations showed up in our data as a series of interrelated failings: "He doesn't press hard enough for immediate results, he doesn't quite get to the heart of a problem, he doesn't confront well enough, he shies away from performance problems, he doesn't provide enough structure for his subordinates, he isn't good at introducing needed change in the face of opposition." A superior ascribed to him "a lack of toughness — not wanting to be overly demanding or critical when the situation demands it." All these limitations add up to a certain lack of aggression. One important consequence is that he is not well equipped as "an agent of major change." He is not an executive to whom it comes naturally to bring about "step changes" in the organization. He finds it difficult to make the unpopular moves that go with change of that magnitude.

It would be easy to overplay this fault. It's not that he never pushes or can't push. It's that, when the pressure's on, he has trouble pushing hard enough. When he quizzes a subordinate on a problem, for example, he does indeed draw out important information; yet sometimes he doesn't go quite to the heart of the problem.

An inhibition seems to lie behind this lack of aggressiveness. Somewhere along the line (we will soon see where) Mark learned not to cross the line with people. An unwritten code of ethics, laced by anxiety, allows him to go only so far with other people, so that in a pinch he surrenders *his* prerogatives to *their* prerogatives. While expansive in other respects, in this respect he is self-effacing and therefore different from extremely expansive executives, whose egos are anything but effaced.

The psychology of his reluctance to push others becomes clear when you hear him talk: "My attitude is: Let's get in far enough to see if something is amiss, and then let's get into doing something positive about it. It comes back to putting someone on the spot: If you go further, you're hammering them." When queried about his use of the word "hammering," he said, "That's what it feels like. That's also related to structuring subordinates' work. To structure more is to intrude on their turf, imposing myself, diminishing their self-worth." Unlike an extremely expansive person, who blithely or inadvertently downgrades other people, he consciously guards against diminishing another person's sense of worth. Feeling freer to make demands on himself than on others, he works harder than his subordinates.

Closely related to his reluctance to assert himself is his inability to express anger. In general, he is unexpressive emotionally, a coolness that is associated in people's minds with the ability to be "absolutely unflappable under tremendous pressure." About expressing anger he said, "I've seen so many cases where people were angry and made absolute fools of themselves. The open expression of anger is threatening to me because it can damage relationships, perhaps irrevocably . . . . In my *head* I know that relationships can be improved by openly expressing dissatisfaction."

In being fearful of expressing anger in any form, Mark gives up some of his power — because emotions like dissatisfaction, displeasure, resentment, and anger, when used appropriately, provide the impetus for action. Mark goes beyond being controlled to being overcontrolled and in the process diminishes his personal power.

Speculating about the causes of this behavior, he said, "Shame may be the thing." Shame in the sense of a fear of exposing others, presumably paralleled by a fear of being shamed himself. The issue of shame appeared to be tied up in a lack of self-confidence: "I know there are things I should take a strong stand on. But deep down I wonder: Am I really prepared? I hold back for fear of looking foolish."

From what Mark reported as his parents' "shoulds" and "shouldn'ts," we get an inkling of the childhood causes of his self-restraint. "First, do well in school. Second, proper behavior in a social setting. Don't be obnoxious. Don't annoy people or damage anything." In addition to what was said, there was his mother's example. He sees himself as having internalized his mother's desire to please: "I got from my mother wanting to please because her aim in life was wanting to please my dad." Her need to please was such that when on rare occasions she and her husband disagreed, she accommodated him. "When my father got mad, my mother would do what he wanted to do. My mother swallowed what she wanted."

Mark Tabor epitomizes the way underexpansive executives avoid the worst offenses of expansive executives and, more than that, bring an abundance of positive qualities to the job. Mark Tabor also exemplifies the losses such executives sustain in keeping themselves too much under control. If, as discussed in the previous chapter, overexpansive executives employ "unsocialized power" (that is, are self-centered and destructive), and if positive executives use "socialized power" (that is, are organization-centered and constructive), then these executives employ "oversocialized power." They are so concerned about committing the offense of intruding on others that they don't permit themselves to push as far as acceptable tolerances allow. A top executive, for example, who had used his considerable skills as a leader to institute major changes in his company, had a streak of this self-restraint that led one of his subordinates to describe him as "passive." In the same spirit, someone else suggested he be more forceful in making speeches. On a psychological test, his score on wanting to exercise control was considerably lower than on wanting others to influence him — a result that disturbed him. Consistent with this sense of himself as not aggressive, he cited as one of his major strengths: "Gives others room."

A second personal commodity that executives of this type sacrifice is anger, which is no more permissible in their eyes than naked power. They may feel it but not express it, or, such are their internal restrictions, they may not even feel it unless it overpowers them. As mentioned, disallowing anger in any form deprives them of an important source of power, since dissatisfaction at its varying levels of intensity often fuels attempts at influence.

In addition, as a general policy of not imposing their own needs on others, these executives systematically avoid calling attention to themselves. The value they place on modesty explains their refreshing lack of the brash egocentrism found in extremely expansive counterparts. To say that these individuals are inhibited in this respect is too weak a term; prohibited is more accurate.

In the feedback session, Mark and I got a glimmer of where this restraint came from — a restraint that makes it difficult for him to push his points forcibly in meetings and to promote himself with higher management. The glimmer came in the form of an extremely low exhibitionism score on a psychological test. I asked him, "What voice from your past tells you not to seek attention?" He responded, "I don't know. . . . Maybe my mother, who always told me, 'Never brag!'" In this stricture we have one indication as to why Mark has kept his light partially hidden under a bushel.

Development for the executive who is not expansive enough to make strong demands on others is a different matter. What seems to be needed is to free the individual somewhat from the inner restraints, the prohibitions, that bind too tightly. These individuals need to understand what makes them self-effacing; they also need to bolster their confidence to demand as much of others as they demand of themselves. In sharp contrast to extremely expansive executives, the challenge for these executives is to unleash themselves personally by learning to push *harder*. This change in their behavior will come more readily if it is accompanied by a revision in their beliefs about how much they must put limits on themselves and how much they must avoid trespassing on the territories of others.

To summarize, there are two broad classes of extremely expansive executives. One class has practically no redeeming qualities: In the hands of such executives, the organization's performance is hurt, and its human capability is degraded. The other class has an adverse effect on the organization in human terms but redeems itself by obtaining good business results, at least in the short term. For the latter class, the danger is that pushing for short term results at the expense of the health of the organization sacrifices the organization's future.

Likewise, there are two broad classes of moderately expansive executives. One class is exemplary in both business and human terms. Members of the other class treat people well but at some cost in business terms. In a sense, they sacrifice results to the scrupulous treatment of people, just as the second class of extremely expansive executives sacrifices people to results.

Chapter Eight

The Expansive Manager at Home

Drive is not something that executives generate to meet job demands and then leave on their desks along with the other accouterments of managerial life. The drive to mastery, along with other expansive characteristics, goes home with executives because it is part of their makeup as people. Even executives who draw strict lines between work and home—by, for example, making a practice of never discussing work with their spouses—don't stop being the essential individuals they are. Try as they might to draw boundaries around work activity, executives cannot compartmentalize their personalities.

This chapter is about the imbalance between work life and private life to which expansive executives are susceptible. The chapter also considers the ramifications of this imbalance back on the job and distinguishes between a workable and an unworkable imbalance.

Manifestations Outside of Work

Executives who make work and career their number one priority in life put their private lives—and ultimately their work

126

lives — at risk in various ways. Of these ways we will discuss three. First, they tend to be "not there"— not sufficiently available — for close relationships. Second, when they are present, they tend to turn both relationships and leisure activities into quests for mastery. Third, because they diminish the importance of non-work life, they tend not to take good care of themselves.

Limited Availability for Close Relationships. Long hours, business trips, and work-related social engagements all combine to keep executives away from home a great deal of the time. At home, the ever-present briefcase, bulging with mail, memos, and periodicals, keeps many an executive occupied on week-day evenings and during the weekend. Voice mail, a great convenience, makes it all too easy to stay in touch with the office during off hours.

The long hours spent working mean that sheer physical fatigue from work-related exertions also limits the executive's availability for close relationships. Long days, short nights, and depletion from more or less continual stress exhaust most executives by the end of the day or the week and leave them with precious little energy for family relationships. Tired out, they may be impatient and irritable; they may take out the frustration caused by problems at work on their family. This is what Bartolome and Evans mean by the "negative spillover" from executive jobs.[1] Executives, who must spend most of their time at work relating to other people, are left with little time, energy, or inclination to relate to the people they claim are the most important individuals in their lives. Though they may be physically at home, their minds may still be at work. They spend time with their children, for example, but their attention drifts, even despite themselves, to some unresolved problem, an important upcoming meeting, a recent triumph. But it is not just their jobs that take them away, it is also their expansive natures — the irrepressible drive for mastery and the organizational and psychic rewards from attaining mastery.

The problem of limited availability for relationships would be relatively easy to solve if it were purely physical — simply a function of time spent at work and time left for family. But the

problem is often at least as much emotional as physical. Many
executives are neither especially willing nor able to participate
fully in close relationships. Why is this?

The principal reason is that executives, especially expansive ones, feel good about themselves chiefly through accomplishment. The attachment to this mode of adaptation and its
satisfactions can be so strong as to be addictive. Hardly a day
can go by without getting a dose of mastery-derived gratification. If an executive's attachment to work in fact reaches addictive proportions, family relationships are virtually sure to suffer.
And when family relationships begin to suffer, the executive's
investment in work often becomes that much greater, as an escape from the unpleasantness at home and as a compensation
for the associated feelings of failure. The wife of an executive
in such a situation described him as follows: "In the office he
was very much in control; he was removed from intimate relationships. It's the one area where he functions superbly. He
doesn't have to worry about hurting anyone's feelings. He handles superficial working relationships really well, where they don't
demand deep emotional give-and-take . . . . He thrived in the
office; he wrapped his whole life there; it was a neat package.
He didn't have to go beyond the office for anything."[2] This was
not a jaundiced view, and in fact it squared with the rest of the
data. In a nutshell, he was experienced as "personable" but not
"personal."

Whether executives are available or unavailable to their
spouses greatly affects their marriages. A study of 325 European managers, all male, found a strong relationship between
"expressiveness" on the husband's part and marital happiness.
Expressiveness was defined as taking an active interest in one's
wife, talking with her about herself and her problems, and expressing affection toward her. Eighty percent of the marriages
in which the husband saw expressiveness as an important part
of the relationship were very happy. On the other hand, 80 percent of the marriages in which the husband did not value expressiveness were unhappy.[3]

Organizations themselves are another factor in the executive's difficulty with close relationships. Large bureaucratic

institutions operate according to a "code of impersonality"[4] and place a value on, and encourage the development of, qualities of the head rather than qualities of the heart.[5] Sex roles also contribute to the difficulty. Most of the executives in our sample took the traditional male role, marked by a paucity of self-disclosure, emotional expression, and the intimate exchange associated with close friendships. What the psychologist Sydney Jourard described twenty years ago as "the lethal aspects of the male role"—referring to the harm done to the man's relationships and body by an inability to be self-disclosing—still persist.[6] There is some indication that women admitted to the executive suite have many of the same characteristics as their male colleagues. One could say that these women have masculinized themselves in the service of ambition.

Finally, many executives have trouble with close relationships because of their personal histories. Certainly not all, but a sizable proportion of the executives we studied had suffered a major disappointment in relationships early on in life: The death of a parent, an abusive parent, chronic difficulty making friends, or the alienation caused by a physical handicap were among the causes of such disappointment. As a result these people had turned away from relationships and transferred much of their emotional investment to the world of achievement and mastery. They were not so scarred that they could not carry on relationships with co-workers or marry and have families. But on close inspection there was something missing in their relationships. There was a basic pessimism about other people, a fear that led them instinctively to hang back and keep from being vulnerable in relationships.

We saw this inhibition in an executive who, though he was otherwise highly effective, lacked a certain something in his work relationships—a spark, a warmth. At home, while devoted to his wife and children, he either engaged in solitary projects or, when he did spend time with his family, was remote emotionally. There is reason to believe that an early trauma impaired his ability to get close to people. At age twelve he contracted a serious communicable disease that hospitalized him for several months and left him with a minor handicap that was

nevertheless sufficient to keep him out of athletics. Recalling
that time he said, "The thing I remember most about the dis-
ease was that friends seemed to abandon me. Up until that time
I was a hotshot in school — smart, athletic, one of the leaders.
After I got sick, no one came to see me. . . . When I returned,
I was still smart — I finished at the top of my high school class,
but I wasn't a hotshot anymore. I had lost my physical talents.
Thinking about it now, I understand why the illness undoubt-
edly complicated the social side of my life, particularly with girls.
But at the time I didn't see it clearly. I was still me." You could
say that he suffered a severe disappointment, which to this day
makes him leery of close involvements and leads him to protect
himself by keeping his distance. He summed it up by saying,
"*I was wounded, so I won't expose myself to that again. I put my energy
into deeds.*" To the extent that he withdrew from interpersonal
relationships, he transferred his investments to the intellectual
and managerial arena. His reaction may have reflected the way
his mother or father handled major disappointments, but we
don't have data on whether they served as a model in this respect.

This pattern of development in which qualities of the head
are valued and developed at the expense of qualities of the heart
was captured clearly by Lawrence Kubie in a study of young
scientists. According to Kubie, the pattern is set initially when
children with intellectual ability run into difficulties in their relationships with emotionally significant others. At the same time,
they receive encouragement for intellectual endeavors, throw
themselves into bookish pursuits, succeed academically, and
withdraw from sports and social life. "As a result, by the time
[the young scientist] reaches adulthood his only triumphs and
gratifications will have been won in the intellectual field, his
range of skills will have become restricted, and the life of the
mind will be almost the only outlet available." These budding
scientists end up "putting every emotional egg in the intellectual basket. . . . The sense of security and the self-esteem of the
young intellectual come to stand on one leg."[7] Executives are
not generally as lopsided as this; they can't function in their jobs
without basic interpersonal skills. But the inhibition and un-
derdevelopment on the interpersonal side often applies to them

and helps to explain executives' lack of emotional availability for intimate relationships.

The Effect of the Orientation Toward Mastery. We have seen how executives have trouble with intimacy in their relationships with spouse and children. How then *do* they approach those relationships? They do what they know best: They deal in achievement.

With their spouses, they are perpetually busy with chores, social obligations, or arrangements for the children. Since family life is full of tasks that need performing, this mode serves a definite purpose. The difficulty, however, comes when tasks fill the void left by the relative absence of intimate involvement with spouse and children. One executive's task orientation was so highly developed that when he left for work he gave his wife index cards with lists of things to do.

In addition to the ordinary jobs with which executives occupy themselves around the house, they have a penchant for devising major projects that, in effect, create part-time jobs for themselves and their wives. One such project is to build a big house. The decision to build is, in our experience, typically more the male executive's than his wife's. In addition to the tax advantages of a large mortgage and the tangible sign of having moved up in the world, the new house seems an obvious expression of expansive urges. It affords the opportunity over a period of many months to conceive of a satisfying outcome and by stages bring it into existence. It also has the effect of turning evenings and weekends into occasions for meetings given over to decisions about design, financing, choice of materials, decorations, problems with the contractor, and so on. Instead of leaving room to deepen relationships or to grow emotionally, these executives elect to pile another expansive project on top of lives already dominated by efforts to achieve.

The mastery orientation of executives is also evident at home in the expectations they have of their children. Expecting a great deal of themselves, they also expect a great deal of their children. Early in their own lives they seized upon high achievement as a way of making their way in the world, and they automatically assume that this way of life also is best for their children. The orientation to mastery is so central to their self-concept that they have little or no perspective on it as they apply it to their children. A perfectionist father requires his children to perform chores with the same scrupulous attention to detail that he brings to his work. Rich Bauer, as we saw, was so concerned about having his children turn out right that he interfered with their attempts to find their own way, even though his own self-turnaround was his greatest developmental achievement. Executives cherishing high aspirations for their children predictably end up closest to the children—often firstborn—who fulfill these aspirations and most distant (or even estranged) from those children who reject the sacred value placed on achievement.

In my own case, I gained a new appreciation for my expansive tendencies when my son was a junior in high school and the question arose as to which college he would attend. He had been an A student. I had believed that it didn't matter to me where he went to college, as long as he got a good education. Suddenly his social life became more important to him, and his grades dropped a notch. As I watched him hurt his chances of getting into a prestigious college, I tried every means available to get him to concentrate on his schoolwork. When, over a period of months, it became apparent I was losing the battle with him, the battle turned inward. Slowly, painfully, I realized that I did, in fact, want him to attend one of the best colleges. I had been trying to impose my aspirations for myself on him. In my own generalized anxiety to acquit myself by doing exceptionally well, I had discriminated poorly between myself and him.

When emotionally distant executives who are away from home most of the time impose on their children their own stringent work ethic and sky-high expectations, the result is a stressful home environment that is harmful to the children. Upwardly mobile executives, especially when they are men, tend not to be involved in their children's day-to-day lives and are most likely to pay attention to their children's successes and failures. Independent achievers themselves, they seem intent on turning their children into independent achievers.[8] One indication of the consequences of all this comes from a survey of companies that provide extensive insurance coverage: Children of executives were more than twice as likely as children of nonexecutives to receive treatment for psychiatric problems or drug abuse.[9]

Self-Neglect. What effect does an expansive personality have on executives themselves outside of work? If they work long hours, if they fill their spare time with more work, if they avoid depth in family relationships, then it is fair to say that they neglect themselves. They deprive themselves of much of what life has to offer outside of work.

Extreme cases are commonplace. One executive, who literally structured his entire weekend with paperwork, family obligations, and household chores, was so dependent on an activity-filled "free" time that he was aghast at the suggestion that, purely as an experiment, he try waking up one Saturday morning with nothing planned for the day. Another executive, who lived on his farm and in his off-hours busied himself with routine maintenance and special projects, came to the realization that "my life is out of balance. I work too hard, and *when I play, I work*" (emphasis added). Another executive took only a few days of vacation a year and even then brought along work and remained in contact with the office. He secretly took pride in this abstinence from leisure as a sign of his dedication to work. Executives like these, who drive themselves practically as hard outside of work as at work, deny themselves the chance to relax, recharge their batteries, or get a fresh perspective on their jobs and themselves.

This tendency to take relatively poor care of themselves may include getting little or no physical exercise. Consumed with reaching closure on tasks and attaining objectives, they disregard almost everything that could interfere — including bodily indications of fatigue, stress, or illness. One executive prided himself on never, until recently, having taken a sick day in his thirty-year career. He was rarely sick, and, when he was, he dragged himself out of bed and went off to work. Another executive with a self-taught high threshold for pain kept up his heavy travel schedule while recovering from a chronic illness. A co-worker told the story of once walking into the executive's hotel room to find him administering medicine to himself with a hypodermic needle. It is almost as if their bodies are beasts of burden to be worked as hard as possible without regard for anything but the beast's minimal physical needs.

Executives who do look after themselves physically and who do get regular exercise use it as a way to release tension and aggression accumulated on the job. They may also turn exercise into another arena for competition and high achievement. I once happened to be in a hotel exercise room while a general manager in his fifties and in tiptop shape put himself through a grueling hour-long workout that included a hard run on the treadmill and a round of rigorous calisthenics appropriate for a football player. He later told me that this was his *daily* regimen. He had taken up tennis in his forties and had drilled himself into becoming a top-seeded player in his age-bracket. Exercise for executives like this individual becomes yet another opportunity to express their urge for mastery. Competitive sports are an obvious way to satisfy the need to prevail. It is common for male executives who played sports in their youth to continue to do battle on the tennis court or the golf course or even the polo field. One took relish in relating how he and a fellow executive went on a vacation with their wives in Mexico where "he and I beat each other's brains out on the tennis court in the hot sun while our wives sipped margaritas in the shade."

Finding a Workable Imbalance

By now it should be clear that expansive executives are capable of creating lives that are markedly out of balance. Striving for mastery takes precedence over practically everything else. I should acknowledge, however, that the psychology of driven executives is such that they may not feel out of balance. Indeed, they may stoutly defend their way of life, arguing that this is the way they prefer to live. On the one hand, they are justified: Who are we to judge what choices and sacrifices they should make? On the other hand, in their righteous defense of themselves is an element of denial of the price they pay. No effective executive can enjoy the balance made possible by a normal nine-to-five job; their heavy job responsibilities coupled with the vigorous work ethic expected by competitive organizations will not allow it. But if imbalance is a given, the extent of it can certainly vary. While expansive executives are susceptible to leading severely out-of-balance lives, with negative effects on family relationships, family members, and their own health and well-being, they are not necessarily doomed to this fate. What makes the difference, apart from contextual factors, is the sort of expansive personality they have.

What we have called moderately expansive executives have a very considerable drive to mastery but keep it sufficiently within bounds to make possible what might be termed a "workable imbalance." Their ambitions for themselves, the effort they expend, their need for control, and their appetite for recognition are all well above average yet do not reach towering proportions. As a result, they have interest and energy left over for nonwork pursuits such as personal relationships. *Despite* their careers they have satisfying marriages — that is, intimate in the interpersonal sense.[10] Perhaps the governing variable that allows them to moderate their expansive drives and place some limit on their expansive investments is a modicum of personal security, a partial sense of self-worth.

On the other hand, the drive to mastery of extremely expansive executives seems to know virtually no bounds. In one guise or another, these executives go in unrelenting pursuit of mastery. Perhaps the measure of that extreme intensity is the underlying doubts they try to quell. Whatever the precise cause, the result is an unworkable imbalance that takes a toll, sooner or later, on themselves or their families. It would seem that the severe imbalance in their lives corresponds to a severe imbalance within. Put another way, their extreme work-absorption stems from an extreme self-absorption, a concern with demonstrating one's worth that is so overblown that it ultimately proves to be the person's undoing.

From the purely pragmatic point of view of the employer, why worry if executives work too hard? They're paid handsomely; they *should* give it their all. As most of us know, this myopic attitude eventually backfires when the individual develops health or family problems that distract him or her from work and undercut his or her performance. This first-stage negative spillover from extreme overwork turns into a second-stage negative spillover *back* to the work setting. Clearly, executives cannot perform well over the years unless they maintain themselves and the family system that, among other things, serves to maintain them.

From the standpoint of job effectiveness, life outside of work can make positive contributions not only to the executive's health but also to his or her development as a person and therefore, ultimately, as an executive. Relationships with one's growing children, for example, offer learning opportunities as rich as any training program or job assignment. The challenge of letting adolescent children take increasing control of their own lives parallels nicely the challenges of granting appropriate autonomy to subordinates. Executives who make the effort to work through the inevitable power struggles with young adult children learn valuable lessons about delegation. They learn to distinguish more clearly between their needs for themselves and their subordinates' needs for themselves.

Another way that private life affects job performance is through personal hardships. No one would wish a family or health crisis on an executive, but when the accumulated effects of years of neglect lead to disastrous problems, there can be a developmental payoff if executives respond adaptively to the crisis. From the damage they've done over time, they can salvage a lesson or two. For executives possessed by ambitions for mastery and success, it may take nothing less than a personal hardship to get their attention and spur an adjustment.[11]

One executive, with a background in the physical sciences, reported that he learned a lot — about personal relationships as well as work relationships — from the painful dissolution of his first marriage. "We had a pretty good marriage for a while, but my devotion to work was a constant source of irritation to my wife. If someone got short shrift, it was her. Our differences led to a lot of spiteful things being done. It got pretty bad with respect to what we would do to one another to make a point.

I learned a lot about vindictiveness and how a person can influence another . . . . I came out of that relationship a lot wiser about what two people have to do to be close . . . . Now when my present wife wants to tell me something, I listen better. I take the attitude 'What can I learn?' instead of being defensive. I was much more defensive with my first wife . . . . At work I can understand the stress people go through. I'm more sensitive, more sympathetic to family situations. . . . *I also feel that through soul-searching and a wrenching experience you know yourself better and see how other people see you"* (emphasis added).

Considerable drama surrounds the question of whether expansive executives, especially the extreme cases, will recognize obvious self-defeating behavior at work as well as the problems they bring on themselves outside of work. But for reasons that inhere in the character of the executives themselves or in their elevated situations, self-awareness can be very difficult to come by.

Besides making time for themselves and their families, executives can do the most good by making themselves available psychologically. At a premium is expressiveness — the ability to share one's own thoughts and feelings and the ability to be responsive to another person's thoughts and feelings. This mutual sharing includes both the good things and the bad, those things that make the person proud and those that worry or deflate the person. The ideal here, however, is not indiscriminate sharing, which can drag a relationship into perpetual scrutiny of everything that beats within each person's breast.

The capacity for expressiveness and intimacy pays dividends for the executive's marriage and for his or her parenting. The individual becomes more understanding and supportive — less a machine and more a human being. He or she learns to give more of him- or herself as a person. This capacity also pays off for the individual in the form of emotional support that he or she is now able to *receive*. In exchange for a willingness to be vulnerable, the individual is much more likely to get taken care of. The need to nurture and to be nurtured may be something the individual is completely unaware of — until he or she begins to meet that need. It's a case of not knowing what you're missing.

When an executive develops a capacity for this sort of human connectedness, the benefit is not only personal. It is just this capacity that is lacking in the work relationships of many expansive executives. This is not to suggest that what is needed on the job is the same kind of intimacy that is desirable in one's family. But a certain competence with emotions, one's own and other people's, is fundamental to effective working relationships.

To conclude: Driven managers are not doomed to have unsatisfactory or failed marriages and troubled children. A busy schedule, combined with heavy traveling, makes family life challenging but hardly impossible. The critical ingredients are that the manager set some limit on the amount of work, in any form, that he or she does and that the manager be capable of close relationships with family members. Many managers who satisfy these conditions have happy marriages.[12]

This capability is in some ways trainable. Managers can learn to listen better, they can be helped to better appreciate individual differences, they can become less a stranger to their emotions and those of others. But there is a limit to managers' educability on this score. The limit has to do with the fact that their incapacity is, in a sense, motivated. It serves a purpose, albeit self-defeating in some respects. It is a learned incapacity that these individuals developed in response to the early conditions in which they found themselves. Furthermore, it is a characteristic that is woven into the very fabric of their expansive natures.

Part Three

Developing Professional and Personal Balance

Let him who would move the world first move himself.
— Socrates

Self-knowledge is not an aim in itself, but a means of liberating the forces of spontaneous growth.
— Karen Horney

Chapter Nine

Changing
Self-Defeating Behavior:
What Works and What Doesn't

In Part Two we took a look at the nature of expansive character. In this part we consider how, through self-understanding,
extremely expansive executives can become less destructive. In
Part One we saw the many ways that criticism can fail to get
through to a senior manager. We also saw that, despite the many
obstacles, some criticism does get through to some executives.
Assuming that an executive truly "gets the message," will he or
she make use of the input or let the opportunity to grow slip
away? Will he or she make the difficult shift from seeing the
need for change to actually changing?

The intention to change is a far cry from the enactment
of change. Of the many reasons why executives prove unable
to make the adjustments they set out to make, one important
reason, in our view, is the overreliance on behavioral methods.
This chapter considers what behavioral methods are and are
not able to do, and it begins to define what an alternative
to an exclusive reliance on the behavioral approach might look
like.

141

Value of Behavioral Methods

When managers attempt change, the method of choice is usually behavioral: their self-improvement projects are straightforward efforts to alter their behavior. There is a lot to be said for a behavioral approach to leadership development: It is practical and eminently reasonable, and its efficiency and businesslike quality recommend it highly to managers. If a manager wants to build a new capacity, one of the best ways to do it is simply to begin exhibiting the new behavior. Actually undertaking the desired role — which means practicing it a lot, with coaching — will often eventually do the trick, whether the goal is to make better presentations, control others less, or delegate more responsibility.

For example, a typical self-improvement project undertaken by executives is to improve their speaking ability. As they ascend to senior levels, they suddenly have much more occasion to make presentations, formal or informal, to large groups of people. How they come across in that circumstance — whether to the board of directors, a large group of subordinates, or a gathering of outsiders — can make a material difference in their ability to move their organizations forward. A sizable proportion of the managers we have studied share the problem of being too stiff, formal, and controlled and not dynamic enough in front of a group. The method many of them prefer to correct the problem is to take a course in communication skills and to get lots of practice. Perhaps public speaking is the sort of skill that is amenable to behavioral methods. With practice the person becomes desensitized to stage fright and internalizes the basic techniques for effective presentations.

John Sculley is a public figure who battled to improve his presentation skills. Consistent with his expansive nature, he brought a zealous determination to the developmental task: "I had to work many hours to improve my skills as a speaker — to overcome my severe stammer as a boy and gain the confidence to speak before large groups of people. . . . When I was named marketing vice-president, I was determined to build a strength out of what was originally a weakness. . . . I became obsessed with the idea that I was going to become better than anyone else . . . a successful communicator."[1]

Mark Tabor—the executive we discussed in Chapter Seven—followed through on his intention to change his behavior by keeping a structured daily diary. He constructed the diary to help him improve in three areas, all having to do with becoming more aggressive. First, he tracked the number of hours spent on high-priority items versus items of less importance. In so doing, he sought to correct a tendency to be too responsive to other people's initiatives. Second, he tracked the number of times he took on work as compared with the number of times he transferred work to other people. In particular, he sought to turn down more of the demands or requests being made of him. Third, he tracked the number of times each day he operated in his "discomfort zone"—specifically, by challenging other people or by initiating (constructive) conflict. The diary lent structure to his intentions by focusing him on his developmental goals and by holding him accountable for progress. The diary was a help, but his reluctance to push other people hard limited his efforts to change.

When behavioral change doesn't work, it may be because it simply isn't enough; some changes in the executive's character may also be needed. Before exploring what character-based change means, let us look more closely at why behavioral change in executives on its own sometimes fails to succeed or only partially succeeds. We will start with an example from our research.

An Executive Who Couldn't Change His Behavior

Hank Cooper is an executive who was aware of a persistent performance problem but was unable to correct it. When we met him, he had been the general manager of a small business unit for eighteen months, after spending fifteen years working his way up the ladder in a technical service function of his company. His promotion to general manager was part of his company's attempt to increase the number of senior managers with strong technical backgrounds. Being highly intelligent and energetic, he had little trouble acquiring the knowledge necessary to make the transition from his functional specialty to general management. He did, however, run into trouble because of the way he treated people. One of the leading causes of executive derailment is abrasiveness,[2] and Hank Cooper's career was side-tracked because of it.

His abrasiveness mattered not so much because it violated a social code as because it cost him some of the support he needed to make things happen. Tied up with his people problem was his arrogance about his exceptional intelligence. The best that could be said about him in this respect is that (to quote a superior) "he doesn't suffer fools easily." Another superior was less kind: "He is an arrogant intellectual type, who treats with disdain those who are not his [intellectual] equal."

Whatever the explanation, and there were others, he regularly mistreated his subordinates, who, even if they saw his behavior as unintentional, described it in vivid terms. His subordinates made references to "acid, sarcastic attacks," "cutting remarks," "berating people in front of others," and "demolishing people." One of his peers said that "he is overly aggressive, and he pisses people off." A superior surmised that "having no manufacturing experience, he never got the rough edges knocked off. If he's going to be a general manager, he must learn to deal with people."

When we reported back to Cooper, the data on his abrasiveness did not come as a surprise to him. He knew going in that he rubbed people the wrong way. In discussing his abrasiveness he had joined everyone else in indicating a need for change. In fact, as he told us in the feedback session, he had long known about his abrasiveness: "I've known these things for twenty years."

With this knowledge, why had the problem persisted? First, Hank Cooper had not fully appreciated the seriousness of the problem. After receiving the report, he expressed a "certain level of surprise at the intensity of the criticism." He added, "One of the illusions I've been operating under is that I'm hard-hitting but fun. I meant no harm, and I'm doing no harm. It's no big deal. When you're in a certain group, people get to know you. They kid me about it, so it's no big deal." However aware of his abrasiveness, he was out of touch with the hurt he caused. He had little sense of what his victims felt. At one point, when a fellow manager and friend told him that it's fine for him to be "right a lot" but not OK to "push it in people's faces" and thereby make himself into "an arrogant SOB," Hank responded by saying, "I see that intellectually but not at a gut level." He (and we) discovered that any feelings he had about hurting people simply did not register. In a session to plan the changes he would make, I read him a long list of things that people had said about him in sharp, graphic language: "Uses a verbal whip, treats people with disdain, makes personal attacks, a wise ass, makes cracks at people's expense," and so on. When I asked him how he felt about hearing those unflattering descriptions of him, he said, honestly, "Nothing." Thus, the basis in his character of his mistreatment of others becomes clear: He was disconnected both from what his targets felt and from what he himself felt about committing his aggressive acts. The abrasive tendencies persisted for a character-based reason, which helps to explain why he had failed to appreciate the seriousness of the problem.

To better understand Hank's character flaw, let us look briefly at the likely origins of his aggressive interpersonal style and his difficulty knowing his feelings about it and its effects. As the only child of now deceased parents, he was our only source of information on his childhood. He remembered his mother as something of an emotional tyrant, capricious, critical, and at the same time overprotective. His father, a shadowy figure during Hank's childhood, allowed himself to be eclipsed for the most part by his wife and did little to moderate her negative impact on Hank.

Recalling those early times with his mother, Hank told us, "Maybe she flared up too easily. As a result, I talked back a tremendous amount. I could tell that I drove her up the wall. As a little kid, my mother might say: 'Take this medicine.' When I balked, she threw it at me. I'd say, sarcastically, 'I guess I can't take it now.' At fifteen it was no longer a contest. If she threatened me, I'd threaten to break a certain vase." It is obvious that he and his mother were locked in a destructive relationship in which he, presumably to cope with her, developed a repertoire of reflex aggressive tactics. He sees the penchant in his present life for repeating that pattern: "I can get into war games easily. There's a strong element of survival."

In addition to learning to counterattack, he evidently adapted by cutting himself off from the hurt inflicted by a mother who regularly criticized him or otherwise aggressed against him. In effect, he built a shell around himself designed to protect him from the pain suffered at the time. Although for years he had been telling friends entertaining stories about his epic struggles with his mother, the stories—including those told us—were not occasions for him to reexperience the pain of those early injurious experiences. Being cut off from his feelings, past and present, Hank Cooper lacked empathy for other people and for the child he had been.

Limits to Behavioral Methods

As Hank Cooper's story shows, executives—like anyone else—sometimes simply cannot produce the desired behavior. Like Hank, they are aware only intellectually of the problem, so they don't fully appreciate its seriousness. Or the offending behavior is so profoundly rooted in the person's character that it cannot simply be removed.

Rich Bauer, for example, appreciating his problem with supporting, praising, and expressing faith in subordinates, made a serious effort to do so, only to find himself in agony when he tried to praise subordinates face-to-face. "Since the last time we got together, I have worked on providing positive feedback to my people. It's almost impossible for me to do it. I experience tremendous emotional turmoil. I try to provide some positive feedback, but I find it agonizing to do it." Reflecting on why this was, he said, "I understand the roots of this. I expect perfection." In other words, his character as a person kept him from making the desired change.

Another limitation of behavioral change is that even when executives do accomplish it, they may not be able to sustain it. One staff executive, for example, reverted to autocratic form under pressure. Before board meetings, at which he periodically makes presentations, he got extremely tense and worried, and he fell back into the old, highly controlling, poorly listening pattern. A subordinate said, "He made a heroic effort to change, and I mean this as an enormous compliment. But in time of stress or challenge, the potential for him to revert is there." Another subordinate distinguished his "good leadership style" from his "bad leadership style," which he said kicks in even today when the executive is under pressure. The executive himself said that more and more he uses a participative style—except when he's defensive.

Yet another limitation on behavioral change is that it may be only skin deep. For change to become permanent, it needs to take root in the personality of the executive. Behavioral change, because it is essentially role taking, will always seem artificial at first, but for it to be successful, the different behavior exhibited on the outside must infiltrate the executive and result in different attitudes and feelings on the inside. When making behavioral changes that went against the grain, one executive we worked with virtually forced himself to act differently. This forced quality meant that his behavior would shift as long as he was vigilant but would revert to old patterns when he dropped his guard.

This executive's co-workers saw some of his change in style as mere role playing because he did not seem to have truly internalized the change. A peer raised the question in the case of the staff executive mentioned above and answered it in favor of authentic change: "One might say: We're seeing an act; will the real Tom Barnett please stand up? In my view, it isn't an act. He says to himself, 'Now I've got several hundred people reporting to me, and I'm going to act differently.' It's part of strategizing, and putting himself in the strategizing. It's unusual for an executive to go through this kind of self-assessment and change." A subordinate, much less generous, suspected this individual of being "a mimic. There's not a core in his professional self to absorb those behaviors. He needs to shape his own style, become a believer in his own beliefs." A human resources staff member commented that after the executive's latest promotion "he became more accepting of feedback, but you really don't know for sure."

The way this executive himself talked about the way he had changed made me wonder whether he had truly internalized the new behavior or was simply playing a part. In recounting how he modeled himself after his boss in a certain way, he described the process in a way that suggested less than full internalization: "It's very effective, so I was able to imbibe his style . . . . I've become a chameleon of all these styles of people I worked for in different areas."

Behavioral methods are limited by the fact that they intentionally keep the person out of it. Change is something that the individual imposes upon him or herself with minimal reference to identity, which after all accounts for the behavior in question. Change like this is essentially impersonal, rational. One senior manager who was considering whether to undertake personal development observed, "The changes I've been making come out of my head. I've been applying techniques that seem to work better than other techniques in the business world. I don't know if something *inside* is changing." In his comment this person reflects a dissociation, characteristic of the purely behavioral approach, between his head, which directs what techniques to adopt, and what is happening inside.

Another major reason that behavioral change alone often fails is that executives, like most people, have a strong attachment to their fundamental way of being, of which the specific managerial behavior is merely an expression. Their way of being represents their identity as a human being. While a strong sense of self is crucial to the individual's well-being, it may be so strong that it becomes rigid and resistant to change. A person's current self-definition is both an achievement and a constraint.[3] Individuals tend to build fortresses around their identities,[4] and, in fact, identity as a mode of adaptation doubles as a means of defense,[5] so much so that it can be difficult to distinguish adaptation from defense.

The attachment to one's character helps to explain the conservatism that frequently surfaces when executives contemplate change. One executive who had recently left IBM and landed a more senior position in another major company with twice the salary told me, "Fundamentally, my management style is cast, and I'm not about to risk changing it and jeopardize the success I've achieved." Executives are reluctant to tamper with their winning formula. As a human resources executive commented, "What's gotten him there has been successful, so why change it?" The reluctance to change can become a superstition. A consultant reported that a hard-bitten client of his had trouble responding to his organization's pressure for a more humanistic style, saying, "If I lose some of my toughness, am I really going to be successful?" Executives are also constrained from trying something different not just by who they have been but by what they *believe* they should be, which rationalizes and reinforces their identities.

A staff executive we worked with who parlayed high principles and perfectionism into a successful career and a rewarding marriage and family life struggled with the question of making basic changes, even though he saw how doing so could improve his effectiveness at work and increase his satisfaction at home. "I have believed that if I stay within the box of what's good, moral, ethical, and proper, then I'll continue to get what I want from work and family. I am nervous about advice that I make the box bigger." The box confined him because it compelled him to spend every waking moment in accomplishing things and in doing them extremely well, even things that were not truly worth doing well or, for that matter, worth doing at all. His "orderly world," as he called it, had proven to be a demanding taskmaster, but obeying it had allowed him to display his "goodness," reassured him of his worth, and, in the end, made him a success. It is understandable, then, that he felt possessive about his identity and even superstitious about straying from his box.

The people around an executive bring a similarly conservative attitude to the prospect of intervening to correct a performance problem in an otherwise effective executive.[6] One executive challenged us: Is the potential improvement worth the risk of losing a reasonably effective executive? A human resources manager reported, "I've seen executives try to change and get lost because they got away from their managerial style—the way they grew up and manage best."

A peer and friend of a high-ranking and highly effective executive expressed concern over the possible harm that could be done to this individual by the extensive feedback he was about to receive and by any attempts he might make to improve. "I am very uneasy. This guy should not be spooked. I don't want him to go into a shell. . . . We are definitely in a fine-tune mode. If he improves, it will be a marginal improvement, not a major improvement. What I worry about with this kind of process is that people are complex packages, and his package has allowed him to be very successful. If you have [a golfer] who shoots 80, and that's better than most, and you say, 'There are a couple of little flaws; let's rebuild a little,' you fix the flaw but undermine the confidence. Everybody wants everybody to be perfect, and they aren't. When you tinker with the swing, the end result may not be better. It may be worse — because the change isn't natural."

This concern is, of course, well placed in general. Executives, like the rest of us, adopt a basic personal strategy that enables them to maintain their self-esteem and make their way in the world. It is no mean feat to find a solution to the problem of being an effective, satisfied person in this life, and executives naturally become strongly attached to their identities because the way they are has brought them so much success. They can be so attached that they become extremely reluctant to make adjustments, even when the solution has become the problem. They may hang on to what got them there even if they are passed over for promotion. Even managers below executive level may adopt this attitude if they feel they are sure bets to become executives.

Thus, of the many reasons why executives fail to produce or sustain change that they do come to see as needed, an important one is that the executive tends to work exclusively at a behavioral level. To confine oneself to intervening on the surface means that one resorts chiefly to willpower. Executives frequently try to erase offending behavior by latching onto something on the surface.[7] But, according to George Vaillant, whose conclusions come from his analysis of a thirty-year study of 100 Harvard graduates, "mature mechanisms cannot be acquired by a conscious act of will. There is nothing more transparent than someone *trying* to use humor or altruism; or someone trying to hold back rage."[8] If an executive wanted to decrease his defensiveness about criticism, for example, he couldn't do it through sheer willpower alone; he would have to see what it was about his sense of self that made him so sensitive. As a senior manager we worked with put it to a few of his peers during a stock-taking session several months after each had received feedback: "I have found that behavioral modification is not lasting. If all we're doing is *acting* differently, then we go back to what we've been, we regress back to what we've been. The key question is: Are we *being* different or only behaving differently? That's an important difference. So far, I don't feel comfortable that I really *am* different."

A lack of attention to who the executive *is* can hinder his or her efforts to alter the way he or she acts, as we saw in the case of Hank Cooper. He remained abrasive even though he had tried off and on for years to change. The inner restraint turned out to be rooted in his character: He knew in his head that people saw him as insensitive, but he had no true appreciation in his heart for what his victims felt. Long ago, he had shielded himself from his own frequently painful feelings, so that now his lack of empathy for others stemmed from his lack of empathy for himself. For him to solve his managerial problem, he would have to grow personally.

The field of executive development has concentrated on task-oriented learning and, in particular, skill development; it has neglected personal learning and, in particular, "identity development."[9] Likewise, executives driven by expansive urges to achieve and advance tend to be motivated to build managerial expertise and to acquire technical, organizational, and industry knowledge. Successful executives do not generally go in for reflection on their identities as people, and "most career development processes reinforce this strong task orientation and low concern for self-reflection in the mobile executive."[10] But the simple truth is that if leadership is in essence a form of self-expression, if it is inescapably personal, then leadership development must, at least at certain times, also be personal. What does this mean?

Combining the Behavioral with the Personal

For a manager to make a genuine, enduring change is truly a tall order. Why, in searching for ways to assist in this process, should we restrict ourselves to one method, as time-honored, popular, and comfortable as it may be? Why not fortify the behavioral approach with personal learning?

In our experience it is an eclectic approach — one that combines intervention on the surface with intervention below the surface — that stands the best chance of producing genuine and lasting change for the better. Significant change can and should proceed both from the inside out and from the outside in.

The executive introduced a few pages ago as someone struggling with whether to depart from his "orderly world" illustrates well the interpenetration of outer and inner change. He entered our program expecting only to modify his behavior but realized during the feedback session that more was involved: "I expected that we would put together a plan [for me] to *act* different. What I got hit with was a challenge to *be* different."

The approach we use has evolved over the last several years and continues to evolve. In addition to varying over time, it varies with what a given client needs and with what a given staff member is able to provide. The program we have developed is just *one* way to depart from a strict reliance on behavioral intervention.

What is different about an approach like ours is that it decompartmentalizes management development. Instead of keeping job performance and the inner person in separate compartments, it considers the relation between the two. Instead of keeping work life and private life separate, it compares the two — as a way of helping the person see how character affects behavior. Likewise, instead of compartmentalizing managerial career and early history, our approach examines parallels between the two. Performance in the present job remains the focus, but examining inner life, private life, and early life gives executives insight into how they perform their jobs and how they can improve.

Besides the utility for us, as researchers, of consulting an executive's upbringing, there is also a distinct developmental value for managers in consulting their own histories. Even when the intervention is chiefly behavioral and no deeper change is being attempted, it is instructive for the executive to take into account the historical antecedents of the behavior he or she intends to alter. This helps the executive to see better what lies beneath the surface.

A turnaround-style executive we worked with saw more clearly in his feedback session that his successful track record had been achieved at the expense of his subordinates, including some that he had hand-picked. His people criticized him for allowing them too little autonomy and influence and for neglecting them and their careers. He admitted that he saw *himself* as the chief agent of change. He entered most meetings with his staff having a preformulated position in mind. His rationale: "With all my experience in problem situations like these, I don't want to mess around."

In the feedback session he immediately and gamely resolved to modify the way he related to subordinates. In true fix-it fashion, he wasted no time in coming to a decision to solve the problem. As soon as he got back he would resist the temptation to make up his mind before a meeting. He would enter with an open mind and give his subordinates a genuine chance to develop solutions. He was sure he could effect this change because he had made similar adjustments earlier in his career.

Not wanting to dampen his enthusiasm but concerned that he underestimated the difficulty of changing in this way, I asked him where he thought his management style originated. The idea was to engender in him a greater respect for the forces that had led to his behavior in the first place. He instantly recalled an early boss with an autocratic style. Using a clue from a biographical questionnaire that the executive had completed, I encouraged him to search his memory for a still more potent influence. After a pause, he said: "My father." His father, a devoutly religious man, had striven to be "perfect in the eyes of God" and attempted to force his children into the same mold. Our conversation was the first time this executive had made the connection between his father's character and his own sense of himself as knowing the right way and imposing it upon his people. This realization helped him to see what he was up against in correcting what he had taken to be merely a surface problem.

Thus, even when the objective is merely to change trouble-some behavior, it is helpful, if not vital, to respect the roots of the behavior. To scrupulously avoid any reference to forma-tive early experiences or to the inner person can lull the execu-tive and helping professionals into a false sense of confidence — a confidence that can, if the individual proves unable to execute the plan, give way to discouragement and cynicism and a reluc-tance to undertake change in the future.

Early history can also be an avenue for promoting deeper change. Executives can usually be helped to see more sharply and experience more poignantly the inner forces that drive them by referring to the significant experiences that set those forces in motion. Rather than understanding themselves and their cur-rent problems in terms of the present only, they learn to see these in the context of their "life trajectory."[11] Executives can gain insight and find comfort in "recognizing that their current situation is a logical and 'inevitable' product of previous life ex-perience."[12] Through self-examination informed by reference to one's upbringing, one can revise ingrained notions of self and ideals for self. To define one's life trajectory in this way is a fairly straightforward task that taps into readily accessible memories. It need not probe early experiences long since repressed; it does not involve delving into the unconscious.

Management development professionals understandably steer clear of their clients' childhoods for fear of invading privacy or because of the stigma associated with psychoanalysis. How-ever, assuming conditions of strict confidentiality, most execu-tives find conversations about their early experience perfectly natural. Under the right conditions, the field of management development would do well to set aside its taboo against refer-ence to the clients' upbringing and allow practical, common-sense reference to a reservoir of clues about the person and the person's inner life.

The Importance of Follow-Through

Besides adding an emphasis on the inner person to the usual emphasis on behavior only, our approach adds follow-through.

It is increasingly common for management development programs to include an assessment of the manager's strengths and weaknesses, often by means of a survey of co-worker perceptions. Participating managers are not simply handed a ream of data; they get help in identifying areas for development and, within those areas, mapping out concrete plans for improvement. But as helpful as programs of this kind can be, they typically stop with planning. Participants do walk out the door with a plan in hand and with some optimism about acting on the plan, but they typically get little or no assistance back on the job.

Our approach decompartmentalizes assessment and follow-through; we continue to work with managers as they attempt to implement their plans for development. The major vehicle for follow-through is a coach, who serves in any of a number of capacities. The coach helps the manager design concrete ways to make improvements in areas targeted for development. The coach might actually sit in when the manager attempts, for example, to improve relationships with certain key peers. The coach is also available to counsel the manager on those underlying beliefs and feelings that may interfere with the individual's efforts to improve. The coach meets at least once with the manager and his or her spouse to help the spouse understand what the manager is attempting and, if possible, to enlist the spouse's help in the process. The coach similarly helps the manager get the immediate superior's input to the individual's plan for development. The coach also acts as broker by arranging for the manager to take part in educational experiences that address developmental needs.

The coach, incidentally, is not necessarily one of us. Sometimes we hand off primary coaching responsibility to someone in the executive's organization who is respected and trusted by the manager and who helps with the behavioral aspects of the change. Even when we do play an active coaching role, we cooperate with someone in the organization who can be available on a daily basis and thus play a role that is complementary to ours. This person can also function as an advocate who puts the word out — especially when the manager is in any kind of trouble — that the individual is taking the process seriously.

One cannot overestimate the importance of follow-through. A project in self-development is fundamentally no different from any other project: It succeeds or fails according to how well it is conceived, organized, staffed, implemented—in general, managed. Unless it becomes and remains a priority, it will fizzle out. Unless the executive follows through, the project—especially an attempt to modify behavior—will amount to nothing. The executive must take responsibility for managing a change project, but it is often desirable for another party—a boss or a consultant or a friend—to share some of that responsibility.

The importance of this project-management aspect of development was brought home to me by one executive's efforts at improving the way he managed his time. Out of a planning meeting came the idea that he would make better use of his executive secretary. A month later, the consultant happened to ask the secretary whether the executive had talked with her. She said, "Yes, he asked me to badger him to do his paperwork." It thus became apparent that, instead of sitting down and discussing and reworking his relationship with his secretary, he had merely made a passing comment. The consultant arranged a sit-down conversation in which the executive clearly stated his need and the secretary disclosed both her interest in an expanded role and her reluctance to take it—arising from the difficulty she had influencing the executive. Out of the conversation came an agreement on how the two of them would work together differently. Although their relationship was slow to change, he had at least clearly defined the role he wanted her to play.

The lesson, then, is that it is unwise to leave even what seems like straightforward implementation to chance. Good intentions are usually not enough. It is vital to bolster good intentions by introducing structure, providing expert resources, holding the manager accountable—in short, by being there.

Setting Limits to the Intervention

Any approach that decompartmentalizes conventional methods of management development needs its own limits and safeguards. One safeguard (as well as a means of promoting the client's growth) is our current practice of using two staff members with each participating manager. One staff member tends to be a management specialist who specializes in leadership issues in the context of the inner person. The other tends to be a clinician who specializes in inner work in the context of leadership issues. In less staff-intensive versions of this service the clinician becomes a shadow consultant who advises the primary staff member. The thornier the issues, the more important it is to involve a clinically well-equipped professional directly.

If an executive turns out to be troubled emotionally, maritally, or parentally, we refer the participant to a therapist. We do not act as therapists ourselves, and we take none of the liberties that are customary in a therapist's consulting room. Although we help managers recognize basic patterns of adaptation and defense and help them see how their childhood experience formed these patterns, we do not engage the individual in reexperiencing pain long since repressed. We do not assume that highly private matters — alcoholism, sexual problems, and so forth — are fair game for extended discussion. On the other hand, and unlike some therapists, we do suggest practical corrective measures. Furthermore, our role as facilitators of personal growth is just one facet of a multifaceted coaching role.[13]

An important self-imposed limit is that we do not force insight or change on executives. If there is one way to create casualties in any kind of intensive development program, coercion is it.[14] We scrupulously hold in check our own need to have an impact, so that it does not turn into aggression toward the participant. Our idea is that whatever we have to offer must be found by the participant.[15] The executive is in control of how deep and how fast he or she goes.

Two Levels of Payoff

Two levels of benefit can result from personal as opposed to strictly behavioral development. At the first level, participating managers can gain a better sense of the inner person that gives rise to the outer person. At the second level, participants can actually *change* the inner person. This second level of benefit, a *shift in character,* is described fully in the next chapter. It has a more dramatic impact and at the same time is harder to bring about. It is important, however, not to overlook the very real and more readily obtainable benefit of the first level.

Executives who manage to gain a better sense of the inner person become aware of the powerful forces within them. They see better what drives them. Rich Bauer came to this sort of recognition during the feedback session as he reflected on comments about his powerful presence. (Note how his comments are riddled with expansive imagery.) "I have created a larger-than-life image — which isn't healthy — with my children and the people who work for me. . . . There was a time when I needed it — ten years ago when I was building the image. [Since then] I've let the inflated caricature get out of control. . . . I want to let some air out of the balloon. . . . I've got an exaggerated image that my kids have to live up to. There's an exaggerated power image the people who work for me have to live with. I can see it creating problems, and it's not healthy for me either." Rich's attempt at internal redefinition is graphic and palpable. He had adopted a heroic role in part as an antidote to insecurity early in his career. To his credit, he has started to get a perspective on his need for heroism as it has become less adaptive for him.

Rich is a good example of first-level benefit in that he came to see more clearly the connection between his inner life and his outer behavior but stopped short of actually altering his inner makeup. He took better account of who he was without actually changing who he was.

The value of first-level personal development is not limited to self-recognition. Once executives see better, in their own cases, how their inner lives influence the way they perform, they begin to see the person-behind-the-behavior in their fellow managers. Stated another way, they develop increased empathy. Having learned to see and accept the person within themselves, they learn to see and accept the inner person in other people. Once again, personal development does not have to result in a change in the inner person for the manager to gain from the experience. This leaves unanswered the question: What exactly is a change in the inner person? The next chapter explains what it means for an executive to undergo a shift in character.

Chapter Ten

Character Shifts: How Managers Change Who They Are

For years Hank Cooper tried to put a stop to his abrasive interpersonal style, but he never succeeded because he treated the problem symptomatically and never at its root. For Hank, as for so many other executives, improvement on the surface is impossible without a corresponding evolution beneath the surface. A change in character is not easy to bring about, but it is possible. This chapter elaborates on what a character change consists of and, in particular, what it means in the case of driven senior managers.

The popular view, widely held in the managerial world, is that while successful adults can perhaps modify their behavior, they can't change their basic personalities. Writing in 1890, the eminent psychologist William James enunciated this view: "By the age of 30, the character has set like plaster and will never soften again. . . . An invisible law, as strong as gravitation, keeps him within his orbit."[1] There is truth to what James said. Character hardens. It is durable. Some people do live their entire lives in one mode, never changing, as if their character is, in fact, set in plaster. Successful and highly placed managers seem especially unlikely candidates for basic change. Too many voices, their own included, whisper to them, "You're great the way you are. Why risk losing what got you here?"

Many people dismiss the possibility of personality change because they have in mind a transformation in a person's makeup, a clean sweep of the person's inner self. They conjure up images of a discarding of the contents of an individual's core self in favor of a new, improved self. But images of radical psychological surgery are seriously mistaken. Even George Vaillant's image of "casting aside ill-fitting identities" is, in reality, more a matter of making alterations than acquiring an entirely new wardrobe.[2]

What is attainable is not a revolution but an evolution. The person's character is not transformed. It shifts. What was very important to the person becomes somewhat less important, and what was unimportant becomes more important. In one sense, character change is a shift in emphasis.

The notion of inner evolution is consistent with the conception of identity as "a unified thing that remains similar to itself and yet changes."[3] This is why your college friend remains identifiable as essentially the same person at your tenth reunion or your twenty-fifth reunion, whether the person has grown or not grown, whether life has treated him or her well or badly. Character change is paradoxical. The adult's core self changes and remains the same. There is continuity, and there is discontinuity.[4]

I take the view that change in adults is neither a rare nor a remarkable occurrence. It happens naturally from time to time throughout adult life as the person moves into different roles, encounters various challenges and crises, and alternates between periods of relative stability and periods of change. Robert Kegan goes so far as to argue that a person is not so much a thing — a fixed entity — as an activity. The person is a process, always evolving.

William James speaks for many of us in pointing out how resistant to change people are, but to me he is overly pessimistic in seeing no potential for fundamental change. Robert Kegan strikes a responsive chord in many of us by pointing up the potential for lifelong evolution, but to me he is overly optimistic in portraying adults as continually evolving. We all know cases of arrested development. Based on our research, I have come to believe that, despite the very real durability of personal makeup, adults—even successful senior managers—can bring about a shift in character. What does such a character shift look like? To answer this question, we must first look at the executive character *before* the shift takes place.

The Problem of Lopsidedness

Many executives who get into difficulty are, in a sense, too specialized for their roles. To play their specialized part at the top of their organization, managers need a generous infusion of expansive characteristics, most notably a not-to-be-denied drive to mastery. But problematic executives are too well endowed with this necessary ingredient. The problem with these overdeveloped expansives is that they are lopsided.

Lopsided was originally a nautical term. It applied to a ship that "loped" or leaned to one side. The reason the boat tilted to one side was that it was constructed in such a way that it was disproportionately heavy on that side. It was unevenly balanced.[5]

Similarly, problematic executives lean heavily to the side of independent achievement. Their sense of worth is so tied up in how they and their organization perform that they live in fear of falling short of the mark and losing all value, managerially and personally. Bobby Knight, the highly successful college basketball coach, was so identified with his team's success that, whenever the team lost a game, it was as if "a giant hunk had been taken out of his self-esteem."[6]

Origins of Lopsidedness. Human beings, from the moment they are born to their dying day, are driven by a need for a sense of worth. All human beings need to feel as if, in some sphere, they count. They prefer *not* to feel inferior, unimportant, insignificant.

The whole dynamic starts at birth. Early in life the child is accorded a certain value by the people around him or her and, in response to this essential treatment, develops enduring beliefs and durable strategies for maintaining a highly valued condition or for reversing a condition of being devalued. Based on this formative early experience of the world, the child instinctively becomes *anxious* — for example, to continue to be treated as a valued object or to avoid being treated as a devalued entity. Early experience also forges the person's beliefs about self and others and, as a result, a set of strategies for getting on in the world. This constitutes much of what is meant by character — the sense of self-worth and the accompanying methods used to maintain or enhance this sense.

Perhaps what children need most is to be valued. Winnicott contends that what children need in a mother is not cleverness or intellectual enlightenment but devotion, meaning that the child is a top priority in the mother's life, ranking high in the mother's scale of values. Even to care for the child physically is a way of conferring value on the child. John Bowlby's much cited research on the iniquitous effects on babies of being separated from their parents and of lying for the most part unattended in an institution probably shows as much as anything how devastating it is to be deprived utterly of parental devotion.

Some lopsided executives were not valued as children or were even actively devalued. But thanks to countervailing influences they managed not to internalize a sense of low self-worth. They did not give up on themselves and the world. Instead, they fought the notion of worthlessness by devoting their lives to proving themselves. This is the self-vindicating type described in Chapter Five.

Other lopsided executives were raised in what many people would look upon as favorable childhood circumstances. Their parents were invested in them — too invested. Out of their own narcissistic needs, these parents treated their children as extensions of themselves and valued their children only to the extent that the children reflected favorably on the parents. People raised under these conditions lack a core sense of worth. Their feelings of adequacy must constantly be purchased through performing well and through looking good in one way or another. There is a painfully *contingent* sense of worth. This is the striver-builder type described in Chapter Two.

This perfectionistic striving, as Marian Woodman calls it, comes from internalizing the demands of influential adults. "Authority figures in our childhood acted out of power, demanding the best little boy or girl, the best little scholar, the best little athlete, so the child introjects that power and constantly criticizes, evaluates, and judges himself or herself. An inner voice is constantly saying, . . . 'I'm not good enough.'"[7] Perfectionists buy the notion that their sense of worth depends on being nothing but the best. Or, as Larry Hirschhorn put it, "The image of the ideal is accompanied by feelings of compulsion to achieve the ideal." It is a compulsion because unless people of this description come close to achieving the ideal they cannot feel good about themselves. They may even feel very bad about themselves.

A Classic Case of Lopsidedness. Diana Dowling had in her early forties reached an executive-level position, and a line position at that, and almost as soon as she had achieved her career ambition she encountered a midlife crisis. The crisis was touched off by her extreme dependence on achievement and status as evidence of personal worth. One day during a tennis game at the prestigious country club she belonged to, she suddenly felt a revulsion toward the country club and all it stood for. Troubled by this eruption of feeling, she sought counseling and soon discovered that she was in rebellion against her own status-consciousness. This insight led to the discovery of a linkage to the periodic bouts of depression that had started in high school.

The first brush with depression happened after her family moved during the summer before tenth grade. "I went from an environment where I was sort of on top, a leader, a popular person and well liked and everything, and I moved to a new environment where I was a nobody. Now that I look back, I see I was depressed and felt awful because I was a nobody, because *I defined who I was by my performance* in school and extracurricular activities — by my achievement. My feeling at the time was, 'Here I go once again. I have to do it again.' So I struggled, and I felt bad. And then came spring, and I made the school newspaper, and I made good grades, and once again I was becoming happy.

"I realize now I had an *incredible* push to be part of the in-crowd, whoever was popular. I would look over people who were not popular and say to myself, 'They're nice people, but. . . . '

"I was pushed [internally] to be around popular people — people who rated, doers, achievers, people who would boost me up a little bit. I am still like that, and I hate it. I think to this day I lose out on relationships."

This cycle repeated itself in college, in business school, and at a couple of points in her career so far. More than the customary reaction to relocation, the depression was evidently touched off in each instance by her sense of herself in the new situation as being nobody, as not counting, as virtually not existing. Talking about going off to college, she recounted, "So I went to high school and succeeded. Then I went away to college, and I joined a sorority. Everybody in the sorority was successful. Everyone had already proved themselves, and once again just like that [snaps her fingers] I was depressed again. And now looking back I can see why: *I was a nobody. A nobody might as well be dead. Because I defined myself by my achievements*" (emphasis added).

Diana traced her insecurity directly to her childhood. "All of this I know came from when I was a baby, when I was told that I need to behave in such and such a way and that I can't be obnoxious and dirty and aggressive and let my mother down and scare her or my father or behave in these ways because my parents were very strict in who they wanted me to be . . . . My mother told me always to smile and told me how to feel, and if I didn't [do what she wanted], it made her nervous, brought out her anxieties. To this day she is putting that message on me."

To her credit Diana did more than see her mother's misguided influence on her; Diana saw the similar influence she has had on her own children. "Of course I am now reliving it with my children. I have a twelve-year-old son who has repeated my cycle to a tee." Diana's son expects so much of himself that he actually gets physically ill out of worry about performing. "If the kids didn't measure up to the same idea I had for myself, then I would have to deal with the feelings that were repressed in myself. Their failure would bring out in me my anxiety, and that's how the pattern is passed on from one generation to the next — the 'witch mother' messages I call them, which I'm sure I have passed on."

Thus, the lopsided overweighting toward performance is very much in evidence in Diana Dowling — not because achievement is part of what she needs to feel good about herself, but because of the extreme extent to which she depended on achievement for a sense of self-worth. Later in the chapter we will return to Diana for a look at how she has attempted to right herself.

Consequences of Lopsidedness. The problem with depending too much on performance for a sense of worth is that distortions creep in. Ironically, the very performance that managers rely on to establish worth gets distorted by excessive concern about performing. We saw in Chapter Six the various ways in which extreme ambition to excel can degrade a manager's effectiveness. By being too concerned with establishing worth on the basis of accomplishment, a certain desperation sets in. Desperate people do desperate things. As managers they care too much about their own welfare and too little about the organization's welfare. They become compulsive and exhaust themselves and their people in a frantic campaign to do well. They so much want to win big that they overextend the organization. They claim competence, importance, and accomplishment that are not rightly theirs. They may stoop to intellectual or emotional dishonesty — by taking credit due other people or by blaming other people for their own mistakes or failures. They may retain control (while purporting to share it) as a way of conferring importance on themselves. Those executives who aspire to stardom and deny their fallibility tend to identify with other stars or potential stars and write off those people who, in their view, are marred by imperfection.

In his play *The Cocktail Party,* T. S. Eliot expressed in poetic terms the pursuit of worth gone wrong:

> Half of the harm done in the world
> is due to people who want to feel important
> They don't mean to do harm,

but the harm doesn't interest them
or they do not see it,
or they justify it
because they are absorbed in the endless struggle
to think well of themselves.[8]

Managers can lean so decidedly to one side that the other side is virtually lost to them. When they put great stock in being independent achievers, they typically sacrifice their capacity for close relationships. The relationship between these two sides of their nature becomes polarized. Lopsided managers prize and therefore develop — develop and therefore prize — one side of the polarity. They devalue, disregard, and perhaps actively suppress the other pole. One side wins; the other loses.

Denying a part of oneself doesn't simply cost a person that part. It forces it underground, where it makes its presence felt in disguised and unhelpful ways.[9] As part of Diana Dowling's training to be a "nice" person, she had her anger bred out of her. Talking with us at the point of realization, she felt the loss of her capacity to make appropriate use of anger. And she recognized that suppressing her anger didn't eliminate it but merely forced it to find alternative avenues of expression. She used sarcasm and other forms of passive aggression.

Lopsided managers also exaggerate the "light-dark" polarity. The light or bright side is what managers take to be their admirable selves, the characteristics worth assigning high value. The light side is what Jung called the "persona," or mask — the side of the person presented to the world to make a good impression. The dark side includes all those parts that, in the person's mind, are inconsistent with this desired impression. Because the dark side threatens what a person is trying to be, he or she avoids the dark side and may reject it outright.[10] But the potential locked up in what the person looks upon as his or her dark side is then lost. Diana Dowling, in disallowing anger, gave up the chance to put it to good use.

So the need for a shift in character arises from an overdependence on high performance as a means of establishing one's worth as a person. If the lopsidedness in an executive's behavior is to be remedied, it may be necessary for the person to correct for the internal overdependence that gives rise to the distorted behavior. Thus a character shift in driven people usually means a move *away* from extreme lopsidedness. A pattern of adaptation, set earlier in life and adaptive for the circumstances at the time, comes to require revision. To respond more effectively to present circumstances, managers *adapt their adaptations.*

However, a shift does not necessarily reduce the force of a pattern of adaptation. A shift can even be a step backward developmentally. In the novel *Oscar and Lucinda,* Lucinda's mother was a neat person even before her husband died and left her overwhelmed by suddenly having to manage a huge farm in the Australian wilderness in the late 1800s. After his death she "became like a caricature of her former self and would demand neatness in the most ridiculous degree."[11] Rather than attenuate the pattern, she accentuated it. She became *more* lopsided.

For expansive executives, especially the extreme cases, a shift in the right direction is one in which they decrease the heavy emphasis on mastery as a means of ensuring a sense of worth. They come to place somewhat less weight on the mastery-seeking side of themselves. They moderate the high anxiety brought to the quest for mastery. They learn to take themselves less seriously. The net effect is that they become less lopsided.

Tackling Lopsidedness: A Case Study

Chris Cramer is a high-potential manager, not quite forty, already a department head, who underwent an inner change. Although his career was in great shape organizationally when he began the process of change, he was a prime example of executive lopsidedness, as his own comments show: "For the last year, I was unhappy in my job. I think I did the job because that's the way I am. I have to *do* — I don't think that will ever change. I have to do and achieve in order to live. But there was no joy in it, and I felt unfulfilled.

"I was my own worst enemy in that I placed tremendous pressure on myself to be perfect. This, I think, led to unrealistic expectations of myself and tremendous frustration when perfection was not achieved.

"I believed that this also played out in my relationship with my boss. I put him in a position where I tried to pretend that he was the one that was expecting the perfection . . . so that whenever he gave any kind of criticism I took it as a tremendously negative thing. . . . If he did not feel I had done well or if I was not perfect in his eyes, I was not perfect in my eyes, and therefore I was worthless. Therefore I was always feeling frustrated, worthless, not good about what I had achieved, even though I had achieved quite a bit within the organization. I couldn't understand why he couldn't give me more credit. I think now it was because I couldn't give myself any credit, and everything he did that was critical was put through the wrong end of a telescope."

He went on to reflect on why it was difficult to come to grips with his own contribution to the jam he was in: "It was almost impossible for me to face up to my deficiencies at that time simply because my deficiencies meant I wasn't a good person, a good soldier, a good boy, whatever you want to call it. So I would do almost anything to try to make those things look smaller in comparison to what I achieved. The problem is that it's almost as difficult for me to talk about [my achievements; it's difficult to say to myself]: 'Well, you've done really well, Chris. You've achieved an awful lot. You started at the lowest rung, you weren't given a boost, and now you're a department head.' It's strange when you can't handle the success and you can't handle the failure."

In recounting the evolution he went through, Cramer traced its beginning to the realization that he expected to be superhuman: "I felt that every day I had to come in here and achieve some astronomical feat. Now that, I will have to admit it, only came from me. I can't blame my boss for this, I can't blame my peers, I can't blame the people who work for me. I think that's what I saw with your help. Finally seeing that and seeing how ridiculous this was — that was the thing, the crack, that kind of allowed me to open all of this up. It was the most insightful thing that you showed me. That's what I have been building from ever since.

"It was this feeling that you don't have to wear your superman suit every day. You don't have to leap tall buildings every day. You can come in and act like a normal person, and you will probably be able, without your superman suit on, to do quite a lot of pretty good things, just because inherently you're capable of it."

The strength of Chris Cramer's attachment to what Wilhelm Reich calls "character armor" became evident to him the first time he imagined removing it: "I thought to myself, Clark Kent wasn't such a bad guy after all; he was able to do a lot of decent things. So I visualized that OK, but I couldn't just take my superman suit off right away. To do that made me feel frightened as hell. This little plucked chicken without his superman suit was totally and obviously ineffectual. Like Clark Kent, bumbling, incompetent, inarticulate. So if I had suddenly taken my superman suit off, I would have felt naked, totally unable to deal with this place."

Cramer undertook the mental change over the next several weeks by removing the suit one piece at a time. First, the cape; then the sleeves; and so on. Chris did not dispose of the suit entirely but kept it on hand in case of an emergency. "I would never get rid of it totally because I do need it. There are still times when I need to leap tall buildings, but I can put it on, do that, and then take it off again. I put it on to give me a little extra courage. But I'm able to take it off again.

"So I think as long as you have your positive feelings about yourself in place and your realistic feelings about yourself in place, then when you put the superman suit on, it is a whole different thing. In the past I used it in a defensive way, and also in an aggressive, negative way towards my peers, and also as a way to try to feel good about myself. To try to be good. To be acceptable to my boss and to myself. But it's not a crutch anymore. I'm using it in a positive way."

The shift took place more quickly than usual because Chris Cramer was primed for growth and because circumstances favored growth. The conducive circumstances included his conscious unhappiness, a breakdown in his relationship with his boss, to whom he had been reasonably close, and an attractive job offer that boosted his confidence.

What benefit did he derive from recognizing and discarding his superhuman aspirations and his secret heroic costume? In Chris Cramer's words: "I think I'm less a striver now. I feel good about me because of me and because I can see I have influence within the organization and people listen and all that. What I don't so badly need is [the high opinion of] the upper guys."

Beyond the inner easing of his phenomenal push to excel, how was his leadership affected? "I was always reactive before, always selling. I spent a lot of time thinking, 'How are we going to sell this to Steve [his boss]? How are we going to sell this to the organization?' Rather than thinking about what *it* is. Now I don't really worry too much about selling it, because I know I can. Because I am so much more confident that people will listen, selling has become a minor thing."

The newly found sense of worth meant that Cramer worried less about the merit of his ideas and, accordingly, felt less compelled to sell them hard, in classic expansive fashion. As he relaxed internally, he took the edge off his aggressiveness and became more receptive. "I feel so much more relaxed. I am much more willing to listen. I am much more willing to let other people take control; I sit back more. I sit back with my peers more, and I sit back with my people who report to me more. I gave them a lot of *operational* freedom before; I didn't give them much strategic, directional freedom. I think I am able to give that now. That doesn't mean I don't have a big impact on them. I certainly do but in a different way that is more subtle. I do more taking input in, thinking about it, putting it in perspective, guiding it.

"I'll give you a recent example. This week my boss sent me in his place to a meeting at corporate [headquarters] with these people who are vice-presidential, most of them, or the tier down from vice-presidential. And I sat in there, and I was relaxed. I didn't feel any anxiety. I didn't feel like I had to talk. I didn't feel like I had to make any points. I only had to say what needed to be said. If it had been six months ago, I would have tried to talk a lot. I would have tried to make a lot of points. There I was without my superman suit on, and I was enjoying it."

As part of the process of seeing the supercharged aspect of his drive for what it was, Cramer delved briefly into his own history. In retrospect it was clear to him that his parents' expectations were a major determinant. According to Cramer, an only child: "Growing up, I can see that I had to be perfect in order to be loved. All my parents' emotional energy and eggs were in my basket, and it was a tremendous responsibility. I certainly got a lot of material things that I probably wouldn't have had if there had been more than one child. But also it put a tremendous pressure on me."

Already affected by his parents' idea of what was best for him, his aspirations for himself were sharply intensified at the age of thirteen when his father died suddenly of a heart attack and his mother became severely depressed and had to be institutionalized. "My father was a very strong figure in my life, . . . but suddenly he has a heart attack and dies. He just disappears from my life. Then my mother, who I learned later had tremendously low self-esteem, got severely depressed. When my father suddenly disappeared from my mother's life, she felt worthless. She even tried to kill herself, and I found that painful, too, because obviously I wasn't worth living for. It has taken me a long time to face up to that." Facing up to the pain of having his mother come close to giving up on her life and on Chris himself was part of the work he had to do to come to grips with his fierce drive to mastery.

Consequences of a Character Shift

If extremely expansive executives can be likened to high-powered engines perpetually in high gear, then a welcome aspect of character shift is that it enables them to develop a kind of mental overdrive — an extra gear that allows them to do just as much but with less wear and tear. There is less wear and tear because, as with Chris Cramer, they are less anxious about how they are doing. There is less performance anxiety.

To develop this extra gear is to achieve a kind of personal transcendence. Overdrive represents a new state of being in which managers shed their excess drive, their excess ambition.

At the same time, they shed the gross distortions in the way they lead an organization, handle people, treat themselves.

When driven managers consider the possibility of easing up, they immediately become afraid that they will lose their edge and become complacent. One young executive felt that it was risky to try to temper his ambition: "I'm concerned that it's an on-off function — not a continuum that you can diminish."

Our experience to date, however, suggests that the fear of losing one's edge is greatly exaggerated. The shift into overdrive enables the manager to continue to pursue goals vigorously and efficiently yet without an acute feeling of urgency. Chris Cramer illustrates this well: Even as he removed the superman suit and its imperative for daily superhuman feats, he remained strongly motivated. There was no real danger of his losing his intensity, his potency. He did rid himself, however, of the excesses brought on by trying too hard.

A shift in character is a reaction against the dominant side of oneself. It is a kind of rebellion against being thoroughly dominated by a set of compelling beliefs and a correspondingly compulsive way of life. The individual fights back against what Karen Horney calls "the tyranny of the shoulds." The manager liberates him or herself somewhat from the demands of a harsh superego.[12] (The superego is the part of the self that, according to Freud, combines one's conscience and one's ideals for oneself.) The superego becomes less harsh, less strict, and less rigid in the demands it makes on the person. In effect, the person adopts a less oppressive stance toward him or herself that makes room for elements out of favor in the prior internal regime. In similar terms, Daniel Levinson wrote of "modulating the tyranny of the Dream."[13] By "Dream" Levinson meant one's wishes for oneself, one's ambitions. Levinson's studies of men led him to conclude that midlife is an opportune time to become "less tyrannized by the ambitions, instinctual drives and illusions of youth."[14]

Diana Dowling, cited earlier in this chapter as an example of overdependence on performance, learned to moderate the inordinate, unremitting demands of her internal parents. Not surprisingly, this internal moderation has carried over to her actual role as a parent: "As far as the children go, [this change in me] is just as cathartic. . . . I try to allow my children to be who they are. At times I am able to allow their emotions to be obnoxious, smelly, dirty, awful, and what we call unacceptable, but which aren't. I can allow the children to be just what they are without saying a damn word to them. And I can say, 'Boy, you feel awful, don't you?' And they will go, 'Yes.' And I'll go, 'Fine. You can't always feel good.'" By freeing herself to be what she had previously prohibited herself from being, she could give her children the same freedom.

Recovering Lost Parts of the Self

If a shift deemphasizes a dominant side of the self, it can also increase the emphasis on a recessive side. Because the recessive side has been pushed into the background, it has in a sense been lost to the person. Growth takes the form of reclaiming these neglected aspects.

The main character in Pat Conroy's melodramatic novel *The Prince of Tides* sets out to find himself in this way. A tortured middle-aged man raised in the low country of South Carolina, he was priming himself to transcend some of the early influences that had made him unsuccessful at work and a mixed blessing at home: "First there had to be a time of renewal, a time to master a fresh approach to self-scrutiny. I had lost nearly thirty-seven years to the image I carried of myself. I had ambushed myself by believing, to the letter, my parents' definition of me. They had defined me early on, coined me like a word they had translated on some mysterious hieroglyph, and I had spent my life coming to terms with that specious coinage. My parents had succeeded in making me a stranger to myself. They had turned me into the exact image of what they needed at the time, and . . . I allowed them to knead and shape me into the smoother lineaments of their nonpareil child. . . . I longed for their approval, their applause, their pure uncomplicated love for me, and I looked for it years after I realized they were not even capable of letting me have it. To love one's children is to love oneself, and this was a state of supererogatory grace denied my parents by birth and circumstance. I needed to reconnect to something I had lost. Somewhere I had lost touch with the kind of man I had the potential of being. I needed to effect a reconciliation with that unborn man and try to coax him gently toward his maturity."[15] This insightful passage evokes the theme of discovering or rediscovering what has been lost. The main character speaks of having lost touch with himself and of reconnecting to something he had lost.

The poet Robert Bly writes evocatively on the same theme. As children we have behind us an invisible bag. To keep our parents' love, we put the parts of ourselves that our parents don't like in the bag. "We spend our life until we're twenty deciding [unconsciously] what parts of ourself to put into the bag, and we spend the rest of our lives trying to get them out again. . . . Sometimes retrieving them feels impossible, as if the bag were sealed."[16]

However, if our parents are the chief culprits, they are hardly the only influence, and they themselves are subject to powerful forces in their own histories and in society at large. Who is to blame matters less than the end result: Certain human potentialities worth having are discouraged and suppressed. We learn to be ashamed of these things and therefore hide them, only later perhaps to go in search of them.

The young executive who spoke of ambition as an on-off function illustrates the problem of recovering a lost self. Asked about how his mother had related to him when he was a child, he made the striking statement: "In a sense, she related to me as a project. In a sense, as a being or thing to fulfill her ideas or ideals or vision of what a number-one son should be. I never felt a strong sense of conflict with what I was demanded to do. I bought into the program." (Note the use of the word "demanded.") In speaking of the extent of her influence on his makeup, he traces to her all of the following: "The goal orientation, the achievement orientation, the standards. Some of the be-perfect syndrome. The get-it-right syndrome." In other words, he was inflicted with a strong case of the performance syndrome. The good news is that he has, in fact, performed superbly. The bad news is that, approaching midlife, he has become unsure whose drums it is he marches to. Although he had never read Levinson's book, he used the same imagery: "I ask myself: Whose dream am I fulfilling? I get a lot of fulfillment from what I'm doing, but the question is: Whose dream is it?"

Recovering the Relational Side of the Self

In emphasizing mastery, expansive executives deemphasize relationships except insofar as relationships are a means to their ends. According to Robert Kegan and several other authors, relationships and independent achievement are two poles of human endeavor. At one pole, called expansive in this book, we have independence, mastery, self-differentiation, self-determination, self-sufficiency, distinct identity, and autonomy. Individuals at or near this pole feel keenly a need for self-respect, respect from others, and personal accomplishment. To satisfy these needs, they seek entry into the world of work and generally want not just a job but a career.[17] At the other pole, which I call "relational," we have interdependence, "a capacity for collaboration," "closely attuned interpersonal relations," intimacy, integration, and self-sacrifice.[18] Individuals at or near this pole feel strongly a need for acceptance, closeness, self-expression, and mutuality. They want to please, and, in being fearful of displeasing, they restrict their aggression.

David Bakan, a psychologically oriented theologian, made a similar distinction between "agency" and "communion." Agency manifests itself in self-assertion, self-expansion, the urge for mastery, separation from other people, and restricted expression of feeling. Communion manifests itself in membership, connection to others, intimate contact, and emotional expression. Carol Gilligan, who saw human development in the same bipolar terms, argued that the emphasis on agency represents, in our society, a largely male psychology and the emphasis on communion a largely female psychology. Similarly, Salvador Minuchin conceptualized families and family members in terms of separation and attachment.

In reality, no one ever occupies one pole to the complete exclusion of the other pole. As Kegan argues, at every stage of life a balance is struck between the two poles. An "evolutionary truce" is negotiated.[19] One side of life is more prominent than the other but never totally eclipses it. When a young person enters a stage emphasizing the differentiated self, other people are not lost; they are simply subordinated to the independent self.[20]

After Chris Cramer's father died and his mother became severely depressed and suicidal, he reports that, traumatized by abandonment, he swore off dependence on others. "[At a tender age] I was suddenly all by myself, and I decided: No way will I ever be dependent on anybody again." Obviously, this is hyperbole because as a manager he has relationships that entail some degree of dependence. But his statement is accurate to the extent that it expresses a wariness about dependence and a determination to maximize independence. In protecting himself from further abandonment, he lost something — the capacity to surrender himself in a relationship — that he has not yet seen fit to recover.

There is no doubt that the prevalence of men in the ranks of senior management contributes to the "masculine" bias so evident in this class of people. One quintessentially masculine executive provides a good example. Physically reminiscent of James Coburn, the flinty actor who played tough-guy parts in movies, he is almost totally identified with agency. Overall, this executive is evidently a good leader, as captured in a comment by a peer: "He has a strong sense of what the organization and the situation require and is unswerving in his commitment to it." In being unswerving, he is tough, aggressive, tenacious, outspoken. On the other hand, he is not warm or considerate or responsive or attentive or interested in his people as individuals. A telltale sign is the fact that his score on masculinity was *three* standard deviations above the mean. If he is to grow, he must overcome his reluctance to exhibit any remotely "feminine" characteristics.

For male executives, a shift in character often means a move in the direction of the "feminine," embracing a reduction (even if modest) in their investment in work and an increase in their investment in personal relationships.[21] For men to make this shift at midlife is to redefine themselves as being less thoroughly wrapped up in the quest for mastery, power, and rationality and more concerned with cultivating close, mutual, emotionally expressive relationships.

The converse of these executives are those managers, like Mark Tabor, whose expansive sides are underdeveloped and whose relational sides are overdeveloped for their leadership roles. They are, to varying degrees, too attuned to how people respond to their initiatives, too reluctant to assert themselves, too eager to please, too self-effacing, too self-minimizing. Their developmental task, the reverse of the extremely expansive executive's, is to rediscover self-assertion and personal power denied them in their youth. In developing, they gravitate away from being, in some respects, overintegrated.

Healing Split Consciousness

Another dimension of a character shift is to reverse the splitting of oneself into sharply bright and dark sides. The bright side is that part of the self that the person believes is worthy of esteem. The dark side — what Jung calls the shadow — is what the person believes will, if revealed, discredit or disgrace him or her. A shift in character is typically a reversal of the highly charged splitting between the bright side (taken to be good) and the dark side (taken to be bad). Melanie Klein used the word "reparation" to describe this process. Reparation is the "tendency to repair, to make *whole* again, that which has been split or torn apart. People enter a stage . . . in which they integrate their once split awareness."[22]

To heal this painful split, the manager must cease to identify so thoroughly with the "good" side. By the same token, the manager must cease to dissociate so completely from the "bad" side. To do this is to become less dependent on how one is performing. Diana Dowling came to understand that she was constantly "trying to impress people, trying to make them think I was something." Of course, she worried that she was impressing people unfavorably. The heavy psychic burden she placed on herself, she realized, depressed her. Growth for her is "allowing myself to be." It is learning not to "condemn

myself if there is a fumble." She recalled that "in the past I wasn't
even allowed to pick up the ball if I fumbled." Notice the use
of the passive voice, "I wasn't allowed." It's as if an outside force
had controlled her.

Diana was tortured by performance anxiety. A big step
forward has been to recognize the anxiety for what it is rather
than be unconsciously controlled by it. She now tells herself,
"*Be* anxious — feel it." Her antidote to the crippling effects of the
anxiety begins with acceptance: "So now I try to allow the anxiety, and I try to nurture it, and I try to nurture myself, and
pretty soon the anxiety isn't there anymore. To see the moments
of anxiety and what brings it on, and to chip away at it, and
acknowledge it, and accept it, and accept me — that's the healing process."

Diana's quest is to make herself whole by permitting herself normal human fallibility — what she had come to treat as
her abhorrent dark side. "What I have missed is being able to
say the wrong things and do the wrong things and still be OK.
God, I have missed that. That's what I am working on now.
That's what I daydream about right now. It's healing. A yearn-
ing for wholeness, that's what it is. It brings tears to my eyes."

Incorporating one's dark side into one's sense of self is made
difficult by the primitive sense of the dark side as tantamount
to evil. Diana reflected this in saying, "A lot of me that I had
repressed I feared would come out as evil." Jung explicates the
phenomenon as follows: "The inner voice brings the evil before
us in a very tempting and convincing way in order to make us
succumb. If we do not partially succumb, nothing of this apparent evil enters us, and no regeneration or healing takes place. . . .
If we succumb completely, then the contents expressed by the
inner voice act as so many devils and a catastrophe ensues. But
if we can succumb only in part and if by self-assertion the ego
can save itself from being completely swallowed, then it can as-
similate the voice, and we realize that the evil was, after all, only
a semblance of evil, and in reality a bringer of healing and illu-
mination. In fact, the inner voice is a 'Lucifer' in the strictest
and most unequivocal sense of the word."[23] (In Latin, *lucifer* means
literally "light-bearing" or "light-bringing." Thus, out of the apparent darkness in oneself can come light.)

One potential evil Diana Dowling experienced was the monstrous rage that welled up in her when she made this previously banned emotion legitimate. "As a kid I would get raging mad for a moment, and I then would immediately repress it. So there is this anger inside that deserves acknowledgment, but I was afraid that, as a result of my growth this year, I would become a monster and kill everybody. . . . A lot of my dreams were about monsters, mean monsters." As if following Jung's advice, Diana escaped this nightmarish prospect by learning to give partial and constructive expression to her anger. "It's a slow process coming to grips with the fact that I can be angry and not hurt anybody, not kill anybody."

To heal the split between bright and dark, good and bad, the highly developed side and the neglected side, the person must abandon the notion that the way he or she has chosen to be is the only way. It is a departure from an absolute belief in one's way of being, a move away from the unquestioned assumption that, as Kegan phrases it, "our way . . . is not merely workable but the most workable way." Growth is "making relative what I had taken as ultimate."[24]

Summary

To review, a shift in character has three aspects — cognition, power, and values. The cognitive aspect refers to the person's act of seeing him- or herself as others do. Subjective experience that had hardly been examined or questioned is now held at arm's length and viewed objectively. Subject is treated as object.[25] The manager does what fish can never do and gets outside of the taken-for-granted water — becomes amphibious, as it were.

A "re-cognition" or "re-vision," as Kegan terms it, is necessary but not sufficient to accomplish a shift in character. The transition in "meaning-making" that Kegan conceptualizes is profound, but the use of cognitive terminology misses an important element — the power dynamic.[26] It is not enough to see oneself — in particular, one's lopsidedness — in a different light. One must *push back* on what one finds. To change, a manager must object to the domination of one side of the self by the other.

To use Fritz Perls's language, the "underdog" in oneself must achieve greater parity with the "top dog."[27] The weak side must assert itself in relation to the strong side. No small matter.

This shift won't happen in the absence of the third aspect of a character shift — values. Crucial to the maintenance of the status quo (or to a reform of it) is the person's system of values, the mechanism for determining the value of one element versus another. A shift requires managers to reorder their hierarchy of values such that their quest for worth can be satisfied by exhibiting qualities previously assigned a low value or no value at all. This happens when executives recognize the costs incurred by having placed a high value on certain things and the benefits foregone by having placed a low value on certain other things. Growth goes well beyond *awareness* of previously disavowed elements of self. What is wanted is genuine *acceptance* of devalued, denied elements.

We saw at the end of the previous chapter that managers benefit from gaining insight into their character and into the connection between their character and their leadership behavior even if their character does not actually change. If what we called a level-one benefit is greater empathy with oneself and others, then the level-two benefits arising from a true shift in character go considerably beyond enhanced empathy. Managers able to achieve such a shift drop their rigid and righteous adherence to a fairly limited band of behaviors. In ceasing to be true believers in their historic modes of leading and being, they open up the possibility of expanding their repertoire. Other modes become conceivable, desirable, and realizable. Managers able to grow in this deeply personal way become more versatile, more flexible, more adaptable — without losing their capacity to be resolute.

Part of the increased versatility comes from the fact that these managers no longer distinguish so sharply between those subordinates viewed as star performers and those viewed as flawed performers. By transcending the tendency to polarize their own bright and dark sides, they likewise transcend the tendency to polarize their view of other people. In this way they become whole. They move beyond experiencing themselves and others in black and white and learn to work better with shades of gray. The process also works the other way. If an executive depolarizes a relationship, it has a reparative reverberation within the executive. Hirschhorn explained that "to repair a present relationship [that is, with an *external* object] is also to do some repair of relations to one's internal objects. The present relationship becomes a symbol of many past similar relationships so that habitual modes of relating are to some extent restructured."[28]

Those several benefits are evident in the case of Lee McKinney, who is featured in the next chapter. The data strongly suggest that Lee McKinney is an individual who actually changed in a fundamental way. He is also representative of a third type of expansive executive—the perfectionist-systematizer.

Chapter Eleven

The Evolution of a Manager: The Lee McKinney Story

The question of personality change in executives is controversial enough that it is worth devoting a chapter to the case of a manager who accomplished such a change. In this way we can understand better what a character shift in a driven senior manager entails and how, in a world that reinforces him for what he is, he was moved to change in a basic way.

This chapter describes an executive, whom I shall call Lee McKinney, as he was before the change. It also gives a description of the nature of the change he underwent, as well as an account of the process by which the change occurred. In addition, this chapter introduces a third type of expansive executive — the perfectionist-systematizer. This type joins the striver-builder presented in Chapter Two and the self-vindicator/fix-it leader presented in Chapter Five as a prime example of the varieties of expansive executive.

Lee McKinney is a senior manager in his late forties who heads a vital area in his large, functionally organized company. He is dedicated, hardworking, results-oriented, effective, durable under stress, loyal, and adept at introducing order and systems. But certain aspects of his leadership style have taken the luster

182

off his performance in his present job and made his ascent to the top rung questionable. These nagging problems, which at the outset he only dimly understood, prove to be rooted in his basic character as a person and reinforced by the life he had made for himself at work and outside of work.

Lee's Drive

Lee McKinney is a company man, a family man, a religious man. For twenty-eight years he has worked relentlessly at a series of professional and managerial jobs, and to the present day he has not let up. He cares about his wife and family, provides well for them, makes a point of being present for important family occasions, and has always been invested in how each of his three young-adult children are doing. Yet in one of his numerous insightful moments with us, he confessed, "I always told myself that family came first and work second, but I didn't practice that." A regular churchgoer, he has for many years taken leadership positions in his church, to the point where he now has been appointed an elder in his region—a responsibility that takes him away from home one weekend a month.

He has driven himself unmercifully—at work, at home, and in his church and civic involvements. He described himself as being "overwhelmingly committed to the company—to a fault. . . . I almost feel guilty getting a paycheck. I've got to earn it twenty-four hours a day, seven days a week." One of his children said that "he has this thing that you should always do the best you can in achieving the highest you can. That's the way he is with everything." This drive has had the advantage of earning him a well-deserved reputation for being thorough, results-oriented, and productive. It has had the disadvantage for him personally that he exhausts himself and barely allows himself the chance to recover. He said in an initial interview, "I wake up drained sometimes but I tell myself: You can't be drained. You have to do this or that." At a later point he told us that if he wakes up feeling flat, he looks at himself in the mirror and exhorts himself out loud. He has gone so far as to slap himself in the face to get himself going. Even this draconian

measure has not prevented him from frequently giving off a sense
of being weighed down and tired. He has worked at his job or
his outside involvements thirteen or fourteen hours a day, six
days a week, and he has still felt as if he was perpetually behind.

There is a superstitious element to his drive. Lee has always worried that his luck, represented by a "white cloud" that
he felt followed him around, would run out if he eased up in
any way. "I'm afraid if I don't work hard, the white cloud won't
be there."

Even during his leisure time he has managed to stay constantly busy. He reported that his family complains to him,
"When do you *not* have something to do?" His heavy involvement in work of one sort or another has bothered his wife who,
according to him, "thinks it's wonderful that I've become a senior
executive, but she detests the company because it dominates
my life." Though he has so far had no major physical ailments,
he understandably worries about his health. He asks himself,
"Will I continue to have the *energy* to contribute?" One wonders,
since he, as a point of pride, has *never* taken a sick day and reports
not liking to sleep—because it's "nonproductive."

Lee has a devoutly religious father to thank, in part, for
his extreme drive. His father's own yearbook said about him,
"He can because he thinks he can." His father's favorite saying
was: "Whatever you do, do with all your might. Things done
by halves are never done right." His mother, who did not hold
a paying job, seemed to pass on to Lee the perfectionism she
brought to keeping the house. Her imperative for him was: "Do
something useful." As a young teen before his work ethic took
hold, he liked to laze around on summer days. But she would
have none of it. "When I was fourteen, my mother would say
to me in no uncertain terms, 'No son of mine will lie out in the
sun.'"

As an executive, his assets—useful in managing his function—include his organizational ability, discipline, structured
approach, and attention to detail. But this set of qualities has
sometimes gotten in the way. A subordinate complained, "As
organized as he is, he imposes this on all the rest of the organization and wastes time." Similarly, another subordinate com-

mented that "he has a very elaborate follow-up system. It's too good sometimes"—in that he "overmanages."

He has taken the same posture at home, where his entire family sees him as a perfectionist. His concern with getting every last detail right has shown up in his expectations for his children. According to Lee, "My style is, when the kid is cleaning the car, I inspect every last bit, and if it's not perfect, I tell the kid it's not perfect and have him fix it." His children agree. A grown child said, "Dad's a perfectionist. He'd always find something wrong with the job that any of us did."

This detail-orientation has been part of Lee's general high expectations for his children, which have mirrored his high expectations for himself. "I want my kids to be perfect—100 percent. . . . I've expected each kid to give 110 percent each day to each thing that child tries. Sandra [his wife] believes that's too much. She's exasperated by that." The children also have seen him as expecting a lot, perhaps too much. As one said, "He wants and expects perfection. No matter how well I do, he is always looking for something to improve on. Sometimes I think you can't ever please him." One of his children confessed to having felt extremely angry: "I used to hate my dad for the way he drove us, and drove us, and drove us. I just despised him for it—for not being able to ease off and for staying on us." Lee's compelling need for his children to be of high worth showed up, predictably, in a close relationship with his high-achieving first child and a problematic relationship with his underachieving second-born.

In fact, this imperative that everything be done well has hampered him at work, where historically he has not discriminated well enough between important and unimportant tasks. His loyal secretary was dismayed with him for being "concerned with trivialities" and "way behind in his mail." When, for example, he returned from a long trip, he felt compelled to read copies of the *Wall Street Journal* stacked on his desk. Since even with his prodigious capacity for work, this proved impossible, the newspapers piled up, first on his desk and later in his coat closet. Besides working longer hours than necessary, an ill effect of his perfectionism has been that he is sometimes inadequately prepared for important meetings. After the feedback session he began to ask himself, "How perfect do you have to be? When I sharpen a pencil, I look carefully at the point. . . . I'm failing to discriminate [between what's worth perfecting and what is not]."

Integral to his perfectionism is a religiously informed devotion to principles — to what he believes is right — that at times make him righteous and difficult to influence. A peer captured this by describing him as "principled, willing to fight — and a pain in the ass occasionally." A subordinate said about him, "Lee is not a good listener." A city official with whom he had worked closely in the community said, "I would like him to be more considerate of other people's opinions — to search more for other people's opinions before dominating the scene with his own opinion." This was not just an issue of giving others a chance to speak; it was also his difficulty taking in other points of view. A fellow board member for a community agency commented, "When it gets to the issue of moral judgments, he can't step out of his own perspective. It's his dogged devotion to principle." At work he is sometimes seen as being too identified with his own function and not sufficiently in tune with other functions. Another subordinate attributed to him a general sense of himself as having "relative infallibility. He thinks he's almost always right." In his feedback report several people referred to him as "self-righteous" and "sanctimonious."

Again, at home the picture was the same. Along with the considerable appreciation of him as a manager, father, and husband, his children made comments to the effect that "he will sit down and listen if we disagree, but he's pretty convinced he's right, and it's hard to get through to him." He has made a consistent effort to "make sure [his children] had values" — what one of his children called "the key words to life."

With his convictions has come an effort to shape his children accordingly. One of the children said, "If he is sure it's right, he'll put a lot of pressure on the person to change." This is perhaps the children's biggest gripe, that "he tries to mold us into his own way of life, instead of letting us have our own." Lee's need for control, which stands out here, is not an end in itself but a means to the end of having his children turn out well — as one said, "to be someone he could be proud of." Thus, his strongly held beliefs at times proved troublesome at home, at work, and in the community.

In a way Lee's life can be viewed as a quest for redemption. In religious terms, he "worried about being accepted by God." Was he good enough? Would he be saved? In secular terms, he sought redemption through career success. Evidently he had long nourished the dream of becoming CEO of his company. When a year earlier he was passed over, his entire family was acutely conscious of his disappointment. One of his children said, "He cried inside when he didn't get the promotion to CEO." His wife Sandra said, "When he didn't get the promotion, he was really down. I told him it wasn't that important, but he didn't have much of an answer." The ascension to that throne evidently loomed for him as the ultimate sign of corporate worth.

He has sought worth in the other spheres of his life as well. He has invested a lot in his children over the years in an effort to have them grow up to be worthy people, individuals "he could be proud of." At one point he declared a bit piously, "Judge whether I've been successful by how I've done with the kids." He also pursued a parallel career in the church and the community, doing good works. In all spheres he has evidently sought a sense of personal worth. When asked early on in the program what motivated him, he answered, "Self-esteem. If I don't feel good about me, I can't feel good about everything. A feeling of worth." Yet despite his considerable success in all phases of his life, he could state flatly, "I've always had difficulty feeling good about me."

The Perfectionist-Systematizer

Lee McKinney is an example of a third type of expansive executive: the perfectionist-systematizer. More than anything, this type of person needs to be right, needs to be beyond reproach. Being right is the way the perfectionist achieves a sense of personal worth, and being right comes from following principles.

The greatest fear of people like this is that they will fail to adhere to their principles, whether lofty or trivial. They continually try to do what is right and expect others to do the same, and they are continually on the lookout for nonadherence in themselves and others. They are vigilant, even hypervigilant. They are attentive to details, even obsessed with details.

Their concern with principle is often associated with a heightened sense of order. Philosophically, whether aware of it or not, they have a strong predilection for Plato's forms—the ideal shape the world should take. They identify fervently with essence (the ideal world) and are troubled by existence (the actual, imperfect world).

Perfectionists are typically the offspring of people very much like themselves—exacting, principled people who hold their children strictly accountable. Growing up with a perfectionistic parent or parents, these individuals develop strong consciences. They internalize the host of "shoulds" coming from the parent. The more punishing the parent, the more self-punishing and punishing of others are the children.

Indeed, Lee McKinney was capable of being a punishing parent when his children were young. A child who in one breath called him a "great father" because "he was always there" said in the next breath that his father was quick to punish. "There would be a spanking, a slap across the face, maybe to excess sometimes. Discipline was never mild." Evidently, something snapped in Lee whenever a child violated one of his cherished principles. In fairness to him, he was most likely to lash out when he was exhausted.

At their worst, individuals of this type are opinionated and self-righteous. They can be oppressive about minor things that to them are matters of principle. The old Lee McKinney was described as someone "who looked for who's in charge so he knows who to shoot if something goes wrong." Prone to finding fault, as Lee McKinney was before the change, such executives leave the impression that their principles are a pretext for elevating themselves over others. Worse than fault-finders or nit-pickers, they can be out-and-out tyrants. As managers they are prone to overcontrolling subordinates in an effort to "get it right" on their terms. Like Lee McKinney before the change, they may feel compelled to do *everything* and to do everything *perfectly*. They are so enthusiastic about having their units run in an orderly fashion that they can lose sight of the organization's purpose. Anything that looks messy to them, they want to clean up, even if doing so serves no useful purpose. Efficiency overtakes effectiveness. Such is their devotion to their principles, and to their image of themselves as principled, that they tend to be impervious to indications of the harm they are doing.

At their best, they are guided by their principles but not tyrannized by them and likewise guide others without turning into oppressors. As managers they lead on the basis of personal integrity and high principles but are capable of accepting different principles and of working successfully with the people who uphold those principles. They harness their sense of order to constructive ends. They get beyond the attachment to form for its own sake and put it to work infusing their units with needed structure and definition. Like Lee McKinney, they typically specialize in systematizing organizations or in running a tight ship. They also excel at implementing a slim-down strategy — at trimming fat and eliminating unnecessary levels, functions, or staff.

Rather than inflict their high standards on their subordinates, they inspire their people to meet those passionately held standards. As leaders they often become, as Lee McKinney did, a moral force within the organization and the community, but they avoid being self-righteous and rigid. Their principles and their image of themselves as principled are not so inviolate that they feel violated by criticism. As was evident from his ability to learn about himself and grow, Lee McKinney was such a person.

What Lee McKinney Changed

Two years after the feedback session, we took stock of the nature and extent of the change in Lee by interviewing eleven co-workers and six family members, including his sister and brother, as well as Lee himself. We asked just one basic open-ended question: "What change, if any, have you observed in Lee McKinney in the last year or two?" We followed this question with probes about what caused, hindered, and aided the change.

There was general agreement on the fact that Lee had changed and on the nature of the change. Of seventeen people interviewed, thirteen noted the same basic evolution in the way Lee behaves: He has become less negative, judgmental, and critical, less difficult to reach; more supportive and open-minded; a better listener. Nine of eleven co-workers and four of six family members noted the change.

The consensus at work was that he has clearly changed for the better. His boss upped his evaluation of Lee's effectiveness "from a 7 to a 9 on a 10-point scale." A direct subordinate concluded that Lee's improved performance "speaks to increased organizational effectiveness. As a result, I don't have to spend as much time composing letters or gathering information. I don't have to spend a lot of time making a case or responding to hard questions."

Many of his associates at work made similar comments. One person noted, for example, that "he's presenting himself in a role of an 'I'm-on-your-side' kind of guy rather than 'I'm a senior vice-president, and I'm a judge.'" Another person described him as "less of an obstructionist and more accommodating to change." A third co-worker said that "in the past Lee was the last person I would call if I had a problem; but now the situation is almost totally reversed. I think he has developed some real listening skills." His boss gave the following assessment: "Basically, not only I but the whole senior management group have noticed a marked change. It's overwhelmingly positive. Lee is now viewed as supportive, as opposed to being just a critic. Before, the talk was that he was only negative. Now he is seen as tough but also supportive. Plus he seems to be enjoying himself more."

One of his peers, who works closely with him, made a telling comment: "There was a time when Lee gave the impression, true or not, that the reason he was asking questions was to be the expert, to catch someone up short. Now, when he asks a question, he frames it so that you know he wants to be part of the solution, not part of the problem. It no longer seems like he extracts information to use it against you. He has recognized — and this is to the credit of your program — that there are more important things in life than being smart; that it is better to be a team player than be the smartest guy on the block."

Thus several co-workers, responding independently, report the same essential change. Further verifying the change, the members of his family say approximately the same thing about him in an entirely different context. A college-aged child, echoing what the last co-worker said above, told us, "He and I are able to talk things out more; . . . I feel it's easier for me to come talk to him if I have a problem." And another child in college credited him with better listening skills: "He is either more understanding or able to listen better. Two years ago if you didn't do well in a particular class, there was no excuse. The grade was the grade. Now you can explain a little more to him, and he'll understand a little better . . . . He is willing to understand other people's points of view better. He listens better. It's always been easier to give him the good news, but now if there's bad news it's a little bit easier to give it to him, to tell him the whole story."

Associated with the change in the way Lee behaves outwardly has been a shift in his inner self. Just as he now relates differently to other people, he also relates differently to himself. To other people, co-workers and family members alike, this inner shift has manifested itself in his being more relaxed. One of his grown children made a connection between his being more relaxed and his being more approachable. Another of his children perceptively observed, "The most overall thing that I can sense is that he is more comfortable with himself." Lee himself made precisely the same comment: "I'm more comfortable with myself. The biggest difference is in the way I feel about myself."

This altered relation to himself is what stands out the most in the new Lee McKinney. He seems to have toned down the harsh demands of his superego. He is no longer so aggressively critical of himself. He is more relaxed in the sense that he is no longer so tense with the effort to prove himself. There is less "self-centeredness," to quote a family member. A grown child observed:

He's more relaxed and less tense. I don't think he
is always trying to prove himself. I see it in the nature of our conversations, and the way he reacts
to comments, even the way he plays tennis. Also,
he's less concerned with me and my career, which
is not a negative thing. My career is not so compelling to him that he ties it in to his sense of self-
worth. We still talk about it because I'm his daughter and he loves me, but it's not so much a reflection on him. It is a welcome change because he's
detached himself a little. He becomes a little less
quick to tell me what I should do and how I should
do it. In the past he almost reacted like I was one
of the people working for him. For me it was like
talking to a senior manager at my corporation.

(Apropos of the comment about the way Lee plays tennis, he
reported that the tennis pro had complimented him on how his
serve had become "more relaxed, more fluid.")

Interestingly, the management development manager also
saw Lee as less anxious to demonstrate his worth through his
children's accomplishments: "I hear him talk less about his family
than he used to. It was almost as if he was too proud of the accomplishments of the family. Somehow he was working too hard
at it. He's every bit as proud of his family as before, but he
doesn't wear it on his sleeve. It is more natural."

Will the Change Last?

Further verification of the change in Lee is the widespread belief that it will last. Fully fifteen of the seventeen people we spoke
to thought the change would be a lasting one. This is especially
noteworthy in light of how skeptical people tend to be when
someone makes an effort to change. Following are sample comments from three coworkers:

Most people don't change. They try, but they run
out of steam. The first time they are under pres-

sure they revert back. . . . It is difficult for people
to change at any age. You don't change really. You
just adjust. Lee is one of the rare ones.

There has been enough reinforcement, enough time
going by, enough critical incidents having occurred
that I say: Lee has changed. Rather than: Lee is
trying to change.

If you had asked me twelve months ago, I would
say maybe we're going through another school of
thought — let's try this, let's try that. Today I would
say it will stay with him.

In a similar vein, a family member commented, "Yeah
I do [feel it's lasting]. I think it has had a profound enough impact on him. He's happier than he was: That's the driving force
that will make it last."

Those who know a person making a change often acknowledge an improvement but express doubt that it is "real"
or "natural." In this regard, twelve people were asked the question: "Was the change internalized?" Eight said yes. One member of his family said: "Yes, I think unquestionably [that he's
internalized the change]. There is no question in my mind."

To summarize: Clearly, Lee McKinney succeeded in
redressing an imbalance in his character. Previously, he had
been trying too hard to establish himself as a person of worth,
he had been too identified with his high standards for determining worth, and he had been too critical and pressuring of other
people in these terms. Following the shift, he remains highly
motivated to contribute, but he is no longer so intensely anxious about his worth or tense with the effort to prove it. Evidence for the changes in Lee comes from both co-workers and
family. In particular, they see him as more effective in relating
to others. He sees the same thing in himself, but he is perhaps
more impressed with his increased comfort with himself — something that a few co-workers and family members have also noted.

His increased comfort with himself has enhanced his relationships by freeing him to be more reciprocal. No longer so

concerned about his worth, he doesn't have to have all the answers. He can *ask* for assistance instead of always having to be
the one who *provides* assistance. "I've found out there's a whole
lot of help out there. . . . It's a big departure—just to ask for
help. That's different for me, really different." To need help has
ceased to be a forbidding sign of unworthiness.

Lee's new comfort with himself has a deeper aspect: He
has learned to recognize emotional needs long since buried. At
first it seemed, in our conversations with him, that he needed
help awarding himself more leisure time. We picked up on his
stated need to be "less driven, less perfectionistic so I can have
more 'me time.'" This was to be time to read, to relax, to play
tennis, all of which he enjoyed but seldom made time for.

Lee's deeper needs became apparent during the group program when one of the staff members asked Lee, who had felt
neglected as a child, what the "Dutch uncle" he never had would
have said to him during a particularly trying hour. Lee's response
was to cry quietly. The staff member asked him how he felt.
"Weak and unmanly," he said—a reference to being embarrassed
about crying. "I'm afraid that the others will think I can't lead."
At the staff member's suggestion, Lee asked each of the other
executives whether they thought he could lead. Each one said
yes and meant it. One hard-nosed executive told him, with moist
eyes, "I'm *more* confident in you now. You're a stronger leader."

So Lee McKinney's unmet personal need went beyond
a need for personal time, recreation, self-indulgence. Lee needed
to permit himself to recognize his own emotional needs, to allow himself to be *needy*—weak, unhappy, vulnerable. He also
needed to allow other people to nurture him at those times. After
receiving several hugs as the session ended, he said, "Except
for my wife, I haven't been hugged in thirty years."

How Lee Went About Changing

The reader may feel that a certain mystery surrounds Lee
McKinney's evolution. I can dispel some of the mystery, but
I don't pretend to have penetrated it completely.

What did Lee actually do en route to his reemergence?
The nub of it is that, in several different settings, he engaged

in intensive self-reflection that became increasingly deep over a two-year period. He used a number of mirrors to reflect on himself—on his behavior and on the motives that prompted his behavior. These mirrors were held up by him and by numerous important people in his life. Thus, over this two-year span he more or less continuously expended considerable psychic energy in various forms of self-reflection. One of his children commented on how seriously he took the program: "He has spent a lot of time cogitating or reacting to it emotionally."

What motivated this self-reflection? A number of things. Principal among them was the sting of being passed over for promotion and the desire to improve his candidacy. But he was also of an age that made him very interested in taking stock. A grown son made the point that "he is in a questioning stage of his life—because of his age, because of where he is career-wise. . . . He's searching: Who am I, and what do I want to do with the rest of my life?" But more than life circumstances, what prompted him was a genuine interest in knowing himself and in growing. The same grown son said about his motivation: "The main thing is that when this started a few years ago it was something he *wanted* to do. It wasn't like someone told him to go find out about yourself and change. He really wanted to know how other people perceived him, and he was willing to change."

Lee wanted to know, but he also felt throughout the process a mixture of, in his words, "excitement and trepidation." He wanted to change, but he was also afraid of changing. As an expansive person, he had a predictable fear of failure: "Can I succeed in changing? Can I do it? It's the lack of confidence."

In taking this sustained look at himself, what did he see? He saw his motives as they were, not as he had believed them to be. He had looked upon all his community service as motivated by principle, but late in the program he realized another motive was operating: "I have gone through many years thinking I was the great giving volunteer when, in reality, I need gratification I couldn't get in other ways." As he implies, the gratification he needed was a reinforcement of his worth as a person. Along this line he concluded in the feedback session, "I have a big ego, but I haven't realized it." By this he meant that he had a big need for ego gratification that he hadn't owned up to. Similarly, he came to see his drive to excel at work in a different light. "I used to say that I was motivated to contribute. Really, what I was looking for was recognition." These sorts of self-realization are very difficult to come to. It is no mean feat to be honest with yourself about what you do to purchase self-esteem. In facing up to what actually drove him, Lee McKinney showed real courage.

To come to this realization, besides being estimable in its own right, was instrumental to his metamorphosis. By opening his eyes to his ego needs, he had a better chance to influence how he went about meeting them. In stepping outside himself and discovering his acute need to prove himself and gain recognition, he diminished the excessive power of that need. Late in the two-year process he discovered that "powerful things are controlling me. I have spent almost fifty years thinking *I* was in control, and now I've found out that things were controlling *me*." By discovering what controlled him, he made it possible to exercise a modicum of control over it.

The story of Lee McKinney's evolution has so far emphasized self-reflection. But man (or woman) does not grow by insight alone. To be sure, Lee's metamorphosis would not have occurred without a full measure of equally brave attempts to act differently. Every time he saw himself in a new light, he looked for ways to translate the insight into an opportunity to improve in some respect. He played with possible improvement, first in his mind and then in actuality. Shortly after the feedback session, for example, he realized that his perfectionism translated into a habit of structuring his weekends in much the same way he structured his workdays. The perfectionistic grip was so strong that at first he literally could not imagine waking up on a Saturday morning without a full schedule of activities mapped out in advance. As time went on, however, he gave "going with the flow" a try and would later proudly report his successful forays into true, unstructured leisure time, along with a reading on whether or not he had felt guilty.

At bottom, Lee's efforts to learn about himself and to try new things were integral to his overall interest in leading better and living better. In what settings did he engage in this search for self-improvement? The settings alternated between those that were formal, structured, and professionally run and those that were informal, spontaneous, and self-administered. The initial, individual program got the evolutionary process going by injecting the perceptions of co-workers and family into his consciousness in the feedback session. As a result he greatly intensified the self-reflection he normally did on his own. He also began what would become a long series of personal conversations with his wife. Each time he came to a fresh insight he immediately checked it out and talked it through with his wife. Along the way he discovered, for example, that he had trouble asking for or accepting emotional support. (The tête-à-têtes with his wife were themselves becoming a notable exception to this rule.) His wife could see the difficulty he had being needy and quickly came up with an example that confirmed what he was learning: "In family get-togethers, you're nice, you ask about everyone, and then you're out to lunch. You're not there anymore. I used to think it was because you have a higher-level job, and all. But now I realize you never tell them what's bothering *you*. If people ask, you say that everything is great. *I* may know you're down, but no one else would ever know it. . . . You're always doing the comforting and never let people comfort you. You feel neglected, but *you* built the wall." Lee's spontaneous conversations with his wife, occasioned by the program, made it easier for him to believe what he was discovering about himself. Conversely, the outside input validated her view of him and her attempts to influence him. The child still living at home reported about her mother that "she has been supportive throughout the process, and he has relied on her throughout."

Whereas the individual program generated *general* perceptions about Lee, the value of a follow-up group program in which he participated was that it challenged the specific ways he acted. For example, the role he took over and over in unstructured discussions was, in a fellow participant's phrase, that of a "Dutch uncle." Ostensibly his motive was to offer advice, much of it in fact useful. But in the process of dispensing advice, he managed to project an image of himself as a seasoned executive —

knowledgeable, wise, and benevolent. At another point in the program, he turned the telling of his life story into a recitation of his career successes. Again he demonstrated an apparent wish to present himself as having his act together. His lack of self-revelation stood out in comparison to what his fellow executives volunteered about their histories, and this was reflected back to him. In a later session of the program, he told the group a story of a recent triumph under the pretext of asking for guidance. Two or three people saw what he was up to and gently but firmly played it back to him. To his credit he was able to see what they saw, painful as it was for him to do so. Thus the group program provided live instances in which his ego needs operated covertly and, more than the individual program, helped him to see those underlying motives for what they were.

If the reader wonders how Lee's change came about, it was largely as a result of little dramas like these last two—revealing and emotionally disturbing episodes. A bit like a tragic hero in an ancient Greek play, he slowly came to see his own hubris. The group program was also a safe place in which to turn insight into action. After being confronted with his covert ways of getting his ego needs met, Lee tried being overt with his fellow participants about his needs. Referring to his request for counsel on how to approach a new assignment, he said, "I felt it was OK to ask for help. And with great care the guys advised me and challenged me." Referring to times when he let his emotions show, he said, "I had never been vulnerable. I discovered that I am vulnerable and that I can be vulnerable and it's OK."

Work relationships represented another important setting for Lee's process of self-discovery. His boss played a critical role in sponsoring Lee's participation in both programs and in providing input personally in a performance appraisal that was one impetus to Lee's decision to take part in the individual program. The human resources manager functioned as Lee's coach and had many helpful conversations with him. In addition, the management team of which Lee was a member went through an extended team-building exercise during the same two-year period.

So Lee's self-development went on in an environment — at work and at home — that actively encouraged openness and growth. What with the legitimacy given to his effort to grow and the abundant resources available for it, the odds were clearly in his favor. Still, favorable conditions are no guarantee of growth. Lee McKinney made it happen. He made it happen by opening himself to new experiences and by making his development a priority. His daughter summed it up well: "I know that he has treated this program as one of the most important things in his life."

Chapter Twelve

The Hero's Journey: How Managers Make Lasting Change

Lee McKinney's story prompts one to ask: How can other managers effect significant and lasting improvements in the way they lead (and live)? While there is no formula for what Lee McKinney did, there is a general process that managers can follow. This chapter lays out the phases of personal evolution, including tasks that must be performed during each phase and resources that must be available. It also shows how character shifts and behavioral change are combined in a sequential process of managerial and personal development.

There are four phases to the journey of self-development. The first is a prechange phase in which the manager puts most of his or her energy into maintaining the existing self. In a sense, then, the journey begins "at home." The individual may experience tensions or receive cues that suggest a need for major change, but these are generally deflected. Whatever adjustments the individual might make in this phase are kept comfortably within the existing system — that is, the existing "self-system." No serious challenge is made to the established "organization of the self."[1]

200

The function of this first phase is stabilization. The function of the second and third phases is destabilization. During the second phase the manager *separates* from his or her old self ("leaves home"). To suggest that this separation is complete is to exaggerate wildly. It is more accurate to say that the individual achieves some distance from his or her preexisting self. In standing outside the self, he or she sees much more clearly the problem with the existing "organization of the self" and develops an interest in reorganization. This is a most unsettling time for the person.

The third phase, often an extended one, is given over to a *search* for a new self. Upon the successful completion of this phase of the journey, the manager has not only discovered the potential to become something new but has actually realized that potential. Instead of settling for self-insight he or she translates insight into action. In discovering a new self, the manager takes on challenges never faced before.

The journey is not truly complete until the individual returns "home" to arrange for an *accommodation* of the new self. After the destabilization of the second and third phases, the function of this fourth phase is to restabilize the individual.

Let us at the outset correct any misimpression that the process of change is something a manager can take on single-handed. Certainly the manager needs to take charge of the process, but change on this order of magnitude is most unlikely to happen without the active involvement of key figures in the manager's life—family members, friends, peers, bosses, and subordinates.

Phase One: Maintaining the Old Self

For most executives explicit indications of a need for change are typically in short supply (see Chapter Two). The executive's elevated situation is responsible for this, as is his or her expansive nature, which prompts the person to resist acknowledging any indications for change out of a need for an undisputed sense of worth.

The manager's existing identity, or character, is held in place by strong forces. All adults have gone to considerable trouble to fashion an identity that allows them to allay anxiety about self-worth and to make their way in the world. They are understandably reluctant to meddle with a workable arrangement, even if in some ways it does not work well. Like any "organization," it has a life of its own. It invests quite a bit of energy in maintaining itself and warding off threats to its continued existence.

The manager's identity is also held in place by the settings he or she has chosen to support that identity — such as tasks to perform, people to perform them with, and norms governing work and relationships. These settings expect certain things of the person and reward him or her for meeting those expectations. Because identity is thus defined both by the individual and by the environment in which he or she is embedded, the person, according to Kegan, is "an 'individual' *and* an 'embeddual.' There is never just a you."[2]

To point out that the person is an "embeddual" is just a technical way of saying that a human being is a social animal. It is perfectly healthy and natural for people to have their identities bolstered by their work and relationships. If not as much as children, adults still need what Donald Winnicott called a "holding environment" — a setting that supports their current definition of themselves. For an identity to work well for an individual, it needs to be stabilized. It is this very stabilization function, however, that may stand in the way of self-insight, often the first step in a process of growth. The manager, and the people in the manager's environment, often do too good a job of defending his or her current makeup.[3]

Phase Two: Separating from the Old Self

To step outside of oneself is one of the most dramatic and threatening things an adult can do. In his classic book *Hero with a Thousand Faces,* Joseph Campbell used ancient myths to show the awesomeness of taking this step in a journey of self-discovery.[4] To embark on such a journey is to "go outside the accepted limits" and is tantamount to "a form of self-annihilation."[5] The mythic analogue is for the hero to be swallowed by a monster and to appear to have died. The "physical body of the hero may be actually slain, dismembered, and scattered over the land or sea."[6] If this seems grossly melodramatic, remember Campbell's raw material is the epic stories of the ancient world. These legends exaggerate to make the point that it approaches being a heroic undertaking for someone to cross this first threshold.[7]

Some expansive managers are moved to cross this threshold by the lure of self-renewal. More often, it is the case that managers have to be virtually driven across the threshold. The more expansive the executive, the more attached he or she is to the mode of worth-through-mastery, the greater will be the pressure that has to be applied. This pressure takes a number of forms, the most important of which may be direct criticism.

Sources of Criticism. People generally "leave home" because they feel they must. The internal pressure to leave can build gradually: Signals accumulate over time to make the individual increasingly uncomfortable with his or her current construction of self. The pressure can also mount suddenly, as when a major event floors the person. A serious setback at work or a troubled or failed marriage, for example, can lead individuals to start asking basic questions about themselves. In this book we are chiefly concerned with the jolt that comes from constructive criticism, especially a concentrated dose of it. It commonly takes being hit over the head for most adults, especially successful adults, to reconsider who they are. But there is no guarantee that hard times — or hard-hitting feedback — will set off hard self-questioning. The threat to the organization of the self may simply be too great.

If a manager is to get the benefit of constructive criticism, then the people surrounding him or her must overcome their inclination to withhold their true feelings. They must likewise not be deterred by the manager's own reluctance to hear what they feel about him or her.

Most executives have a close associate or two from whom they get occasional candid output about themselves. Frank Lindler, a young general manager, found it easiest to hear criticism from women subordinates. One of them, who was not reluctant to take him on, said, "People don't generally say a lot about how they feel about others. I always felt free to do that with Frank, to express whatever I was thinking."[8] Lindler would also, on rare occasions on the road, sitting in a bar late at night, initiate a personal conversation with a member of his inner circle. One such individual, a man, said, "Every time we go somewhere—every six months or so—we stay up late talking one-on-one. Once he asked how he was perceived by the division. He's curious, just like anyone else. We all have insecurities. He needs some feedback that he considers genuine. It only happens over a drink."[9]

Superiors can be a good source of input, but careful critiques from bosses are rare, except, perhaps, in the case of individuals in their late thirties or early forties who are relatively new to executive-level positions. Frank Lindler, reflecting his personal need to get "adopted" by top management, managed to get coaching from both his boss and his boss's boss. If such input is not available from line managers, it can come to the executive from the human resources staff. Bill Flechette struck up a relationship with an internal consultant who "has always seen me as a diamond who needed cutting and trained himself as the diamond cutter. He has brought me face-to-face with some issues I wanted to face and others I didn't want to."

Spouses can be excellent critics and sounding boards if this channel of communication is open. Bill Flechette used his wife as a confidant: "My wife will tell me if I am getting obsessed with trivialities, overreading a situation, overworking myself. She also points out what I am doing well." Sometimes the executive is only willing to truly listen to his or her spouse *after* receiving outside input. One executive, having had his eyes opened by a lot of criticism in his feedback report, talked it over with his wife. According to him she said, caringly, "There is smoke, so it's worth seeing if there's any fire. You are intense, results-oriented, and sometimes you look upon the results as more important than the people. I could have told you that twenty years ago."

Whatever an executive's sources of data on him or herself, the information only has an impact if the executive accepts the criticism as valid. One manager with severe interpersonal problems at work, although generally not receptive to feedback, had two subordinates whom he respected and trusted enough that he could at least sit still when they talked to him. One of these individuals reported that "whenever I have a problem with him, I tell him to his face. He may shrug his shoulders and think I don't know what I'm talking about, but he doesn't challenge me." What defensive executives like this usually take away from such a conversation is that *other people* see a need for change. But the stimulus by itself guarantees nothing. The governing internal variable is whether the executive takes responsibility for his or her piece of the problem.

Naturally, executives, like the rest of us, must sort through the criticism they receive and separate the wheat from the chaff. It takes a combination of street smarts and self-honesty to cull out the false praise and the false blame. One executive, when asked how he responded to feedback, showed that he very much considered the source: "It depends who is giving it. If [it is] someone I trust, like my wife and [a certain trusted subordinate], I take it seriously. I would be suspicious of [a certain distrusted subordinate] because there is so much self-interest involved and because he is attempting to manipulate the situation. With [the personnel manager], a genuine soul, I take it straight from him. With [a trainer], an enthusiast, a stream of consciousness, I go away and think about it."

The Role of Disconfirmation. Criticism contributes to development only if the executive allows it to be *disconfirming*. What gets disconfirmed is some aspect of the way the executive leads and perhaps also those aspects of his or her character that account for that behavior. For disconfirmation to occur executives must see something wrong or missing with respect to their ability to meet the demands placed on them by a present job or potential future jobs. They must see themselves as, in this sense, having a problem. As we shall see later, they must also have a strong enough sense of self to take the blow that disconfirmation delivers to their system.

Disconfirmation is always accompanied by a certain amount of discomfort or pain. Recognizing that he or she has a problem can hit an executive hard. Starting out the feedback process with us, one high-potential manager explained in a telephone conversation how it felt to learn from his boss that he had a problem serious enough to warrant a development program: "It hurts, to be real frank with you. It really hurts. It's very difficult to deal with. A guy tells you, 'There are some things you do well, but there are some other things you don't do well — around dealing with people.' I went home smarting." The feedback provided in development programs like ours also can be hurtful. One department head reported six months after receiving an extensive feedback report that "the process has been *extremely* valuable. There's been lots of growth. But the process has been internally, personally destructive at times. The book [feedback report] comes like a slug between the eyes. Early on in the process I resisted the idea of flaws, but I have since realized I *do* have flaws."

The extent of the pain varies with the executive's sensitivity and the extent of the problems revealed by the report. Another executive, Russell Wright, participated in the same program because, after being promoted to his present large-scope job, he developed performance problems that threatened both his job effectiveness and his career advancement. He made it clear how painful the experience of receiving the feedback had been; he called it "devastating" and pronounced it "one of the worst days of my life." The reasons for the pain were threefold. First, he had known the problems existed, but they were far more serious than he had realized. Second, he was someone whose sense of self-worth was thoroughly tied up in his career and to whom appearances meant a great deal. Third, being especially sensitive to contraindications of his worth, he keyed on the criticism in the report and disregarded the praise. By the next morning he had done an admirable job of recovering from the shock, with the help of a long phone conversation with a loving wife who saw the feedback as valid but not devastating. Much to his credit, he was able to absorb the significance of the report. In fact, he was even relieved to know exactly where he stood. With the pain of recognition can also be mingled a certain comfort in seeing clearly what one is up against. There can also be a feeling of release from relieving the tension that comes from sustaining an illusion.

In actuality, much of the pain of hard-hitting criticism results from the *loss* brought about by disconfirmation. The executive at first experiences the disconfirming feedback as wounding because it cuts into his or her favorable definition of self. It strips away the good opinion of others that he or she had imagined existed. Expansive executives are particularly prone to experiencing a sense of loss and the associated pain because they are so highly invested in mastery, and feedback may pierce the illusion of mastery. Russell Wright reeled, as anyone would, from the news that he was in deep trouble at work, but the emotional impact was magnified by his extreme need to look good — something that was touched on over and over again in his feedback report. In his interview with us he had, in passing, made a connection between his immense drive to succeed and a sense of insecurity he had had as a teenager. After his long climb up the hierarchy, to be confronted with grave shortcomings put him back in close touch with the feeling of insecurity. It deflated him. It was a loss in the sense that it robbed him of some of his sense of how competent and valued he was.

The Importance of Support. The amount of support a manager receives is a key factor in determining whether he or she can accept criticism or responsibility for failure. All managers on the threshold of a major personal transition need emotional support. Extremely expansive executives, with their pronounced vulnerability and defensiveness, stand little chance of learning from adversity in the absence of strong support. The data challenging a manager's existing view of him- or herself and the pressure to take the data seriously may themselves be insufficient to produce self-insight. If all managers get is criticism and pressure to own up, they may well respond to the call to developmental battle by giving up. Hooked on mastery and the heady rewards that come with it, they respond to such a crisis by getting discouraged or depressed. The potential vision of a re-created self can easily get obscured by pain, anger, and self-loathing.

Executives going through the hurtful diminution that comes with criticism or failure need expressions of support for their inherent value as people and as professionals. Without this support, which can come from within as well as from other people, executives find the encounter with their weaknesses unbearable and escape through some defensive maneuver. They discount or attack the source ("kill the messenger") or insist that the problem has gone away since the data was collected. For executives to face up to their failings, they need to be reassured of their fundamental worth, faults and all.

Support is important because no matter how strong, intact, self-confident, and even invincible executives may seem to be, they are vulnerable when they expose a weakness and start struggling to overcome it. In fact, the more brazenly self-confident they appear to be, the more unsure of their worth and the more vulnerable they probably are. As they undergo disconfirmation, they need a steady dose of confirmation of their value as an executive and a person. In the crisis precipitated by heavy disconfirmation, the executive's vulnerability can turn into an availability for change, provided that the environment is supportive and "solidifies the individual's view of himself as worthy, loving, strong, and capable of overcoming adversity."[10] Like anyone attempting to grow, the manager needs to be "held" in a maternal way—reassured that his or her emotional needs will be met, that he or she is secure. As the manager separates from the old self, he or she experiences separation anxiety—a bit like a toddler venturing out from its mother.

One way to offer support is to point out to managers that the weaknesses they are uncomfortably facing up to are, in fact, consequences of their very real strengths. Another way is to demonstrate that the parties doing the disconfirmation are for them, not against them; that the attempt to confront them is motivated by an interest in building them up, not tearing them down. To take this constructive stance is difficult for people whom an executive has victimized, since the temptation is to respond in kind. Having been treated by the executive as if they were worthless, they may judge him or her in the same polarized way. But if the executive is to be receptive to hearing about transgressions, he or she must feel that the critics' intent is constructive.

Emotional support can also come from within the person. When it comes from within, we call it ego strength, a strong enough conviction in one's inherent worth that the individual can take the blow to his or her self-esteem and before long bounce back.[11] This ego strength can build as a manager gains mastery and advances organizationally and sheds some of the doubt about his or her abilities common in young adulthood. It was said about one young department head who had recently turned forty that, early on, he "didn't accept criticism, but he's better able to tolerate it now. He's matured." To say that managers gain ego strength over time means that they become more confident in their abilities and in themselves, but it does not mean that the insecurity goes away. The two psychological states — comfort with one's ability and anxiety about inadequacy — coexist. When an individual's sense of self-esteem is too weak to tolerate a blow, the defenses kick in, and the developmental value of disconfirmation is lost.

Russ ended the feedback session by anticipating his return to work, where he expected a cool reception from his boss, who had not coached Russ nearly as much as he would have liked. But he was in for a pleasant surprise: "The first couple of days back were difficult, but it got progressively better. I wasn't looking forward to my first meetings with Zack and Susan [the division manager and human resources manager, respectively, both of whom had criticized him roundly in the report]. The first morning back Zack came into my office and said, 'How did it go?' I told Zack, 'Good stuff, and I'm committed to working on it.' Zack said, 'I knew it would be difficult. But I wanted to get your attention, and I wasn't getting it in the subtle ways. When I'd bring something up, you'd explain it away or in some way vindicate yourself. What I said in the report is between us. What I am saying to corporate [headquarters] is, 'I've got a bright, capable person, and he and I are going to work together to make it happen.' It *appeared* sincere but things have a way of changing. Then he came over to me and put his arm around me and said, 'I'm going to help you get promoted.'" Russ's superior gave him emotional support and came across as working from seemingly trustworthy, constructive motives. But perhaps more important to Russ, who had all along feared career-jeopardizing exposure, Zack provided political support: He let Russ know that he had kept his criticism confidential and had left Russ's high standing with the top executives intact.

Russ went on to describe his encounter with Susan, the human resources director: "Then shortly after the talk with Zack, the scenario with Susan Elston was much the same. I told Susan, 'They were a difficult two days. There was more there than I had expected to see. . . . I've identified a couple of areas to work on.' Susan said, 'Great. You've got my total support. I'll help in any way I can.' I felt she meant what she said. She and Zack are like-minded in what makes me tick and what I have to do organizationally. . . . I'm past the point of challenging their perceptions because the evidence is overwhelming."

Russ Wright trusted the human resources director's overture, and his trust in his boss's benevolent posture solidified further when they ran into each other at the office over the following weekend. Russ: "I went in on Saturday to see how a major project was going and to show support, be visible. Zack came in. I gave him a status report on what was going on. Zack said to me, 'That's [the kind of thing] that I want to see.' Then he told me a lot about how he wanted projects to be managed. He sat down with me and started mentoring. He did some coaching and teaching. That's not common. That felt good. [My trust level] went up. . . . He told me, 'You have to give more, and I'll do more.'" At another point in our session Russ volunteered, "Things are coming together in a way that suggests he means what he says. It's not a ploy. It's beginning to look like his motives are pure. That's comforting."

On top of the strong support from these two key individuals with control over his fate, he received "even *stronger* support from the subordinate group." Myron, a key subordinate, for example, "really extended himself. My second day back he came to me and said, 'You're going to get through this thing and be a stronger person because of it. I've already seen noticeable things you're doing better with others that you have done with me. You'll be all right.' We talked about social things, which we hadn't done before. He'd just joined a country club and asked me, 'When can you play tennis?' That was a key change." Russ clearly appreciated the triple affirmation he received from Myron — as a person, a manager, and a friend worthy of being invited to a prestigious club that Russ did not belong to.

In addition to all the support that quickly formed at work, Russ had the benefit of his wife's honesty and caring. He also had the active interest of two close friends, whom he had involved in the process and who called the night he got home and coached him about the mental attitude to take during the difficult return to work.

In the end Russ was able to face the people who had made him face up to his shortcomings: "I've concluded that they were sincere in their motive to have me go through this as a corrective. The process helped because they didn't see me as approachable. . . . They're not playing games." The key ingredient that gave him the heart to come to terms with them and their message was their strong support. "So I mustered enough to get through the day. I realized I'd elevated the thing to a life-and-death thing, but I had time to scale it down the night before going back to work. The calls from friends came that evening, and they helped. What really helped the next day was Zack coming to me. So a lot of the emotions started to subside."

The average manager may not be as fortunate as Russ Wright. It is critical, though, to determine what support is available. It is also important to remember that, as in Russ's case, people who have not been supportive may come out of the woodwork to bolster a manager who takes a heavy dose of criticism.

It has been said that "no creature can attain a higher grade of nature without ceasing to exist."[12] The relevance of this baldly stated truth for our subject is that managers can't develop significantly without ceasing to exist in their present form. To grow is to experience a "little death."[13] To survive this little death so that they have a chance to be reborn, managers must somehow be sustained as they go through it. The sustenance comes in the form of reassurance of their worth as individuals and as organization members. Support of various kinds — social, emotional, and political — gives them some sense of security, some feeling of psychological safety, even as they give up certainty as to who they are.

As a result of separating from their old self, managers *change what they see* in themselves. Hyperexpansive executives, for example, see the gross excesses. They open their eyes to the damage they've done as managers, and they open their eyes to the damage done to them as children such that, as adults, they do what they do. They recognize the extent to which they have been villains as well as the extent to which they have been victims.[14]

As part of changing what they see, managers call into question cherished beliefs about what they must do to feel good about themselves. Actually, they first come to recognize that they hold those beliefs. Then, as they make the connection between what they believe and the damage they do, they start questioning their beliefs. Part of shedding impossibly high expectations for themselves may be an increased ability to appreciate the value they do possess as managers and human beings. What can help here is the confirmation, received in the feedback report, of their very real strengths.

The outcome of the separation phase, then, is self-insight. By standing outside themselves, they see themselves as they have been. In coming to this disturbing recognition, they may begin to change what they believe. They may also begin to change what they do — how they actually behave. However, it takes the third phase to put these changes in place.

Phase Three: Exploring the New Self

In phase three the manager enters a new world, one filled with many tests and ordeals. There are dragons to slay, perils to avoid. In meeting these challenges, the manager discovers latent capabilities. The essence of this phase is action. By doing what may seem impossible, the manager becomes what it may seem impossible to become.

If there is a dragon to slay, it is the notion of what one isn't and can't be. "The hero . . . discovers and assimilates his opposite (his own unsuspected self). . . . He must put aside his pride . . . and bow or submit to the absolutely intolerable. Then he finds that he and his opposite are not of differing species, but one flesh."[15] Ironically, as Joseph Campbell pointed out, the makings of the new self are contained precisely in what the old self looked upon as intolerable. This is consistent with character shifts as recovering lost, devalued parts of the self and as healing the split between the light and dark parts of the self.

One of the most trying challenges of this phase is that, as the executive explores a new self, the old self continues to exist and, in fact, influences the way the individual goes about exploring. One executive, after a feverish unremitting campaign to get to the top of his company, decided once he arrived to ease up somewhat. In fact, he yearned for a deliverance from his burning need to excel. He wanted to achieve this change as badly as he had wanted to have a triumphantly successful career. As he put it, "I am driven to be at peace." Thus, even as he discovered a need to become something different, his first impulse was to accomplish it in the old way. This is not simply an intriguing irony; it can actually defeat a manager's attempt to change. As I learned in my own case, there's something untenable about trying really hard not to try so hard.

Another senior manager, who had also enjoyed enormous success, woke up to the disturbing fact that in his "great drive to be perfect" he became estranged from other people and from himself. He was far enough along in this process of standing outside his existing self to know that underneath the drive to impress others was a profound lack of trust. The irony in his case is that when he told the story of his growth to date, he told it impressively. Just as he performed at work in a way that inspired awe, he described his journey of self-discovery in a way that could easily be awe-inspiring. It wasn't just what he said; it was the way he said it. The pitfall, though, was that the people listening could potentially have aided him in his attempt to grow, and to impress them with how well he had managed the process of growth was, in effect, to exclude them from any role in that process. It was also to duck his true developmental challenge, which was to learn to depend on others.

The Importance of Play. A manager incorporates his or her opposite by actively experimenting with it. In a real sense this ex-
perimentation is play, very much akin to what children do as
they try new things and develop new skills. Adults may underes-
timate the importance of the free play of children, but for children themselves play is serious business. It is a primary arena
in which they extend themselves and discover themselves. Likewise, when adults venture into strange territory requiring new
capabilities, they are engaged in a form of play. They make it
up as they go along, and they repeat a new thing over and over
again until it becomes comfortable and manageable.[16] What is
more, this play on the road to forging a new self can be exhilarat-
ing, even fun.

The play of the exploration phase is a long series of experiments in becoming something new. The objective is to test
out aspects of the new self. In John Gardner's view, self-renewal
is the result of self-testing.[17] Managers dare to place themselves
in situations that require recessive parts of themselves to come
forward (and dominant parts to recede). To do this they must
typically overcome considerable reluctance and even fear.

An experiment can be as simple as reading a book in a
different way. One senior manager told me that he had trouble
keeping up with all the reading material that crossed his desk
because he was a slow reader. It turned out that he was a slow
reader because he wouldn't allow himself to pick and choose what
to read in an article or book. He felt he had to read it from beginning to end. An experiment for him was to allow himself
to read just the parts that looked interesting.

For Mark Tabor, described in Chapter Seven, an experiment consisted of overcoming the inhibition that kept him from
pushing sufficiently hard on his people. He hit upon the idea
of having his subordinates set three-month goals, to which he
would hold them accountable. He also resolved to look for
chances each day to probe his subordinates' thinking deeply,
not just superficially as he had done, and to engage in conflict
rather than avoid it. To encourage him in these experiments,
he kept a daily tally.

Shortly after the feedback session, Lee McKinney took

a vacation without introducing the customary degree of structure and, although it was something of a struggle, permitted himself to relax and be spontaneous. His daughter, a college student who joined her parents on this vacation, found the change remarkable: "On the way to Florida I was bracing myself because I don't look forward to vacations with my dad. Everything is highly structured. We know what we're doing every hour. I was really surprised with how he went with the flow all week! I could tell it was a struggle for him. . . . I don't know how much of it has to do with the work with you folks, but he's a much more reflective individual. He's consciously trying not to be as much in control."

Managers like Lee McKinney use recently gained self-insight to inform experiments in being different. By trying out a new side of himself, Lee sharpened his understanding of it. To appreciate what it means to give expression to a previously suppressed aspect of the self, it helps immeasurably to gain firsthand experience with it. To comprehend better what it meant to free himself from the strict dictates of his orderly world, Lee needed to leave the realm of abstract reflection and enter the world of concrete action. So experiments with new behavior can serve as important tests of new constructions of the self. By the same token, an executive's effort to break an old pattern is aided by appreciating the pattern's deep personal significance. If Lee McKinney had responded to his daughter's request by trying to restrain himself simply through an exercise of willpower, he probably would have met with less success than he did by understanding the effort as a battle against his perfectionist temperament.

Embedding the New Self. Just as the old self was embedded in a culture that supported it, the new self needs to be embedded in a culture supportive of it. The culture of embeddedness is not simply a setting for tests of the manager's growth. By its nature, it actually *produces* challenges that require the manager to exhibit the new capabilities. Thus, the experiments don't have to be authored entirely by the manager, as long as he or she is in an environment that as a matter of course produces the necessary kinds of challenges.

To be specific, let us briefly consider the growing-up experiences of men and women in Western society. Although the
situation is changing, the cultures of embeddedness available
to boys and girls differ somewhat.[18] Boys and girls are subjected
to somewhat different expectations and are also given (and
choose) different things to do. The tasks contain challenges that
develop certain skills and personal characteristics. The result
is that men generally tilt more toward independent achievement
and women toward close relationship. Men are generally more
capable of autonomy but less capable of intimacy; women, more
capable of intimacy but at risk of losing their independence.[19]
Quite apart from any genetic differences, men and women turn
out differently because their opportunities to develop are different. (We speak of men and women in general: Women managers are often as aggressive and autonomous as their male
counterparts — sometimes more so.)

If male senior managers are to become more relational,
then they need to embed themselves, at least some of the time,
in a culture that values and expects close relationships. This
could be a brand-new setting like the group program in which
Lee McKinney participated — a kind of cultural island where
self-disclosure and supportiveness were at a premium. Several
of the participants in this program formed close friendships such
as they had not had before in their entire adult lives.

Where does a manager in search of a new self find a compatible environment? He or she can change jobs, change careers,
change friends, even change spouses. These new activities and
new relationships then stimulate development by calling upon
the side of the self the manager is bringing to the fore. But it
is also possible to *convert* one's existing settings into ones that
are supportive of one's emerging self. People who had accommodated to a manager's current character, weaknesses and all,
may be happy to participate in the manager's evolution. Colleagues who were a bit reluctant to offer criticism because the
manager seemed closed may become willing sounding boards.
Friends who kept their distance from a person who seemed unin-
terested in close contact may prove quite willing to move closer.

Of course, some of the people in a manager's world do
not readily take parts complementary to the self the manager

is becoming. These others resist the change because it upsets *their* equilibrium. They can't easily adjust to the change because it calls for responses that are presently missing from their own repertoire. To play their new complementary role in relation to the manager, they themselves would have to change.

How Pressure Promotes Real Change. For managers to explore a new self, they need, as we have seen, a set of challenges that bring out the developing self. They also need, in this altered environment, a set of people who will cooperate with the manager as he or she tries to be different. They cooperate because they place a value on the manager's emerging self. Managers need support during this phase, which is unsettling and destabilizing, just as they did during the separation phase. Kegan spoke of the painful predicament of being oneself and at the same time composing oneself anew. These are "the moments when I face the possibility of losing myself. The moments that Erikson refers to hauntingly as 'ego chill.' The chill comes from the experience that I am not myself, or that I am beside myself."[20] Managers in an exploratory mode also have a continuing need for criticism. As they attempt to change, what success are they having? Are they, in fact, changing, or is it wishful thinking? What remnants of the old self persist?

For managers to go beyond exploring a new self and actually bring it into being requires a critical ingredient — pressure. Pressure was also important in the separation phase, when the manager was forced to take the data seriously. Pressure is, if anything, more important at this juncture because it determines whether the manager stops at insight, good intentions, and fitful exploration, or completes the journey of self-development.

The possibility of significant, lasting change hinges on overcoming the executive's ambivalence about change and the ambivalence of those around him or her at work and at home. All must overcome their mixed feelings about acting on data that indicate a need for change so that the balance tips to the side of a vigorous, sustained effort to change.

Pressure turns the potential for development into reality. Pressure is generated when the executive or those around the executive decide that the need for change is compelling enough to warrant making it a priority. This judgment is informed by beliefs about what is important. In this sense, the decision to apply pressure has a moral aspect to it.

It is certainly the executive's prerogative to elect to put pressure on him- or herself. However, if other people take it upon themselves to pressure the executive, the question may arise: What right do they have to force someone else to change? It is one thing to require certain business results but quite another to require a change in the manager to get those results. It is understandable that objections might be raised when someone, in a work context, is told to behave differently or suffer the consequences — such as missing out on a salary increase, losing a promotion, or even being fired. In my view, however, the constructive use of pressure is justified when change is critical to the executive or to the organization.

Few executives armed with fresh indications of their shortcomings will automatically make a commitment to change. They are likely to start by considering whether it is worth trading the security of standing pat for the possibility of improvement. They will wonder: Are my current strengths sufficient to outweigh my weaknesses? Are the potential payoffs worth the effort? If I try to change, will I succeed? This last was one of Lee McKinney's concerns once he understood the sort of change he might make. This anxiety is heightened in expansive executives who want to be as masterful in developing themselves as in managing others.

Executives can bolster their confidence in their ability to effect the change and free themselves to commit to it by referring to previous successes in self-development. Hank Cooper took heart that he could change interpersonally from the fact that he had once succeeded in changing physically. As a child, laid up in bed in a body cast, he had resolved to go on a campaign of health and fitness, and for thirty years he had carried on that program. In contrast, another executive had difficulty changing a leadership style that had remained virtually unchanged over twenty-five years because he had no dramatic early successes in self-improvement to demonstrate to himself that he could do it. Adaptability begets adaptability.

Executives can also bring pressure to bear on themselves. One department head took advantage of the boost that superiors can give to a developmental effort by meeting with three levels of his superiors to discuss his plans for developing himself as a corporate leader. Although none of these bosses had previously come forward with their plans or wishes for him, they all responded to his initiative and helped him set priorities for his development. By sharing his intention to change with these superiors, he thus arranged to have pressure applied to himself to make good on his promise.

What can members of the executive's work and family systems do to help the executive reach the threshold necessary for change? First, as we discussed earlier, they must overcome their own reluctance to see the executive change. A superior, especially someone at the highest level, can be among the most effective in exerting pressure on an executive. For an executive to hear from a top executive, perhaps the CEO, that he is in danger of topping out or even of losing his job can do wonders for the executive's motivation to change. Russ Wright, for whom the feedback report was devastating, is a prime example. This can be acutely true for executives for whom the high opinion of their superiors is especially important.

Getting the manager to *fulfill* the commitment to change is just as important as getting the manager to make the commitment in the first place. For change to occur, the effort must remain a priority for the manager and for the other stakeholders. This is asking a lot since the change process can take months or years, but without the continuing investment of key people close to the manager, progress can easily stop. One executive illustrated graphically how the presence or absence of pressure can prove decisive in making change. Out of the blue, his boss, with backing from the CEO, had strongly encouraged him to get extensive feedback preparatory to adjusting his style. The executive told me that he "was forced" to go through the assessment-and-development process, but that having done so he now realized, a year later, how "valuable the experience was." His boss, whom he trusted and who had recently had a similar experience of stock-taking and change, did the forcing. In the preceding year this same executive had had occasion to go over his data with three other senior managers who, like him, "faced a comeuppance, people who had been in the company for a number of years, who are suddenly in need of change." They too were being pushed into self-assessment and readjustment because their styles were interfering with their effectiveness in current jobs or threatening progress to more senior jobs.

Just as the presence of pressure spurred this executive to introspection and led him to make changes at work, the *absence* of pressure at home was associated with a lack of change there. During the feedback session it had come to light that he had partially disowned his son for marrying beneath himself, despite the fact that his son had otherwise followed in his father's footsteps, including getting a degree in engineering and going to work for the same company. As the executive explained, "[My son] did extremely well in school, and I was very proud of him. But on a personal basis I'll never accept that he married as he married. So that's gotten in the way of our relationship. I keep him at arm's length." I suggested that this was a form of punishment, and he responded, "Yes, in a way it is. It's my way of saying, 'This is how I'll treat you for doing what I didn't want you to do.' I've chosen not to get over it." Note that he admits to deliberately harboring his displeasure. I next asked him how it felt to have estranged himself from his pride and joy. His response: "I feel very uncomfortable." In fact, he was troubled by the fact that he had been able to adjust his behavior at work but had made no such adjustment at home. "It should be *easier* to move in this way in one's private life. But in the work environment I've been forced to change. No, I had an option when they told me—change or else. I could have told them, 'Screw you, I'll see you!'—which I would have done without this process. But I've not been *forced* to make changes in this other situation."

Why has he been unable to make changes at home? A traditional male, he is the patriarch of his family and as such possesses relatively uncontested authority, even with his wife. Speaking of the position he has taken with their son, he said, "My wife doesn't oppose me, though she doesn't necessarily accept it. Eric [his son], who is never reluctant to say what he

thinks, is the strongest of my children. But he's not said anything. He seems to accept it. He has not made a fight of it and
continues to be friendly." So what force keeps this man from
reconciling himself to his son's choice of spouse? "I've examined
it, and I've seen that it would be relatively easy to change, but
there's another force greater than the change. An element of
the force is what I perceive to be a rejection of my authority.
Another element is: I know what's best for you! At work I don't
respect blind loyalty. I respect people who will challenge me.
It's very interesting. But the way I conduct myself in my family
is according to a model: The decisions I make are right, and
if I back away, I am rejecting the model."

   This executive yearns to make peace with his son but can't
release himself from the grip of his principles and, in particular, his operating principle for running the family. To relent
in this instance would be to revise his role as the figure of high
authority in the family. What makes the change especially
difficult is that the executive borrowed the "model" from his own
father, whom he admires uncritically to this day. Still, the change
could happen, along with healing effects on his relationship to
his family, if only there were an effective pressure pushing for
it. The change would involve a shift in his relationship to his
father as an *internal* object, as something his father represents
psychologically. This revision in the way he relates to his father
internally would be part and parcel of any revision he might
make in the way he relates to his son.

   Pressure, then, is necessary to significant development.
Pressure is the imperative to change, whether it comes from outside or from inside. As Jung wrote, "Without necessity nothing
budges, personality least of all. It is tremendously conservative,
not to say torpid. Only acute necessity is able to rouse it. . . . It
needs the motivating form of inner or outer fatalities."[21] At the
same time, if external pressure must be applied to get the individual off dead center, the pressure must also ultimately be internal. As Jung argued, "Personality can never develop unless
the individual chooses his own way, consciously and with moral
deliberation. Not only the causal [i.e., external] motive — necessity — but conscious moral decision must lend its strength to the

process of building the personality."[22] Lee McKinney's wife, speaking of his willingness to change, said, "You can't force somebody to change unless they want to." The individual must come to feel that the change in question is the right thing to do and that for moral reasons it must be done. Only a moral imperative will motivate the individual to battle through the numerous tests and ordeals that the process of change entails.

A successfully completed exploration phase results in a change in what the manager actually does. Managers who have thus changed have broken old habits and substituted new. They have altered their pattern of investments — where they invest their time and energy.[23] They have modified their life structure — the settings in which they do what they do. They have revised their beliefs, or values, as to what they must do to obtain a sense of self-worth.

The change in what such managers do and believe is predicated on a change in what they see in themselves. By swinging into action in this phase, they succeed in making the abstract insights of the last phase concrete. They see their lopsidedness for what it was, stripped of the former self's illusions and ideology. In becoming aware of the destructive effects of the dominant side and the creative potential of the recessive side, these managers discover new strength: "Long lost forgotten powers are revivified to be made available for the transfiguration of the world."[24]

Phase Four: Reinforcing the New Self

Phases two and three together constitute a period of destabilization — a departure from one's organization of the self and an initiation into a reorganized version of the self. Phase four is a stabilization of the newly emergent self. Its function is much the same as that of phase one — to firm up and defend the self. In other words, phase four can later become a new phase one, the springboard for another period of destabilization and reorganization. Such is the rhythm of stability and change in a growing person.

The function of phase four, then, is to cement and maintain the reorganized self. As before, the self consists of a set of beliefs or values about what the person needs to do to feel a sense of worth and a repertoire of habits and skills for acting consistently with those beliefs. Stated another way, character consists of strategies for getting on in the world, tactics for enacting those strategies.

The new equilibrium is maintained as the old one was. It is maintained to the extent the person arranges to play roles for which the new self is well suited, has relationships that are in sympathy with the new self, plays those roles and conducts those relationships in a way that confirms the new self, and generally manages to minimize the pressure to be something he or she is not.

Even when the new self is more or less solidified, the job of keeping it so never ends. Extremely expansive executives who reform are particularly liable to a relapse. The mastery-seeking part that dominated the person so thoroughly can reassert itself if the new self comes under severe pressure and falters or fails to deliver.

For Joseph Campbell, the hero's journey ends with a return and a reintegration with society in an altered form. The trick is for the hero and society to find appropriate new settings in which the hero can become once again embedded.

Professional Assistance

Development of the kind described here can and does go on naturally, without the benefit of professional assistance, provided that the manager and key people in his or her life cooperate in instigating it and then ushering the person through a period of transition. If anything, the natural process is preferable because there aren't enough helping professionals to go around and because natural processes are more likely to happen preventively and not just remedially. Vaillant conceived of the development process as an apprenticeship in which the focal person grows by means of a close relationship with people who themselves employ more mature coping mechanisms. Such people are less inclined to experience others in black-and-white terms; they are less split, more integrated as people. They can be anyone—family members, friends, therapists.

If there is ever a time in a manager's life to call upon professionals, however, it is when a major transition is happening or needs to happen. When professionals get involved, their role is to help the manager on his or her way, developmentally speaking. They perform this function by arranging for data to surface, for support to become available, and for pressure to be applied. They may undertake all these tasks themselves or pass them on to others. To intervene in a person's life is to have considerable power, so the professional bears a heavy responsibility to use that power cautiously, conscientiously, competently, and caringly. The professional who assists an executive's personal growth takes a role described in metaphorical terms by Herman Hesse in his novel *Narcissus and Goldmund*. Narcissus, the young teacher, said to Goldmund, his teen-aged student and friend:

> I am superior to you only in one point: I'm awake, whereas you are only half awake, or completely asleep sometimes. I call a man awake who knows in his conscious reason his innermost unreasonable forces, drives, and weaknesses and knows how to deal with them. For you to learn that about yourself is the potential reason for your having met me. You've forgotten your childhood; it cries for you from the depths of your soul. It will make you suffer until you heed it.
>   . . . Being awake, as I've already said, makes me stronger than you. This is the one point in which I am superior to you, and that is why I can be useful to you. In every other respect you are superior to me, my dear Goldmund — or, rather, you will be, as soon as you've found yourself.[25]

This passage highlights a major aspect of the professional's competence: acquaintance with the inner life — "the innermost forces, drives, and weaknesses." In fact, the professional's role is not to assume a posture of superiority but to join with the executive on his or her journey of self-discovery and evolution.

In mundane terms, the professional serves in the capacity of coach. In mythic terms, the professional is "a benign power supporting [the hero] in his superhuman passage."[26] If the manager is fortunate, the coach comes along at just the right time in the journey. Perhaps it isn't luck; perhaps, as the saying goes, the teacher appears when the student is ready.

A completed journey of self-development is a heroic feat. To face up to the problems with one's present organization of self and to take on the risky job of reorganizing it is truly admirable. Those managers who perform this feat do so by mixing insight with action and by cooperating actively with key people who are willing to get involved and stay involved throughout the journey.

Chapter Thirteen

The Challenge
of Personal Growth:
Developing Balance
as a Leader

In this book we have put forward the notion that the performance problems found among executives are often due to a condition of imbalance. The drive to mastery is overdeveloped even for their specialized roles as institutional leaders. Their anxiety about their worth gets into the high ranges, and they become prone to taking extreme and often self-oriented measures to allay the anxiety—to demonstrate their worth. This is hardly a new phenomenon, as Joseph Campbell showed in his study of myths, legends, and folk traditions. The absolute worst of this breed is what Campbell called the "tyrant-monster." If an exaggeration, the idea of the tyrant-monster is nevertheless useful in pointing out the sort of harm that excessively ambitious executives do. In Campbell's dramatic language, "the havoc wrought by [the tyrant-monster] . . . may be no more than his household, his own tortured psyche, or the lives he blights with the touch of his friendship and assistance; or it may amount to the extent of his civilization. *The inflated ego of the tyrant is a curse to himself and his world, no matter how his affairs seem to prosper.* . . . [He is] the world's messenger of disaster, even though, in his mind, he may entertain himself with humane intentions" (emphasis added).[1]

If out-and-out tyrant-monsters are rare nowadays in institutional life, tyrannical and monstrous *acts* are hardly unknown.

In addition to identifying serious imbalance as a major source of performance problems, we have advanced the idea that executives can grow and improve by redressing imbalances. The dominant parts of the self, in which so much is invested and in which the person so strongly believes, lose some of their power and preeminence. The submerged parts of the self, in which so little has been invested and which have gone undervalued, gain favor and are given increased expression. All the mastery-oriented "shoulds," which have virtually tyrannized the executive and, in many cases, led him or her to tyrannize others, are relaxed somewhat. For most — but not all — executives, to develop means to tone down the excessively expansive drive. William James reported that "the transition from tenseness, self-responsibility and worry to equanimity and peace is the most wonderful of all those shiftings of inner equilibrium . . . [achieved] by simply relaxing and throwing the burden down."[2]

If leadership development can be a matter of redressing imbalance, then what sort of balance can we expect? What balance is attainable and desirable? From James and some contemporary writers on management, one gets the impression that people can achieve balance in an absolute sense. When it comes to senior managers, however, it is more realistic to expect not complete balance but *better* balance. To expect complete balance, whatever that may be, is to risk imposing a new ideal on this population. If there is one thing that people with high aspirations for themselves do not need, it is the replacement of an oppressive work-related ideal with an equally oppressive humanitarian ideal.

Moreover, even if complete balance were attainable, it would be unworkable for people who retain highly responsible positions. Executives must, at least at times, get carried away — and in this sense be unbalanced — if they are to lead their organizations to high achievement. As one executive told me, "lopsidedness is *necessary*." Thus, the so-called balanced executive is, in reality, simply less unbalanced. The move away from extreme imbalance typically signals a greater acceptance of one's

self—one's "true self," if you will—especially the heretofore neglected and undervalued aspects of the self. Executives no longer
identify so thoroughly with their persona, the impressive accomplished face they wish to show the world. Part of what they learn
to accept better is their anxiety to accomplish and impress. As
unhappy as they may be to acknowledge this unseemly emotion, to do so enables them to manage it rather than to act on
it reflexively.

The notion of a better-balanced executive may seem to
imply a single best way to run an organization. Let us quickly
dispel any such implication. There is no one best way, no best
style. Even if one were to come up with a template on theoreti-
cal grounds, the template would be useless because human beings and managers will always vary greatly. Rather than an ideal
balanced leader, the best we can hope for is more balanced or
better adapted versions of the various types of manager. We
can only hope that executives will continue to evolve toward
higher levels of adaptation so that we get the more constructive
and flexible versions of the various types. We would want, for
example, an immature fix-it executive to temper his ruthless,
nonsupportive style *not* so that he will become well rounded and
join a pool of managerial look-alikes but so that he will mitigate
some of the destructive effects of his particular style. Leaders
who strike a balance between striving for results and investing
in people are highly desirable, but even they are not men or
women for all seasons. There are organizational circumstances
in which what is required is an executive who is clearly over-
balanced on the side of results. Obviously, managerial capabilities need to be fitted to organizational circumstances.

For senior managers to achieve a better balance in their
work and in their lives by striking a better balance within themselves, they and the people around them must contend with what
I call the Big Doubt and the Big Worry. The Big Doubt is the
widespread skepticism that adults—particularly adults in high
positions—can change. The Big Worry is the executive's own
anxiety (and that of others) that any change might be for the
worse.

The Big Doubt

In my experience many people in institutional settings are prepared to believe that senior managers can make needed adjustments in their *behavior*. Such stylistic change is conceivable, assuming that the person somehow gets the message that an adjustment is needed. But many fewer people seriously entertain the possibility that senior managers can change who they are as people. Such a shift seems improbable to them: How can managers use their basic character to alter their basic character? There is also pessimism about the possibility of personal development as an avenue to more effective leadership.

These doubts are warranted in the case of the most extreme executives, for whom this kind of development is, as a practical matter, extremely unlikely. As defensive and aggressive people, they respond to challenges to their identity very defensively and very aggressively. One such executive, who tended to take an embattled stance toward people outside his organizational unit, had put his relationships with key superiors in jeopardy, even though he had performed admirably in a new corporate venture. The problems arose because he walled off his organization to protect it from the threat of outside invasion, some of it real and some of it imagined. He had great difficulty seeing this about himself because his leadership strategy arose from his personal strategy of vigilant self-protection. Unfortunately, executives like this one represent classic cases of self-perpetuating cycles that are extremely difficult to break.

At stake for such executives are the constructions they long ago adopted to organize their life experience.[3] Consisting of beliefs about themselves, other people, and the world, these concepts of self and the world took shape as a workable response to early experience. As maladaptive for present circumstances as they may be, the individual resists changing these concepts because they were learned too well initially. The extent to which an adult clutches a self-defeating construction and its associated pattern of behavior seems a rough and ready measure of the pain suffered at the time the person made the original adjustment. In the case of the executive described above, we never learned — because it remained inaccessible to him — what childhood experiences led him to adopt his beleaguered view of the world, but it was evident from indirect data that as a child he must have found the world a very unsafe place. For him and executives like him, it seems that the pain was so intense that they put in place exceptionally strong defenses designed to prevent a reoccurrence. When threatened, these individuals become so rigid and the measures they take to pursue the cause of protecting their esteem so extreme that they unwittingly sacrifice another good cause — their continued growth and adaptation.

The doubt that a senior manager, or any manager, can make basic personal changes for the better is also understandable in light of the fact that many people who set out to change fail to do so. Often the intervention used is too weak to do the job. When a manager proves problematic in some way, a coworker may give feedback, but it is doubtful that such a conversation will cause the manager to call his or her basic character into question. Isolated events, whether an informal conversation or the traditional once-a-year performance appraisal or even a week-long training program, are unlikely to lead to a shift in character.

Despite all these doubts, however, profound personal change is possible if the manager is not beyond reach and if the intervention is fairly powerful. An intervention potent enough to shift a person's center of gravity can be a naturally occurring event. This could be any of the commonplace trials and tribulations of midlife and midcareer — a career problem, a marital problem, a health problem, difficulties with one's adolescent children, the death of a parent or other loved one, disaffection with a life dominated by work, and so on. Such hardships normally do not happen by design, except perhaps when an organization places a manager in a stiffly challenging job intended to provoke his or her evolution personally and professionally.

The class of intervention with which we have been principally concerned in this book is deeply introspective self-development. This is self-development precipitated by a concentrated dose of constructive criticism. What the dose of criticism does is force an issue that, if left alone, is likely sooner or later to grow to crisis proportions. Thus, forcing the issue can be seen as a way of anticipating a natural crisis of adult life.

Some of the Big Doubt stems from skepticism that successful managers would be willing to undergo the self-questioning integral to personal change. This doubt has a basis in reality: To examine one's basic motives is unquestionably anxiety-provoking. The first time Lee McKinney discussed his ego needs with us, we asked him how he was feeling. The answer: "There is fear rumbling around my stomach." When Bill Flechette was asked what motivates him in life, he responded first in terms of the external world. He mentioned noble motives such as helping mankind and the like. When asked to consult his inner world, he said that to look inside himself is "like lifting a trap door that opens onto dark water with all kinds of things swimming around down there." Another upper-level manager, unpracticed in self-inquiry, told us, "If you ask me about bringing the *whole me* to the table, I have trouble responding. When you ask me, 'Who are you?,' I can't answer. What makes me tick that makes me do and say what I do and say, I can't answer easily. In the old days, when my wife was depressed after our first child was born, I couldn't understand [the way she felt]. I thought to myself, 'Pull yourself together. . . . ' I can do that: I push feelings like that into the deepest recesses and never deal with them." I asked him, "Can you shine a light on that part of you?" He exclaimed, "Whew! Show those [feelings] to other people?!" "No, to yourself." He exclaimed again: "Worse!"

But, as ambivalent about delving into their inner lives as senior managers may be, the need to know can prevail over the fear of knowing. Fearful as he may have been, the second manager quoted above went ahead with consulting his inner life: "For the first time in my life, I've started to look at my feelings." The fear is an aversion to face up to what one is doing to obtain a feeling of personal worth. The picture, when one strips away the illusions and rationalizations, may not be pretty. The main character in a novel observed that "although people talked to themselves all the time, never stopped communing with themselves, nobody had a good connection or knew what racket he was in — his *real* racket. Did [he] actually know? For most of his life he had had a bad connection with himself. There was just a chance, however, that he might, at last, be headed in the right direction."[4] No one enjoys owning up to a racket, but that may be a prerequisite to leadership development.

Sometimes executives decline to do inner work and later change their minds. One man, coming out of his feedback session, insisted on handling his problem with anger by, in effect, placing a tighter lid on it. He was a self-pressuring person who, not surprisingly, suffered from high blood pressure. Initially he was not receptive to the suggestion that he accompany his efforts at self-control with introspection into the origins of the anger. We respected his wishes. Three years later he called to say that he was still having the same problem and that he was now ready to talk more personally.

So even after receiving a heavy dose of criticism, some executives decline to look inward, at least initially. They typically take the position: "I am willing to fix this problem or that problem, but I'm not open to questioning my motives or my makeup. I'm reasonably happy with who I am, it's *worked* for me, and I prefer to leave well enough alone." Yet a sizable proportion of other senior managers come out of the feedback session with the attitude that everything is fair game. They enter into a prolonged period of self-examination in which they probe their basic motives, gain an appreciation of the oppressive power of those motives, and make a sustained effort to break their hold. As painful as it is for these individuals to discover what truly motivates them, they persevere. The result is a fresh perspective on themselves, a new, bracing honesty with themselves. If they keep at it, the result may also be an actual reconfiguration of the self.

As one researcher surveying the literature on adult development observed, "Change in personality during middle age is not only possible, but it may be required in order to survive."[5] Executives, and adults in general, evolve out of necessity. Even people with so-called character disorders (self-defeating patterns that antagonize and frustrate other people and that resist change) can grow out of the worst of these patterns. As George Vaillant concluded from his longitudinal study, "immature mechanisms of defense . . . are not always the incurable bad habits they appear on the surface."[6] Any help they get from professionals in doing so is simply a way of enhancing or accelerating the natural processes of maturation.

Anyone who has actually gone through a significant personal evolution — or who has been close to someone who has — is no longer so susceptible to the Big Doubt. But no one but the naive or the evangelistic ever loses his or her healthy respect for how formidable a task it is to change in this way.

The Big Worry

Those who are not so doubting as to dismiss out of hand the possibility of significant change may succumb to the Big Worry: the concern that if a manager does indeed change, it will be for the worse. The Big Worry is an instance of the natural reluctance to tamper with a winning formula, and it is particularly easy to understand when the executive in question possesses strengths that clearly outweigh his or her weaknesses. John Warren, the well-balanced senior manager who got great results and also handled the human side well, is a good example. An individual close to John compared him to a very good golfer whose swing could get thrown off by an attempt to improve it: "John is an 80 golfer, so you have to be careful tinkering with his emotional makeup."

However, people worry about intervening even when a given executive is manifestly flawed. Whenever a manager is highly productive, even if at a considerable human cost, there is a concern that any change will cause the individual to lose effectiveness. Furthermore, if an executive seems crucial to the organization's success or survival, people will come to count on him or her, and they will be that much more anxious about anything that might reduce the executive's effectiveness.

The Big Worry frequently takes the form of a fear that personal development leading to better balance will take the edge off the executive's motivation. As much as being too driven may be a problem for the individual and the organization, both parties are liable to the fear that the executive will cease to be driven *enough*. One top executive, who had recently become aware of just how driven he was, and why, and who was in the midst of his own much-desired personal transformation, nevertheless fretted about the consequences of moderating his ambition. Keenly aware of the extreme difficulty of leading a company in what he considered "chaotic times" — with the U.S. economy in decline and global competition very much on the rise — he reasoned in the following way: Most leaders are driven to succeed because they're flawed, so if they become more "normal," won't they lose the ability to lead?

My response to this question is that much of the worry is a result of not understanding what it means to become less driven. One misconception is to understand the change as a binary function, whereby the alternative to total dedication to work is hardly any dedication at all. A second misconception is to equate less drive with more leisure time or more time with one's family. Managers return from self-awareness programs saying they want to stop neglecting their families, and their superiors say to themselves, "Oh no, we need him to keep working sixteen hours a day!" One consequence of personal development *could* be more hours spent with spouse and children, but this is just one of the most obvious, external ways to redress imbalance. A much subtler way is to create a greater balance within, one that makes the executive capable of higher performance with less strain. Lee McKinney captured such a change in himself well: "The key is I'm not trying so hard at everything. I'm not trying too hard to be the perfect husband, and I'm a better husband. I'm not trying so hard to be a good tennis player, and I'm a better tennis player. I'm not trying so hard to be an outstanding manager, and I'm a better manager."

What it really means to be less driven is to eliminate just the excessive portion of one's drive to mastery. The executive remains highly motivated to do well and to have his or her organization do well. The executive continues to try as hard as necessary to lead but no longer tries too hard. Instead of losing his edge, Lee retains it and, in addition, gains the ability to use it better.

What does it mean to make better use of one's edge? First, high-intensity managers use their abundant energy more economically. Less emotional energy is wasted worrying about how well they will perform or how well they have performed. Second, they use their edge more deftly, do a better job of picking their challenges. Less concerned about their own importance, they are better able to judge the organization's priorities. Furthermore, they become better able to judge when to insert themselves into a project or a conversation — so that the difficult task of empowering others becomes more manageable.

If people could understand better what it means to moderate ambition, they would probably worry less. However, it takes experiencing this evolution, at least vicariously, to understand it. Since this experience is not widely available, there is no easy way to dispel the Big Worry.

In point of fact, organizations could stand to worry about the opposite problem — expecting too much of their managers and thus feeding their boundless appetites for accomplishment. Anxious to succeed, organizations are susceptible to pushing people beyond the point of diminishing returns.

Questions Executives Should Ask

Clearly, personal development is not for everyone. What points should executives consider before taking part in a performance improvement program that includes personal development?

Do I really want this feedback? Can I handle it? This first question is one potential participants should ask *themselves*. A "whole-life assessment" — one that collects data from co-workers and family — drops a heavy load of feedback in the manager's lap. To hear from so many people close to the individual at the same time is a once-in-a-lifetime experience that will seem in the end either a bane or a boon, depending on the recipient's readiness to receive that input. The words of praise are typically easy to take. The real question is whether you are prepared to face up to criticism from your co-workers, your family, and yourself.

Am I truly open and committed to my own growth and development? It is socially desirable for managers to say that they want to develop and improve, but it's one thing to give lip service to growth and development and quite another to embark on an arduous journey of self-discovery and self-development. Many managers are used to going on heroic quests to accomplish organizational objectives. They should bear in mind that it is no less heroic to go on a quest to become a better person and a better leader.

Am I prepared to take charge of my development? Some managers enter a development program expecting that the staff will transform them. Certainly the staff members have an important role to play, but ultimately the individual must take responsibility for his or her own growth. No one, no matter how expert or helpful, can do this for the individual. To the extent that the manager overrelies consciously or unconsciously on the experts, he or she squanders the chance to grow.

Rhetoric aside, are my co-workers and organization truly committed to change? Managers who let themselves in for this kind of comprehensive self-assessment and searching personal development need the support of their co-workers and organization. If managers are to make a significant change, they need the commitment of those around them to back up the change and to make needed adjustments to accommodate it. There is nothing more demoralizing than to be encouraged to grow and change and then to have one's fellow managers resist the change once it occurs. Naturally, not everyone will necessarily welcome a change with open arms, but there should be some basis going in for believing that there will be appreciable support for the adjustment that people say they want.

What is the experience like? To make an informed decision about an intensive program, a prospective participant should find out not just what the sequence of steps is but also what it typically feels like to go through such a program. What sorts of emotions do you have when you receive the feedback? What is the experience of actually making changes, outward and inward? Perhaps the best way to prepare for the emotional impact of the program is to talk to former participants. In organizations that use a program like this, it is usually easy to locate veterans. For someone lacking easy access to firsthand reports, it is worth seeking out former participants from other organizations.

Who are the staff members? It is often helpful in pursuing one's personal development to use a professional from outside one's organization. In that case it is highly advisable to check out the reputation of the sponsoring institution as well as the staff members with whom you would work. Do these professionals have a reputation for helping people to grow and improve?

What happens to the information? In our experience there is only one fair position on this issue, and that is for the participating manager to have total ownership of the data. Otherwise the manager runs the risk, with all the exposure, of hurting him- or herself organizationally. In addition, total control of the data gives the manager the psychological safety necessary to concentrate on the development task at hand. Once the individual has worked through the contents of the feedback report, it is up to him or her to divulge whatever information seems appropriate.

Is this a good time to go through something like this? If all hell is breaking loose in your life, the last thing you should do is pile on another stressor. On the other hand, the complete absence of stress is not the ideal condition for a program of personal development. For someone to make something of a program like this, there should be a felt need to change, and that felt need typically arises out of a sense that all is not right with one's world. Of course, if you have an appetite to grow yet no clear idea of how you might go about it, a thoroughgoing assessment is a way to define a specific agenda for development.

Questions the Organization Should Ask

If an organization is thinking about a program in personal development and performance improvement for one or more of its executives, it needs to determine if the program is appropriate and, if it is, how best to use it. The following questions should help the organization make this determination.

What is the benefit of going through an intensive assessment? Except for the most defensive individuals, the manager is bound to appreciate better how he or she affects the organization and what it is about his or her character that causes that impact. Experienced managers tend to find relatively few big surprises in the data but get strong confirmation of what they knew or suspected about themselves. One's strengths and weaknesses are driven home, not just cognitively but emotionally, in a way that leaves an indelible impression and that provides a springboard for developmental action. One human resources manager said, "Once you get the data, you've *got* to do something with it. That's why the program is so valuable."

Will the program hurt the person? There is inevitably some temporary pain in having one's shortcomings pointed out. But no lasting harm is likely to be done to the person if certain precautions are taken. First, no one with a history of psychological problems or in severe distress at the time should be enrolled in the program. Second, the staff and the sponsoring institution should have an impeccable record of giving safe passage to people participating in intensive development programs. Third, the staff members must not only be technically equipped but also be individuals who can be counted on to *care* about the client as a human being. Fourth, the design of the program should include ample opportunity to work through the issues raised by the report and the emotions stirred up by it. It is a mistake to dump a lot of sensitive information in someone's lap and leave. Fifth, participation in the program should be voluntary. That doesn't mean that the initiative can't come from the organization. Nor does it mean that the manager cannot be told that his or her job or future advancement is in jeopardy unless he or she changes. Ultimately, however, the decision about whether to participate in a program of personal development should be the individual's. At a minimum, the decision should be made on the basis of informed consent. Moreover, if the individual doesn't feel there is a real choice, he or she is liable to play games or to merely go through the motions.

I might add that an antidote to the hurt of being criticized is the satisfaction, even joy, of having one's managerial virtues extolled. Virtually every executive has real strengths that get underlined in a feedback report along with the weaknesses.

If the report is confidential, how do we know what the executive should work on? The contract with the executive and the staff member should, in addition to protecting the individual's privacy, call for some way of informing certain predefined parties, usually the individual's boss and coach, what came out of the assessment. At a minimum, the manager should be expected to let key individuals know what his or her development needs are. As it happens, managers usually turn over their co-worker data to these key individuals but withhold the family data.

Who's running the program? In addition to placing managers in safe hands, an organization will want to be reassured that the psychologists on staff know the world of management and organizations. The client organization will not want to expose its managers to psychologists who speak in psychobabble and know only their own highly specialized concepts and techniques. In the right hands, a program like this places equal emphasis on leadership and the person behind the leader.

Will the program work in our organization or our industry? There is no wrong *type* of organization or industry for a personally oriented leadership development program. The only organization that is wrong for a program like this is one that is in crisis and therefore so thoroughly in a survival mode that it cannot do its part in supporting the individual's participation in the program. Its part consists, first, of making the time available for fifteen to twenty people to take part in interviews on a given executive and, second, of having key people like the boss, coach, or human resources manager take an interest as the manager takes the zigzag path to personal development. This is by no means a full-time job, but it does absorb energy and distract the manager temporarily from his or her usual complete absorption in work.

If the organization is not in crisis, it can make effective use of the program, assuming that the program is part of a larger context for management development. That context includes bona fide performance reviews of senior managers, preferably very good performance reviews; a succession planning process that includes reviews of each of the members of senior management; an organization willing to invest in the development of its people; and a willingness on the part of some top managers to invest personally in this sort of assessment and development — to hold up a mirror and see how they affect the organization.

What is the best way to position the program? In our experience it is not desirable to use the program exclusively for managers in trouble. It is far better if participation in the program is a badge of honor rather than a badge of dishonor. In one company, successful positioning of the personal development program was evident in a memo from the division president announcing various programs upper managers would be attending. The personal development program was listed alongside advanced management programs at the Sloan School, the Harvard Business School, and the Stanford Business School — a clear message that to participate was an indication of the organization's investment in your future.

The stress and strain of a journey of self-development are nicely captured in the experience of the cantankerous, violence-prone protagonist of Saul Bellow's novel *Henderson the Rain King,* who pursued his development in a remote African village by, of all things, receiving lessons in how to act like a lion. He was tutored in these matters by a Western-educated philosopher-king, who himself was in superb harmony with a lion with which he kept daily company in the dark basement beneath his primitive palace.

For his first lesson, Henderson had to feel his way down a staircase in utter darkness. Much to his consternation, once he reached bottom he had to run in a tight circle behind the king, who ran immediately behind the lion. At first Henderson balked with his entire being. The king chided him: "You are avoiding again . . . change does not lie that way. You must form a new habit. . . . All the resistances are putting forth their utmost. . . . Well, we shall let them come out."[7] Terrified, Henderson ran some more. Then the king explained, "I intend to loosen you up . . . because you are so contracted. This is why we were running. The tendency of your conscious [mind] is to isolate self. This makes you extremely contracted and self-recoiled."[8]

The next lesson required Henderson to assume the posture of a lion. Henderson more or less managed to do this by using what flexibility he had available to him, or, as the king put it, by "laying aside his former attitude of fixity."[9] Next came the roaring, intended to help him "feel *something* of a lion." After a slow, reluctant buildup, of which the lion took no notice, Henderson gave himself up to it completely: "And so I was the beast. I gave myself to it, and all my sorrow came out in the roaring. My lungs supplied the air but the note came from my soul. The roaring scalded my throat and hurt the corners of my mouth and presently I filled the den like a bass organ pipe."[10]

Henderson's harrowing experience, although a far cry (as it were) from anything a typical executive would go through, does symbolize well the major components of coming firmly to grips with one's profound personal pattern. Henderson's descent down the unlit stairs to the basement, not knowing what awaited him, is suggestive of a journey inward, beneath one's surface. Henderson's "attitude of fixity" describes the prechange rigidity of many senior managers. The resistance Henderson instinctively put up to the developmental exercise assigned him squares with the difficulty everyone has in parting with the old self and trying out a new self. The emotional energy that Henderson expended is an exaggerated indication of what a journey of personal development takes out of the average person. The catharsis produced by the roaring is indicative of the release that comes from liberating oneself from an entrenched pattern. Henderson's eventual success in filling the den with his roaring, once he broke free of his usual contracted posture, reflects the newfound power available through personal development. The king's role as someone who stood for what Henderson wanted to become, who believed in Henderson, who put growth-promoting challenges before him, who told Henderson the truth about himself as he, the king, saw it, who would sit by Henderson's side as he struggled, is an archetype for the various parts that other people play in supporting personal development.

What came of Henderson's Herculean struggle? Henderson concluded: "I believed I could change: I was willing to overcome my old self; yes, to do that a man had to adopt some new standard: he must even force himself into a part; maybe he must deceive himself for a while, until it begins to take; his own hand paints on that much painted veil. I would never make a lion, I knew that. [But] I might pick up a small gain here and there in the attempt."[11]

If managers are willing to enter their equivalent of the lion's den, then significant gains are possible. How else can they prepare themselves to lead in the 1990s and beyond except by taking on personal and leadership challenges? How else can they expand their repertoires, acquire added flexibility, share power with their fellow employees, act in an honest and ethical manner even when the stakes are high, and otherwise do what it takes to lead the organizations of the future? How else can they learn to lead better and live better?

Optimism is warranted if managers will open themselves to developmental adventures. As Joseph Campbell said of heroic quests for self-transcendence, "We have not even to risk the adventure alone, for the heroes of our time have gone before us; the labyrinth is thoroughly known; we have only to follow the lead of the hero-path. And when we thought to find an abomination, we shall find a god; where we thought to slay another, we shall slay ourselves; where we thought to travel outward, we shall come to the center of our own existence; where we thought to be alone, we shall be with the world."[12]

Studying Executives Using Biographical Action Research

We call our method of investigation "Biographical Action Research." It is *action* research in as much as it combines research on individual executives with service to each of them. And it is biographical in as much as we collect data on the individual's early history and current private life as well as on the work situation. To some extent, the research encompasses the individual's entire life. Although the accounts of family life and early years are sketchy, they are useful nevertheless as a way of providing clues to a given executive's personal makeup.

The data collection in biographical action research is predicated on three principles: (1) study the executive from multiple perspectives; (2) study the executive in multiple settings; and (3) study the executive while helping him or her in attempts to learn and grow.

First, we viewed the executive from *multiple perspectives* so as not to limit ourselves to the executive's own view of him- or herself, no matter how honest it might be. We looked closely at the similarities and differences among the various perspectives, such as those of superiors, peers, and subordinates. What initially may have seemed contradictory frequently turned out

243

to help us understand the individual better. For example, early in this study we were puzzled in our work with one executive by the widely discrepant reports we got from his superiors and his subordinates.[1] It seemed that his superiors held him in high regard, while his subordinates, especially those two levels down, were highly critical of him. On closer examination it turned out that he showed up differently to the two groups because, for character-based reasons, he behaved differently with each group. As a carryover from childhood, he had a marked need to please authority figures. He made sure that his relationships with superiors were good but paid little attention to relationships with some key subordinates. The difference in his emotional investment upward and downward gave us a clue to his character.

Second, we studied the executive in *multiple settings.* This involved going beyond the work setting — though we concentrated the most effort there — to consult the executive's life in general, including something of his or her past. We believed that our grasp of the executive's basic character would be firmer if we also saw something of how the person's character manifested itself in other settings, especially at home.

To get this reading we interviewed the executive and members of the immediate family. Several comparisons between work life and family life suggested themselves. If the executive's expectations for subordinates were extremely high, was this also true for children? If the executive had trouble delegating to subordinates and tended to take over in a crisis, did this also happen at home? If an executive had trouble with conflict and emotion-laden issues at work, did the same pattern show up in a reluctance to deal with emotionally charged problems at home? We found many such parallels, and some contrasts as well. For example, the executive who is emotionally distant at work may turn out to have touchingly close relationships at home.

Another of the multiple settings we looked into was the executive's family of origin. Where possible, we interviewed parents and siblings as well as longstanding friends. Although it is unusual for management researchers to investigate childhood, early history provides another comparison point and reveals something of the forces that have shaped the executive's character. Most important here were the parents and what they stood for, how they treated the executive as a child, what they wanted him or her to become, and how they related to each other.

The third operating principle governing our research was to *understand executives by helping them to learn and change.* At a minimum, the intervention consisted of a day-long feedback session in which we reviewed the data (compiled so as to give anonymity to our sources). In some cases, we continued to work with the executives after the feedback session as they attempted to act on and deepen their self-insights. This continuing involvement lasted anywhere from several months to several years, with the average being about a year.

As must be apparent, biographical action research is not remote or impersonal. The researchers, often working in teams of two, formed personal relationships with participating executives. We gained unusual access to the executive's work life, private life, and inner life; the executives received the benefit of our data, our involvement, and our help.

As of this writing, I personally have applied biographical action research to forty-two executives, nearly all from Fortune 500 companies. Thirty participated in the full-scale version of the research or something quite near to it. The remaining twelve took part in a slimmed-down version created to accommodate groups of executives. Two-thirds of the forty-two were in positions ranging from general managers, or an equivalent level in staff roles, to chairman, CEO, president, group vice-president, and the like. One-third held positions one level below general manager; they were department heads in charge of a research function, a companywide quality improvement effort, and so forth.

In addition, approximately fifty other executives have participated in this research without my direct involvement. This book is based upon the executives with whom I have been directly involved (in several cases working with Joan or Bill or both).

Due to the scarcity of women and minorities at senior levels, all executives but one were white; all but three were male. They ranged in age from their late thirties to their mid-sixties, with a heavy concentration in their mid-forties to mid-fifties. The several companies participating were nearly all based in the United States, and most of the participants were born and raised in the United States. Several executives, however, were from the European community. Our research process generated a considerable volume of data, much of it qualitative. It was a tough job to find order in all of that. We analyzed each case by searching for patterns that emerged clearly and strongly from the data, patterns that repeated in the case and therefore could be corroborated. First we generated hypotheses about individual cases: What were the links between the person's character and leadership behavior? What were the links between the person's character and the question of continuing development? Then, at a higher level of analysis, we looked for patterns that transcended individual cases. As a theory of executive character and development began to take shape, augmented by other research literature, we used it to further shape and guide the analysis of individual cases. Thus we developed a grounded theory — a theory that grew from the data — by continually going back and forth between ordering our data and constructing a theory.

Notes

Preface

1. M. Lombardo and R. Eichinger, *Preventing Derailment: What to Do Before It's Too Late* (technical report no. 138) (Greensboro, N.C.: Center for Creative Leadership, 1989), 9.
2. M. Sorcher, *Predicting Executive Success* (New York: Wiley, 1985). Cited in *Preventing Derailment: What to Do Before It's Too Late.*
3. S. Butler, *The Way of All Flesh* (New York: Penguin, 1903).
4. R. Ochberg, *Middle-Aged Sons and the Meaning of Work* (Ann Arbor, Mich.: UMI Research Press, 1987).

Chapter One

1. R. E. Kaplan, W. H. Drath, and J. R. Kofodimos, *High Hurdles: The Challenge of Executive Self-Development* (technical report no. 125) (Greensboro, N.C.: Center for Creative Leadership, 1985).
2. W. R. Torbert, *Managing the Corporate Dream: Restructuring for Long-Term Success* (Homewood, Ill.: Dow Jones Irwin, 1987), xiv.

3. M. W. McCall, Jr., and M. M. Lombardo, *Off the Track: Why and How Successful Executives Get Derailed* (technical report no. 21) (Greensboro, N.C.: Center for Creative Leadership, 1983).

4. A. M. Morrison, R. P. White, and E. VanVelsor, *Breaking the Glass Ceiling: Can Women Reach the Top of America's Largest Corporations?* (Reading, Mass.: Addison-Wesley, 1987).

5. A. Maslow, *Toward a Psychology of Being* (Princeton, N.J.: Van Nostrand, 1968).

6. A. Angyal, *Foundations for a Science of Personality* (New York: Commonwealth Fund, 1941).

7. L. S. Kubie, "Some Unsolved Problems of the Scientific Career," in *The Irrational Executive: Psychoanalytic Explorations in Management,* ed. M.F.R. Kets de Vries (New York: International Universities Press, 1984).

8. G. Vaillant, *Adaptation to Life* (Boston: Little, Brown, 1977).

Chapter Two

1. E. Becker, *The Denial of Death* (New York: Free Press, 1973).

2. The three types of expansive executives described in this book are based on our research as well as a theory of personality types called the Enneagram. Two sources for the Enneagram model are: M. Beesing, R. Nogosek, and P. O'Leary, *The Enneagram: A Journey of Self-Discovery* (Denville, N.J.: Dimension Books, 1984); D. R. Riso, *Personality Types* (Boston: Houghton Mifflin, 1987).

3. M.F.R. Kets de Vries and D. Miller, "Narcissism and Leadership: An Object Relations Perspective," *Human Relations* 38, no. 6 (1985): 583–601.

Chapter Three

1. R. Rosenbaum, "Acting: The Method and Mystique of Jack Nicholson," *New York Times Magazine* (July 13, 1986): 12–13.

2. D. A. Schon, *The Reflective Practitioner: How Professionals Think in Action* (New York: Basic Books, 1983).

3. W. Bennis and B. Nanus, *Leaders: The Strategies for Taking Charge* (New York: Harper & Row, 1985).

4. F. Steele, "The Ecology of Executive Teams: A New View of the Top," *Organizational Dynamics* 11, no. 4 (1983): 65–78.

5. Steele, "Ecology of Executive Teams."

6. D. L. DeVries, A. M. Morrison, M. L. Gerlach, and S. L. Shullman, *Performance Appraisal on the Line* (New York: Wiley, 1981).

7. T. Burns and G. M. Stalker, *The Management of Innovation* (London: Social Science Paperbacks, Tavistock Publications, 1961).

8. M.F.R. Kets de Vries, "Managers Can Drive Their Subordinates Mad," *Harvard Business Review* 57, no. 4 (1979): 125–134.

9. W. Shakespeare, *King Lear.* Houghton, R.E.C. (ed.) (Oxford, England: Clarendon Press, 1960), 31.

10. Shakespeare, *King Lear,* 37.

11. Steele, "Ecology of Executive Teams."

12. A. S. Grove, "Breaking the Chains of Command," *Newsweek* (October 3, 1983).

13. K. Auletta, "Profiles: A Certain Poetry (part 1); *The New Yorker* (June 6, 1983): 98.

14. J. P. Kotter, *The General Managers* (New York: Free Press, 1982).

15. C. E. Larson and F. M. Lafasto, *Teamwork: What Must Go Right, What Can Go Wrong* (Newbury Park, Calif.: Sage, 1989).

16. C. Argyris, "Interpersonal Competence and Organizational Effectiveness," in *Interpersonal Dynamics,* eds. W. G. Bennis, E. H. Schein, D. E. Berlew, and G. I. Steel (Homewood, Ill.: Dorsey Press, 1964).

17. P. F. Drucker, *The Effective Executive* (New York: Harper & Row, 1966), 87.

Chapter Four

1. P. Block, *The Empowered Manager: Positive Political Skills at Work* (San Francisco: Jossey-Bass, 1987); R. H. Waterman,

The Renewal Factor: How the Best Get and Keep the Competitive Edge (New York: Bantam, 1987).

2. C. C. Manz and H. P. Sims, *Superleadership: Leading Others to Lead Themselves* (New York: Prentice Hall, 1987).

3. J. Pfeffer and A. Davis-Blake, "Just a Mirage: The Search for Dispositional Effects in Organizational Research," *Academy of Management Review* 14 (1989): 385–400.

4. J. P. Kotter, *General Managers.*

5. J. P. Kotter, *The Leadership Factor* (New York: Free Press, 1988), 30–31.

6. V. J. Bentz, "Research Findings from Personality Assessment of Executives," presentation to Human Resource Planning Society, Scottsdale, Ariz. (1986), 1–80.

7. Bentz, "Personality Assessment of Executives," 61.

8. Bentz, "Personality Assessment of Executives," 32.

9. D. W. Bray and A. Howard, "The AT&T Longitudinal Studies of Managers," in *Longitudinal Studies of Adult Psychological Development,* ed. K. W. Schaie (New York: Guilford Press, 1983).

10. Bray and Howard, "AT&T Longitudinal Studies," 40.

11. Bray and Howard, "AT&T Longitudinal Studies," 40.

12. Bray and Howard, "AT&T Longitudinal Studies," 40.

13. H. Lasswell, *Psychology and Politics* (Chicago: University of Chicago Press, 1970/1977).

14. G. Burrell and G. Morgan, *Sociological Paradigms and Organizational Analysis* (Hants, England: Gower, 1979).

15. M. Kundera, *The Unbearable Lightness of Being* (New York: Harper & Row, 1984), 193.

16. C. Flake, "Profiles: The Intensity Factor," *New Yorker* (December 26, 1988): 37.

17. Flake, "Intensity Factor," 46.

18. K. Horney, *Neurosis and Human Growth* (New York: Norton, 1950).

19. G. Sheehy, *Character: America's Search for Leadership* (New York: Morrow, 1989).

20. Sheehy, *Character.*

21. J. F. Rychlak, "Life Themes: Enlargers and Enfolders," in *Formative Years in Business,* eds. D. W. Bray, R. J. Campbell, and D. C. Grant (New York: Wiley, 1974), 82–128.

22. Bray and Howard, "AT&T Longitudinal Studies," 103.

23. Bray and Howard, "AT&T Longitudinal Studies," 103.

24. P. Carey, *Oscar and Lucinda* (London: Faber and Faber, 1988), 141.

25. J. D. Barber, "Classifying and Predicting Presidential Styles: Two 'Weak' Presidents," *Journal of Social Issues* 24 (1968): 51–80.

26. Horney, *Neurosis and Human Growth.*

27. F. Fitzgerald, "A Critic at Large: Memoirs of the Reagan Era," *New Yorker* (January 16, 1989): 71–94.

28. Fitzgerald, "Memoirs," 87–88.

29. Fitzgerald, "Memoirs," 88.

30. Fitzgerald, "Memoirs," 88.

31. Fitzgerald, "Memoirs," 88.

32. *Economist* (January 21, 1989): 13.

33. E. Drew, "Letter from Washington," *New Yorker* (January 27, 1989).

34. R. Kegan, *The Evolving Self: Problem and Process in Human Development* (Cambridge, Mass.: Harvard University Press, 1982).

35. R. E. Kaplan, W. H. Drath, and J. R. Kofodimos, *High Hurdles: The Challenge of Executive Self-Development* (technical report no. 125). (Greensboro, N.C.: Center for Creative Leadership, 1985).

36. D. Kipnis, *The Powerholders* (Chicago: University of Chicago Press, 1976).

37. A. Rabinovich, *Jerusalem on Earth: People, Passions, and Politics in the Holy City* (New York: Free Press, 1988).

38. E. Drew, "Letter from Washington," *New Yorker* (December 26, 1988).

39. Kipnis, *Powerholders,* 169.

40. Kipnis, *Powerholders.*

41. M. Maccoby, *The Gamesman* (New York: Simon & Schuster, 1976).

42. D. J. Levinson, C. N. Darrow, E. B. Klein, M. H. Levinson, and B. McKee, *The Seasons of a Man's Life* (New York: Ballantine Books, 1978).

43. S. Bellow, *Henderson the Rain King* (London: Penguin, 1959), 88.

Chapter Six

1. L. Iacocca (with W. Novak), *Iacocca, an Autobiography* (New York: Bantam, 1984), 62.
2. K. Horney, *Our Inner Conflicts* (New York: Norton, 1945).
3. R. A. Caro, *The Years of Lyndon Johnson: Means of Ascent* (New York: Knopf, 1990), 22.
4. D. C. McClelland, *Human Motivation* (Cambridge, England: Cambridge University Press, 1987), 244.
5. M. Argyle, *Social Interaction* (Chicago: Aldine Publishing, 1969).
6. R. White, "Motivation Reconsidered: The Concept of Competence," *Psychological Review*, LXVI (1959): 297–333.
7. K. Goldstein, *Human Nature in the Light of Psychopathology* (Cambridge, Mass: Harvard University Press, 1943).
8. E. Becker, *The Denial of Death* (New York: Free Press, 1973), 21.
9. Becker, *Denial of Death*, 3.
10. Becker, *Denial of Death*, 3.
11. Becker, *Denial of Death*, 21.
12. A. Adler, *Practice and Theory of Individual Psychology* (New York: Harcourt, Brace, 1929), 13.
13. Becker, *Denial of Death*, 29.
14. Becker, *Denial of Death*, 54.
15. Adler, *Practice and Theory*.
16. M. Eagle, *Recent Developments in Psychoanalysis: A Critical Evaluation* (Cambridge, Mass.: Harvard University Press, 1987), 53.
17. H. Kohut, *The Restoration of Self* (Madison, Conn.: International Universities Press, 1977).
18. B. Bettelheim, *A Good Enough Parent* (New York: Vintage Books, 1988).
19. Kohut, *Restoration of Self*, 172.
20. J. Sculley, *Odyssey: Pepsi to Apple* (New York: Harper & Row, 1987), 79–80.
21. Bettelheim, *A Good Enough Parent*, 232.
22. A. Miller, *Drama of the Gifted Child* (New York: Basic Books, 1981).

23. Miller, *Drama of the Gifted Child*, 32.
24. S. Wegscheider, *Another Chance: Hope and Health for the Alcoholic Family* (Palo Alto, Calif.: Science and Behavior Books, 1981), 107–108.
25. R. L. Ochberg, *Middle-Aged Sons and the Meaning of Work* (Ann Arbor: UMI Research Press, 1987), 136–138.
26. Ochberg, *Middle-Aged Sons*, 138.
27. Kohut, *Restoration of Self*.
28. Kohut, *Restoration of Self*, 172.
29. R. D. Laing, *Self and Others* (London: Penguin, 1967).
30. Horney, *Inner Conflicts*; Miller, *Drama of the Gifted Child*.
31. C. Bonnington, "My Deadly Love Affair," *London Times* (section 3, October 7, 1989): 1.
32. Bellow, *Henderson*, 210.
33. Bellow, *Henderson*, 185.
34. Sculley, *Odyssey*, 16.
35. Sculley, *Odyssey*, 51.
36. C. G. Jung, *The Basic Writings of C. G. Jung* (New York: Random House, 1959).
37. Horney, *Inner Conflicts*.
38. O. F. Kernberg, "Regression in Organizational Leadership," *Psychiatry* 42 (February 1979): 170.
39. J. Feinstein, *A Season on the Brink: A Year with Bob Knight and the Indiana Hoosiers* (New York: Macmillan, 1986), 170.
40. Lasswell, *Psychology and Politics*, 60.
41. Bennis and Nanus, *Leaders;* Waterman, *Renewal Factor;* J. P. Kotter, *Force for Change* (New York: Free Press, 1990).
42. Horney, *Inner Conflicts*; Miller, *Drama of the Gifted Child*.
43. Larson and Lafasto, *Teamwork*, 137.
44. F. Fitzgerald, "Reflections: Jim and Tammy," *New Yorker* (April 23, 1990): 45–87.
45. Horney, *Inner Conflicts*.
46. C. Bruck, "The World of Business: Undoing the Eighties," *New Yorker* (July 23, 1990): 61–62.
47. Bruck, "World of Business," 62.
48. L. Hirschhorn, *The Workplace Within* (Cambridge, Mass.: MIT Press, 1988).
49. Horney, *Inner Conflicts*, 35.

50. R. M. Kanter, *Work and Family in the United States: A Critical Review for Research and Policy* (New York: Russel Sage, 1977); P. Evans and F. Bartolome, *Must Success Cost So Much?* (New York: Basic Books, 1988); J. R. Kofodimos, *Why Executives Lose Their Balance* (technical report no. 137) (Greensboro, N.C.: Center for Creative Leadership, 1989).

51. Sculley, *Odyssey,* 4.

52. Sculley, *Odyssey,* 16.

53. Caro, *Lyndon Johnson,* 37.

54. T. J. Peters and R. H. Waterman, Jr., *In Search of Excellence* (New York: Harper & Row, 1982).

55. Waterman, *Renewal Factor,* 75.

56. Manz and Sims, *Superleadership.*

57. D. C. McClelland, *Power: The Inner Experience* (New York: Irvington, 1975), 263.

58. McCall and Lombardo, *Off the Track.*

59. L. Butcher, *Accidental Millionaire: The Rise and Fall of Steve Jobs at Apple Computer* (New York: Paragon House, 1988), 139.

60. Caro, *Lyndon Johnson,* 119.

61. Sculley, *Odyssey,* 34.

62. Bonnington, *Deadly Love Affair,* 1.

63. Kernberg, "Regression."

64. Kohut, *Restoration of Self.*

65. R. A. Emmons, "Factor Analysis and Construct Validity of the Narcissistic Personality Inventory," *Journal of Personality Assessment* 43, no. 3 (1984): 291–305.

66. B. Bursten, "Some Narcissistic Personality Types," in *Essential Papers on Narcissism,* ed. A. T. Morrison (New York University Press, 1986), 387.

67. Miller, *Drama of the Gifted Child.*

68. Butcher, *Accidental Millionaire,* 138.

69. Horney, *Inner Conflicts;* Miller, *Drama of the Gifted Child.*

70. Becker, *Denial of Death,* 4.

71. J. Sonnenfeld, *The Hero's Farewell: What Happens When CEOs Retire* (New York: Oxford University Press, 1988).

72. Sculley, *Odyssey,* 29–30.

73. W. E. Henry, "The Business Executive: The Psychody-

namics of a Social Role," *American Journal of Sociology* 54, no. 4 (1949): 286–291.

74. Caro, *Lyndon Johnson.*
75. Kernberg, "Regression," 34.
76. Sculley, *Odyssey,* 234.
77. Sculley, *Odyssey,* 271.
78. Becker, *Denial of Death,* 6.
79. Becker, *Denial of Death,* 6.
80. A. Maslow, *Toward a Psychology of Being* (New York: Van Nostrand, 1968).
81. R. A. Emmons, "Narcissism: Theory and Measurement," *Journal of Personality and Social Psychology* 52, no. 1 (1987): 11–17.

Chapter Seven

1. J. Littman, *Once Upon a Time in ComputerLand: The Amazing Billion-Dollar Tale of Bill Millard* (Los Angeles: Price Stern Sloan, 1987).
2. McCall and Lombardo, *Off the Track.*
3. R. Kaplan, *The Expansive Executive* (technical report no. 135) (Greensboro, N.C.: Center for Creative Leadership, 1989), 21.
4. J. Conger, *Charismatic Leadership: The Elusive Factor in Organizational Effectiveness* (San Francisco, Calif.: Jossey-Bass, 1988).
5. Feinstein, *Season on the Brink.*
6. J. Newhouse, "The Tactician," *The New Yorker,* May 7, 1990, 51 and 54.
7. D. W. Winnicott, *Playing and Reality* (London: Pelican, 1971).

Chapter Eight

1. F. Bartolome and P. Evans, *Must Success Cost So Much?* (New York: Basic Books, 1988).
2. Kofodimos, *Executives Lose Balance,* 17.
3. Bartolome and Evans, *Must Success Cost So Much?,* 114.

4. Ochberg, *Middle-Aged Sons.*

5. Maccoby, *Gamesman,* 172.

6. S. Jourard, *The Transparent Self* (New York: Van Nostrand Reinhold, 1964).

7. Kubie, "Some Unsolved Problems," 174–175.

8. Bartolome and Evans, *Must Success Cost So Much?,* 114.

9. B. O'Reilly, "Why Grade 'A' Executives Get an 'F' as Parents," *Fortune* (January 1, 1990): 36–46.

10. Bartolome and Evans, *Must Success Cost So Much?*; Vaillant, *Adaptation to Life.*

11. M. W. McCall, Jr., M. M. Lombardo, and A. M. Morrison, *The Lessons of Experience* (Lexington, Mass.: Lexington Books, 1988).

12. Bartolome and Evans, *Must Success Cost So Much?*

Chapter Nine

1. Sculley, *Odyssey,* 113.

2. McCall and Lombardo, *Off the Track,* 113.

3. Kegan, *Evolving Self.*

4. F. Friedlander, in *The Executive Mind,* ed. Srivastva, S. (San Francisco: Jossey-Bass, 1983).

5. G. E. Vaillant, *Adaptation to Life* (Boston: Little, Brown, 1977).

6. Kaplan, Drath, and Kofodimos, *High Hurdles.*

7. M. Woodman, "Addiction to Perfection," *Yoga Journal* (November/December 1988): 51–55.

8. Vaillant, *Adaptation to Life,* 84.

9. D. T. Hall, *Leadership Succession: Dilemmas in Linking Succession Planning to Individual Executive Learning* (New Brunswick, N.J.: Transaction Books, 1986).

10. D. T. Hall and J. Richter, "Balancing Work Life and Home Life: What Can Organizations Do to Help?" *Academy of Management Executive* 2, no. 3 (August, 1988).

11. M. Viederman, "The Psychodynamic Life Narrative: A Psychotherapeutic Intervention Useful in Crisis Situations," *Psychiatry* 46 (1983): 236–247.

12. Viederman, "Psychotherapeutic Intervention," 236.

13. G. Mechanic, Wharton School of Business, personal communication.
14. Kaplan, 1983; Lieberman, Yalom, and Miles, 1980.
15. P. Casement, *On Learning from the Patient* (London: Tavistock, 1985).

Chapter Ten

1. W. James, *The Principles of Psychology* (New York: Dover, 1950), 121–122.
2. Vaillant, *Adaptation to Life,* 224.
3. V. P. Gay, "Philosophy, Psychoanalysis and the Problem of Change," *Psychoanalytic Inquiry* 9, no. 1 (1989): 26–44.
4. R. Kegan, *Evolving Self.*
5. *The Compact Edition of the Oxford English Dictionary* (London: Oxford University Press, 1971), 1663.
6. Feinstein, *Season on the Brink,* 161.
7. Woodman, "Addiction to Perfection," 51–55.
8. T. S. Eliot, *The Cocktail Party* (Orlando, Fla.: Harcourt Brace Jovanovich, 1964).
9. Jung, *Basic Writings.*
10. Jung, *Basic Writings.*
11. Carey, *Oscar and Lucinda,* 82.
12. A. Cooper, "Concepts of Therapeutic Effectiveness in Psychoanalysis: A Historical Review," *Psychoanalytic Inquiry,* no. 1 (1989): 5–25.
13. Levinson and others, *Seasons,* 243–244.
14. Levinson and others, *Seasons,* 243–244.
15. P. Conroy, *The Prince of Tides* (Boston: Houghton Mifflin, 1986), 95.
16. R. Bly, *A Little Book on the Human Shadow* (New York: Harper & Row, 1988).
17. Kegan, *Evolving Self,* 211.
18. Kegan, *Evolving Self,* 101.
19. Kegan, *Evolving Self,* 44.
20. Levinson and others, *Seasons;* Vaillant, *Adaptation to Life.*
21. Kegan, *Evolving Self.*
22. L. Hirschhorn, *The Workplace Within,* 205.

23. C. Jung, "The Development of Personality," in *The Es-sential Jung,* ed. A. Storr (Princeton, N.J.: Princeton University Press), 191–210.

24. Kegan, *Evolving Self,* 207.

25. Kegan, *Evolving Self.*

26. Kegan, *Evolving Self.*

27. I. Plster and M. Plster, *Gestalt Therapy Integrated: Contours of Theory and Practice* (New York: Random House, 1974).

28. Hirschhorn, *The Workplace Within,* 211.

Chapter Twelve

1. Kegan, *Evolving Self.*

2. Kegan, *Evolving Self.*

3. Winnicott, *Playing and Reality.*

4. Campbell, *Thousand Faces.*

5. Campbell, *Thousand Faces,* 252.

6. Campbell, *Thousand Faces,* 252.

7. Campbell, *Thousand Faces,* 252.

8. J. Kofodimos, R. Kaplan, and W. Drath, *Anatomy of an Executive* (technical report no. 129) (Greensboro, N.C.: Center for Creative Leadership, 1986), 64.

9. Kofodimos, Kaplan, and Drath, *Anatomy of an Executive,* 64.

10. Viederman, "Psychotherapeutic Intervention," 246.

11. Vaillant, *Adaptation to Life.*

12. Campbell, *Thousand Faces,* 92.

13. Friedlander, in Srivastva, *Executive Mind,* 217.

14. Levinson and others, *Seasons.*

15. Campbell, *Thousand Faces,* 97.

16. Bettelheim, *A Good Enough Parent* (New York: Vintage Books, 1988).

17. J. W. Gardner, *Self-Renewal: The Individual and the Innovative Society* (New York: Norton, 1963).

18. Kegan, *Evolving Self.*

19. Kegan, *Evolving Self.*

20. Kegan, *Evolving Self,* 169.

21. Jung, "The Development of Personality," 203.

22. Jung, "The Development of Personality," 203.

23. Evans and Bartolome, *Must Success Cost So Much?*
24. Campbell, *Thousand Faces,* 29.
25. H. Hesse, *Narcissus and Goldmund* (New York: Farrar, Strauss & Giroux, 1968).
26. Campbell, *Thousand Faces,* 29.

Chapter Thirteen

1. Campbell, *Thousand Faces,* 15.
2. Cited in A. Storr, *Solitude: A Return to the Self* (New York: Free Press, 1988), 195–196.
3. Kegan, *Evolving Self.*
4. S. Bellow, *The Dean's December* (New York: Pocket Books, 1982), 35–36.
5. H. Thomas, cited in A. Howard and D. Bray, *Managerial Lives in Transition* (New York: Guilford, 1988), 398.
6. Vaillant, *Adaptation to Life,* 158–159.
7. Bellow, *Henderson,* 297–298.
8. Bellow, *Henderson,* 264.
9. Bellow, *Henderson,* 266.
10. Bellow, *Henderson,* 267.
11. Bellow, *Henderson,* 298.
12. Campbell, *Thousand Faces,* 25.

Appendix

1. Kofodimos, Kaplan, and Drath, *Anatomy of an Executive.*

Index